Priscilla and Conrad Reining
Minneapolis , 1957

THE ITESO

ERIA PAULO ENGULU, M.B.E.
Chief Judge of Teso, for whose people this book was written

THE ITESO

FIFTY YEARS OF CHANGE IN A
NILO-HAMITIC TRIBE OF UGANDA

BY

J. C. D. LAWRANCE

WITH A FOREWORD BY

SIR ANDREW COHEN
K.C.M.G., K.C.V.O., O.B.E.
Governor of Uganda

LONDON
OXFORD UNIVERSITY PRESS
NEW YORK   TORONTO
1957

Oxford University Press, Amen House, London E.C.4

GLASGOW NEW YORK TORONTO MELBOURNE WELLINGTON
BOMBAY CALCUTTA MADRAS KARACHI
CAPE TOWN IBADAN NAIROBI ACCRA SINGAPORE

———

PRINTED IN GREAT BRITAIN

FOREWORD

I AM delighted to write this foreword to a book written by a serving member of the Uganda Civil Service. The Iteso are the second largest tribe in Uganda, but very little has so far been written about them. Mr. Lawrance's book will therefore fill an important gap.

The book describes and analyses changes which have taken place in the life of an African tribe during a period of fifty years. To appreciate the advances made by the Iteso—now a wealthy and progressive community—it is necessary to trace their development in all its aspects from the time of their first contact with Western civilization. This is what Mr. Lawrance set out to do and he has achieved his object admirably.

The book will be of value to research workers, for whom it will provide a foundation on which to build future studies of the Iteso. It will also be of value to administrators, who will find that the chapters dealing with law especially will repay careful study.

Mr. Lawrance is well qualified to have written this book. He was District Commissioner of Teso for five years and knows the Iteso well. The life of a District Commissioner nowadays is both a busy and an active one which leaves little time for detailed research. But Mr. Lawrance, as well as guiding the people forward in a period of rapid development, has succeeded in finding time to study their background. I believe that the book will be of great interest not only to all those who know Teso, but to many others who, from various points of view, are interested in the effects on an African tribe of contacts with modern development.

A. B. COHEN

Entebbe
21 December 1955

PREFACE

WRITTEN information about the Teso tribe, one of the largest in East Africa, is very limited. The accounts left by early missionaries and administrators are inadequate and sometimes superficial and no detailed studies have yet been made by anthropologists. I hope that this book will help to remedy this deficiency by collating, while it is still available, the evidence of early writers and of old men's memories in order to present some account of customs and beliefs current at the beginning of this century. At the same time I hope that the book will give for purposes of comparison and record a general picture of contemporary (1955) Teso life. From this comparison may be gauged the effect on an African tribe of fifty years of contact with a European race.

At first sight the Iteso[1] today appear to have little in common, apart from their language, with their kindred tribes of the Nilo-Hamitic family such as the Karamojong, Turkana, and Toposa, or with their more distant relatives the Masai, Nandi, and Suk. Although the Iteso own large herds of cattle they no longer depend on them for their livelihood, nor do they lead the semi-nomadic lives of pastoralists; they have in fact become a sedentary tribe of cultivators. A cotton cash crop in a fertile and well-watered country has brought them wealth[2] and a comparatively high standard of living[3] and, with this rise in standards, they have adopted many European fashions and largely abandoned the spectacular clothing styles and body ornaments retained by the Karamojong or Masai. The economic prosperity of their country has resulted in an impressive development of services, particularly in the adoption of new agricultural techniques and in the provision of water-supplies, good roads, and permanent buildings; Teso district has the highest school population of any district in Uganda outside Buganda Province.[4] Nevertheless, in spite of all these material differences there remains considerable similarity in customs, culture, and social organization between the Iteso and certain other tribes of the Nilo-Hamitic family. The degree of this similarity and the extent to which differences in custom are due to historical accidents, environment, or other causes, must be gauged by more competent judges than me. I have no anthropological knowledge and have therefore had to avoid all theoretical anthropological discussion. If this book provides the information on which such a judgement can be based, it will have served its purpose.

[1] On the analogy of the use of the plural form *Baganda* to describe the Ganda people, the plural form *Iteso* is now in general use. A single Teso man is *Etesot* and the language is *Ateso*.

[2] For instance the cotton crop in 1952 brought £1,282,630 to producers in Teso district.

[3] Judged on cash returns to producers from economic crops and cattle, on clothing and housing standards, on the amount of meat consumed locally, and on the quantity of consumer goods, particularly bicycles and ploughs, sold in the district; for instance, Teso district was in 1953 the largest cigarette-consuming district in East Africa.

[4] 17,464 children in grant-aided primary schools in 1954.

The Teso tribe in 1948 numbered 511,271, of whom 42,288 lived in the North Nyanza district of the Nyanza Province of Kenya and the remainder in Uganda's Eastern Province.[1] They are thus Uganda's second largest tribe, only the Baganda being more numerous. The great majority of them live in Teso district[2] and the information in this book is based entirely on material collected in Teso district. There are, however, large groups of Iteso located in the neighbouring districts of Bukedi (106,844) and Busoga (25,840). This book is limited to an account of the people and provides no details of their environment.

Material for this book was collected and the book itself was written in the five years during which I was District Commissioner of Teso district. I am aware that a District Commissioner by the very nature of his duties can rarely hope to establish the same degree of confidence as can a person who is not a government official, and that in consequence answers to his questions may not always be sincere; it is also true that he can rarely devote sufficient time to inquiries of this nature to ensure that they are exhaustive. On the other hand, a District Commissioner's everyday work brings him into close contact with the native courts and enables him to visit every part of the district; he has direct access to papers and records in the District Office, which is the repository for most of the unpublished information on the tribe. Moreover, I am by no means certain that those questioned were in fact reticent in their replies. All over the district I found people interested and forthcoming; in Usuku one of my informants himself insisted on writing down fourteen pages of information lest my memory or my notes should prove inadequate; I was freely given the full findings of the *Amootoi ka Etesot* society in its inquiries into past customs and history; most of the senior chiefs of the Teso African Local Government showed their personal interest by doing everything possible to further inquiries, either by providing information themselves or by contacting local experts in a given subject.

The form of this book altered as it grew. It started in 1949 as an administrative exercise, to record the then existing law on marriage, adultery, and divorce. The many district council resolutions on these subjects needed collation and there were signs that interpretation of this law differed throughout the district. There are some 9,000 suits filed in the native courts in Teso each year, of which about 750 to 1,000 concern marriage, adultery, or divorce. All these cases are examined, albeit cursorily, by an administrative officer, and I arranged that any case files of interest were collected by administrative officers on tour and examined by me. The resulting draft recording was then sent to several experienced native court judges for comment. It is impossible to acknowledge all the help given by all these assessors, but the comments of Messrs. E. P. Engulu, M.B.E.,

---

[1] This is no longer wholly true. There is an increasing population of immigrant Iteso in Buganda Province, some of whom have made their permanent homes there.
[2] 308,429 and 49,161 Kumam, a closely related tribe.

Chief Judge of the District Native Court; N. Esunyet, Secretary-General
of the Teso African Local Government; E. A. Ejoku, M.B.E., County
Chief of Kumi county and later Secretary-General; J. E. I. Ogaino,
formerly permanent Deputy Judge of the District Native Court and
County Chief of Soroti county; and P. E. Esabu, County Chief of Usuku
county and later of Serere county, were particularly useful. Long before
these drafts were approved and in their final form I had decided to include
other aspects of native law under the chapter headings of Inheritance,
Contract, Real Property, Criminal, and Courts. I followed the same procedure, but the task was more difficult, for inheritance disputes are usually
settled by clan leaders, who keep no written records, and few cases reach
the native courts. Within the last few years the time-established rules of
contract have been shaken by the introduction of a money economy and
by the spread of literacy; the courts have as yet evolved no rules to deal
with written wills or contracts. The law of real property was the hardest to
record. Innumerable economic impacts have affected ideas on this subject
differently in different parts of the district. The change from shifting to
rotational cultivation, increases of population, the introduction of cash
crops, ox or tractor ploughing, the construction of houses in permanent
materials, and the planting of trees have inevitably caused traditional ideas
of tenure to change. The native courts tend to be conservative and slow to
accept new conceptions. I could never have attempted this recording but
for the help and advice of Mr. D. D. Campbell, M.C., District Agricultural
Officer of Teso from 1948 to 1953. We made many inquiries together and
he put at my disposal his copious notes on land tenure and agricultural
customs.

   This recording of Teso law forms Part VI of this book. Its form and
layout is based to some extent on *Customary Law of the Haya Tribe*.[1] The
intention is to give as complete an account as possible of all law which is
administered in the Teso native courts today (1955), not only the unwritten
or common law based on custom but also the written law newly devised to
meet modern conditions. I have classified and arranged these laws in
sections for ease of reference. I am well aware of the arguments against
codification of native law, but if the policy of integration of the native
courts within the judicial framework of the Protectorate is to become a
reality in Uganda, some form of codification will inevitably become essential. I hope that this part of the book will be of direct and practical use to
those concerned with the working of native courts.

   The history of Teso district, which forms Part I of this book, is based
very largely on an essay submitted for the Uganda Government Essay
Competition in 1953, which has already been published.[2] It was written
at a time when I had access only to the records in the Soroti District Office,
none of which is dated earlier than 1909, the year in which the first

---

[1] By Cory and Hartnoll, International African Institute, London, 1945.
[2] 'A History of Teso to 1937', *Uganda Journal*, vol. 19, 1955.

administrative station was opened in Teso at Kumi. If I had had the opportunity of searching through the archives of the Mbale District Office or of
the Secretariat, my account of the early history between 1899 and 1909
might have been more detailed and authoritative.

The remaining four parts of the book were originally designed as a short
introduction to the law recording in Part VI, to give readers some background knowledge of the customs and institutions of the Iteso and thereby
to ensure a better understanding of their contemporary law. I soon found,
however, that the recording of present-day customs and institutions was
impossible or meaningless without a study of the past. What was intended
as a short introduction grew into Parts II, III, IV, and V of this book,
Social Organization, Social Ceremonies and Customs, Mode of Living,
and Culture. The intention throughout these four parts is to give a comparative account of contemporary and pre-British ways of life of the Iteso,
from which the effects of the impact of Western civilization over a brief
fifty years can be judged. The rapid assimilation of European learning,
techniques, and living fashions have had virtually no effect on the culture
of the tribe. In spite of the spread of Christianity, beliefs in the power of
witchcraft, of rain making, of divination, and of mystic healing remain
unaltered. In marriages the social guarantee of bride-price is invariably
given and the ritual of clan ceremonies is nearly always observed. The
binding force of clan institutions such as the observance of taboos has
remained when the need for it is by no means apparent, whereas the age-
set system, which is the dominant feature of most Nilo-Hamitic social
structures, has vanished completely.

The account of Teso life and culture in Parts IV and V is designed not
only as comparative data but also as a record of a way of life which will
rapidly disappear. With the continuing rise in material living standards the
Iteso themselves are already beginning to forget the clothing fashions of
the past and the many varied uses they made of wild trees and plants in
the preparation of medicines for themselves and their livestock, in magical
ceremonies, and in the construction of implements or of houses. I realize
that in recording these uses I must inevitably include much information
that is common to tribes other than the Iteso. I am aware also that my
treatment of such subjects as religion or the social customs observed at
birth, marriage, or death is apt to be cursory. The degree of detail depends
partly on the direction where my own knowledge or interest lies, partly on
the help that was available from other people, and partly on the time that
could be spared for inquiries.

I have already acknowledged the help received from Teso assessors in
checking the law recording in Part VI. The information in Parts I to III is
based largely on written records named in the text, particularly on *The
Lango* by the late Mr. J. H. Driberg and on Bishop A. L. Kitching's *On the
Backwaters of the Nile*. I am grateful to Messrs. Ernest Benn and to Bishop
Kitching for permission to quote from these two works. Many helpers

have contributed towards Parts IV and V, foremost among whom is Mr. C. Vickerman, who during the three years he was an Assistant District Commissioner in Teso collected for me considerable information on musical instruments, household implements, pots, and other artifacts; the two maps on pages 14 and 20 and nearly all the drawings in this book are his work. Much of the information on house building, preparation of food, and agriculture has been gleaned from the notes, preserved in the Teso District Agricultural Book, of sundry agricultural officers, many of them anonymous. The scientific names of trees and plants have been checked by Mr. I. R. Dale of the Uganda Forests Department. Many of the details of age-set ceremonies and the words of age-set and rain-making songs have been taken from the field notes of Mr. F. Lukyn-Williams, which he made in 1921 when serving as an Assistant District Commissioner in Teso. Most of the administrative officers who served with me in Teso have made notes at my request on a variety of subjects, all of which have proved useful. For the recordings of song music I am indebted to various Native Anglican Church school-teachers, particularly Miss Margaret Malinga, Mr. M. E. Ojirot, and Mr. J. Osilon; to Mrs. G. Calcraft of the Church Missionary Society, and, above all, to Dr. K. P. Wachsmann who checked the recordings. The plant remedies used to heal the sick were collected largely by Brother K. Ludger of the Mill Hill Mission at Toroma. The translations from Ateso are for the most part the work of Mr. C. J. W. Okello, Head Clerk in the Soroti District Office, or of Father J. H. Hilders of the Mill Hill Mission at Soroti.

Many people have provided useful criticism: in particular, Dr. K. P. Wachsmann of the Uganda Museum on the chapter on music; Dr. A. N. Tucker of the School of Oriental and African Studies, London University, on the chapter on language; Dr. L. A. Fallers, East African Institute of Social Research, on the chapter on kinship groupings; Mr. J. G. Ross, Department of Veterinary Services and Animal Industry, on the chapter on animal husbandry; and Mr. D. D. Campbell, M.C., Department of Agriculture, on the chapter on agriculture.

The photographs, with one exception, are the work of the Department of Information, Uganda, and are published with the permission of the Director of Information. The map inside the back cover was produced for me by the Director of Surveys, Uganda. These and other unnamed persons gave very considerable help. The book could not, however, have been published but for the generous financial help given by the Uganda Government.

J. C. D. LAWRANCE

Entebbe
September 1955

CONTENTS

II. THE HOME

III. FOOD AND DRINK

IV. WAR, HUNTING, AND FISHING

V. AGRICULTURE

VI. ANIMAL HUSBANDRY

PART V. CULTURE

PART VI. LAW

LIST OF ILLUSTRATIONS

PHOTOGRAPHS

NOTE

The measurements given below the drawings between pages 117 and 163 are, unless otherwise stated, those of the particular objects used as models for the drawings and are not necessarily average measurements.

PART I
HISTORY

CHAPTER I

ORIGINS AND TRIBAL MOVEMENTS
1700–1895

1. *Introduction*

THE story of the development of Teso district and of the social, economic, and political advance of its peoples covers only a short space of time. Only fifty years ago these peoples were in a state of naked barbarism, existing by a precarious and primitive system of shifting cultivation, ravaged by famine, disease, and inter-tribal warfare. Since the beginning of this century Kakunguru's Sniders have established peace and ordered government; the missionaries have brought the benefits of Christian teaching and education; and the introduction of cotton and the plough and the improvement of farming methods under the British administration have raised standards of living and resulted in rapid development of communications and trade, bringing wealth to the district and removing the constant threat of famine and disease. These efforts of outsiders would have achieved scant success had not the Iteso themselves readily and quickly accepted and assimilated these new ideas and techniques and used them to the best advantage. The resultant wealth has been wisely invested in further improvements by Teso's progressive local government.

Yet, only forty years ago, Bishop Kitching expressed surprise that the name of such a large and progressive tribe as the Teso had not appeared in any of the works on the peoples of the Uganda Protectorate.[1] His was one of the first published works to use the name 'Teso'. Captain Kirkpatrick recorded that in 1898 the northern, eastern, and south-eastern shores of Lake Kyoga were populated by Wakedi.[2] When Speke reached Uganda in 1862 this name, *Kedi* or *Kidi*, was known throughout the western Lake Victoria region as applying to the unsubdued and unclad tribesmen who lived on the east side of the Nile opposite Bunyoro; and in course of time the Baganda used the name to cover the whole of the similarly unclad peoples who extended eastwards to Mount Elgon. The Iteso, however, claim that the name comes from *Ikidea*, the people of the east (*kide*), the inhabitants of modern Bukedea.

At the turn of the century Sir H. H. Johnston published his comprehensive *Uganda Protectorate* in which there is no mention of Teso. The country then termed Bukedi was inhabited mainly by Lango and Miro tribes. 'In the southern part of Bukedi are those extraordinary marsh-lakes Kwania, Kamoda and Kioga (sometimes called Choga).'[3] At that time, therefore, Bukedi referred to what is now Lango district.

[1] Kitching, 1915.   [2] Kirkpatrick, 1899.   [3] Johnston, 1902.

This condition of constant swampiness—of rivers that are narrow marshes and of lakes that may have open water at their centre but are belted round the sides with untraversible swamps—appears to extend from Bukedi across the plains to the very verge of Elgon's foothills and thence again westwards to Muruli on the Victoria Nile. Between Elgon and Bukedi, however, though the land is occasionally swampy, it is excellent soil and a good proportion of it has been put under cultivation by the fine, tall, naked tribe of the Elgumi, a race speaking a language closely allied to the Suk. Elgumi is the name given to them by the Masai. I believe they call themselves Wamia.[1]

Nevertheless, in 1901 in *The Church Missionary Intelligencer* the pioneer missionary linguist, the Rev. W. A. Crabtree, had reported from Semei Kakunguru's headquarters, 'There is a people who I find are called Teso. I should think about two-thirds of the people in Kakunguru's district speak Teso . . . (which) is strikingly akin to Bari in many of its roots and forms. I have been able to draw up a *Mateka* (first reading-book), and have sent it to Mengo. Couldn't someone definitely take up this Teso work? . . . visiting districts unknown to any white man but undoubtedly belonging to Teso.'

As late as 1908 the country now known as Lango district was still called Bukedi. In the Intelligence Report for that year is an account of a journey by the Sub-Commissioner, Unyoro district, across the Nile to 'the Bukedi and Achopi Countries'.[2] In another Intelligence Report of the same year is an account (accompanied by a map) by Captain Johnston of the 4th K.A.R. of the country round Bululu and Lake Salisbury. In it is the first published mention of a country named Teso: 'I heard there was not much cultivation at Tesso, but a lot of cattle and sheep and the country north of that grass lands with few inhabitants.'[3] 'Tesso' is shown on the map close to Abela Rock. It is not clear whether the name refers to the area north-east of the rock or to the rock itself, probably the former, although Sir Albert Cook in 1909 believed that 'Teso mountain, an imposing mass of granite rocks' gave its name to the whole country. The inhabitants of Teso Johnston called Wakedi: 'The soldiers I saw at Angorla (Ngora) on leave said the greater part of the Wakeddi of A Company, 4th K.A.R., came from there.'[3] Captain Johnston also names the language Teso. 'Between Seroti and Chooroo the language changes, the language to the east being Tesso, whilst to the west it is Umiro.'[3]

There is an earlier appearance of the name Teso on a War Office map dated 1905 (Old Africa Series T.S.G.S. No. 1539: Sheet No. 86), but it is unobtrusively inserted to the south-west of Lake Salisbury among a series of locality names and does not appear to refer to the whole country. The same map in the area north of the lake bears the legend 'Natives rich in flocks, herds and food but reported treacherous'.

In the Kumi station diary for 1909 touring by administrative officers

[1] Johnston, 1902.
[2] Uganda Protectorate, 1908 (ii).   [3] Ibid. (i).

north of Lake Salisbury and the Agu channel is referred to as 'visiting Teso'. The name had at that time a localized meaning: 'there was only one part of the district which was, and is still, called "Ateso" i.e. the land of the Iteso, and that is the area of Usuku or Napak.'[1]

A map printed in 1913 shows Teso as a separate district with (somewhat prematurely) a government station at 'Siroti'.[2] The district was bounded on the south by Bukedi which corresponded roughly with the modern Bugishu and Bukedi districts without the southern county of Samia-Bugwe, and on the north by Lango district. The boundaries of Teso district when first constituted in 1912 approximated to the present ones except that Kaberamaido county was in Lango and Omoro county of Lango was in Teso. The people became generally known as Teso about the same time as the district was so named. A writer in the 1913 Handbook in an account of Teso district refers to its inhabitants as Bakedi, while elsewhere in the same book there appears an anthropological account of the Bateso.[2]

Both the district and its people have been known by the name Teso since that time. The Luganda form Bateso was normally used to describe the people till Luganda went out of vogue about 1937, and now the Ateso form, Iteso, is in general use. Of the former names, Bukedi has been bestowed on the neighbouring district to the south, the name Wamia persisted in the Tororo area and in Kenya until recent times, though the people formerly known as Wamia have now been officially renamed Itesio. The name Elgumi is no longer used.

Although the Iteso have managed to shed their foreign nicknames of Wakedi, Wamia, and Elgumi, their neighbours in Teso, the Kumam, have not been so lucky. Driberg states that Kumam is a bantuized form of Akum, which was a nickname given to the tribe now known as Kumam.[3] The Kumam themselves claim Lango as their real name and still refer to themselves as Lango. 'They say in ordinary conversation "we Lango do such and such a thing" and refer to bush paths as "yo Lango", to native medicines as "yat Lango". They speak of "lep Lango" (Lango language), "paco Lango" (Lango home), "pone Lango" (Lango customs).'[4] Some Kumam believe the nickname was given because they used to grieve over their cattle stolen by the Lango; kumo means 'to grieve'. The Kumam recognize and accept this nickname and have on several occasions attempted to alter the name of Kaberamaido county to Kumam county; but the Iteso-dominated District Council has resisted this change.

Equally well known is the title Ikokolemu or Lango Ikokolemu. Various derivations have been suggested for this name: Driberg believes them to have been the 'children of Olemu'. (Ikoku means 'child'.) Father Walshe records the story of how 'many years ago, far away in Karamoja or beyond, a certain member of the Lango family stole a head-dress of honour—alem—and with some other relations fled towards Lake Kyoga where they settled down

[1] Wright, 1942.   [2] Uganda Protectorate, 1913.
[3] Driberg, 1923.   [4] Walshe, 1947.

among the Jo Wer (Chopi) and learned their Nilotic language. They were called *Ikokolemu* by the rest of the family, *akoko* in Ateso meaning "to steal".[1] The Iteso usually call the Kumam by the name *Ikokolemu* which is the title used to describe one of the four main divisions of the Teso tribe, the other three being the *Ingoratok* of Ngora, Kumi, and Bukedea counties, the *Iseera* of Serere, Soroti, and Amuria counties, and the *Iteso* of Usuku county. The name is probably first recorded by Captain Johnston, 4th K.A.R., in the 1908 Intelligence Report: 'It is understood that the people round Chooroo are called Cockalerumo, they however speak Umiro language.'[2]

The title *Kumam* was, however, in current use when the 1913 Handbook was published and, though best known to themselves as *Lango* or *Lango Ikokolemu* and to the Iteso as *Akum* or *Ikokolemu*, the people have retained the name *Kumam* to this day.

2. *Early inhabitants before the Teso invasion*

Because there are no traditions of wars with previous occupants, it has often been assumed that the Iteso found their present country empty when they first arrived in it within the last 250 years. There are, however, stories of a strange, dwarf race of pale-skinned people who lived in the rocks at places as far apart as Achuloi, Asuret, and Nyero. Uganda was at one time peopled by the Bushmen, whose features and habits correspond with these accounts.[3] The well-known bent of the Bushmen for rock paintings has been demonstrated at Nyero, Asuret, and Ngora in Teso.[4]

The largest group of paintings is at Nyero and consists mainly of naturalistic drawings of men, canoes, leaves and flowers, and of geometric designs among which concentric circles predominate. There is considerable superposition of designs and two different colours of pigment are used. As a general rule naturalistic are older than geometric drawings and the use of red pigment was common before that of white pigment. These changes in technique and style were very gradual and it seems likely from the evidence of the paintings alone that the shelters at Nyero were occupied for a considerable period of time. There is a thick deposit on the floor of the main shelter which also indicates a long occupation, for it has yielded rough lava implements, better-shaped obsidian and quartz implements, and pottery. There are also numerous bones in the deposit. From this evidence it may be surmised that these early inhabitants were hunters and, if the canoe paintings are any indication, fishermen. It is probable that the Iteso on their migrations found the last survivors of this race of stone-age men still lurking in the rock outcrops which are a feature of the Teso countryside. With their stone implements they would be no match for the Iteso and their disappearance has been complete.

[1] Walshe, 1947.　　　　　　　　　　　[2] Uganda Protectorate, 1908 (ii).
[3] Seligman, 1930.　　　　　　　　　　[4] Lawrance, 1953 (i).

3. *Origins of the Iteso*

It is generally accepted by all authorities that the Iteso belong to the Nilo-Hamitic or Half-Hamitic family of tribes. This is a linguistic grouping of little value by itself for historical deductions. But within the Nilo-Hamitic family is a small group of contiguous tribes with a common culture and origin.

Wright includes in this group the Karamojong, Teso, and Lango in Uganda; the Turkana and Suk in Kenya; the Toposa, Donyiro, and Jiye in the Sudan, and possibly the Buma and Karo in Abyssinia. He names the group *Itunga* (people) on the analogy of the use of the words *Bantu* and *Ji* or *Jo* to represent groups of peoples.[1]

Father Tarantino lists a more comprehensive group which he chooses to call the 'Lango Family'. It contains:

In Abyssinia: the Dime and Bako.
In the Sudan: the Toposa, Dongotono, Lotuko, and Lango.
In Kenya: the Suk, Turkana, Nandi, and Masai.
In Uganda: the Lango, Kumam, Teso, Abwor, Dodoth, Jie (or Lango-Olok), and Karamojong (or Lango-Dyang).[2]

Gulliver limits the tribes comprising the group to the Teso, Karamojong, Jie, and Dodoth in Uganda; the Turkana in Kenya, and the Donyiro, Jiye, and Toposa in the Sudan. This group he names the 'Teso Dialect Cluster' from the biggest tribe in the group. But because the Teso people now have a different social system and culture from those of the other tribes in the group, all of which have close affinities other than linguistic ones and an account of common origin, he excludes the Iteso and names the remaining tribes the 'Karamojong Cluster' because all the tribes in it trace their origin from the Karamojong.[3]

I do not consider this exclusion is justified. The Iteso have many cultural and social features in common with the Karamojong and a tradition of origin in Karamoja is universally held. It is, indeed, one of the few historical traditions which the Iteso have.[4]

This tradition has been assembled and recorded.[5] The ancestors of the Iteso came from the direction of Abyssinia through Karamoja district. Their travels lasted through six generations or ages. The first generation was known as Ojurata's tadpoles; they were men of short stature with large heads, who lived among swamps and on lakesides. Okori's generation followed Ojurata's; they were the men who first began to till the ground and grow crops. During the third generation, Oyangaese's, people began to keep livestock and the custom arose whereby men take their name from the cattle they own. During Otikiri's generation which followed, various crafts were learned, such as bead making, tanning, and the construction of musical instruments. By the fifth generation, Arionga's, the people were

---

[1] Wright, 1942.   [2] Tarantino, 1949 (i).   [3] Gulliver, 1952 (i).
[4] Lawrance, 1953 (ii).   [5] Amootoi ka Etesot, *c.* 1946.

established in Karamoja and known as Iworopom. Their centre was Mount
Moroto and Okong, a place which has not been identified.. They were
subjected to steady pressure from the Turkana to the east; grazing and
water were insufficient for the increased herds and so the tribe split into
three groups. The first, led by Okong and Angisa, penetrated into what is
now Teso district at Angisa near Magoro. From this first group a subsidiary group went farther afield and settled near Tororo. The second
group colonized the slopes of Mount Kamalinga (Napak) and Mount
Akisim. One of these colonizers was Alekilek, who has given his name to
the curiously shaped volcanic plug of that name. The third group stayed
in Karamoja. They are the Karamojong (*aikar* 'to stay'; *imojong* 'old men'),
the tired old men who stayed behind. Perhaps the name *Teso* is derived
from the word *ates* meaning 'child'; Teso is the land of the children who
left the old men behind. Other traditions, however, assert that the name of
the tribe comes from the name of a leader of one of the early expeditions,
who was called Etesot. During the sixth generation, Asonya's, the Iteso
spread farther westwards and occupied most of the modern Teso district.
This is the generation of the second migration which will be described later
in more detail. It will later be shown that the movement from Karamoja to
Teso in Arionga's generation and the spread westwards and southwards
over the whole district during Asonya's generation each lasted about
100 years and it may therefore be surmised that the first four generations
each correspond approximately to a century span.

The only other recorded traditions are that the Iteso 'came from the
East' and that the place of origin was Iworopom, due east of Usuku. The
split may have occurred at a point on the Loyoro river in Karamoja,
possibly at Koten Hill, the former home of the Jie, within the last 250 years.[1]
Karamojong traditions as related to Captain Turpin in 1916 show that the
country between Mount Kadam, Mount Elgon, and the Suk Hills was
formerly occupied by a tribe called the Oropom, which had similar habits,
customs, and language to those of the Karamojong.[2]

There are remarkably close affinities between the Teso and Toposa
languages although these two tribes are separated by hundreds of miles of
territory. How close the two languages are may be seen from a comparison
of a few words denoting animals, parts of the body, and household and
natural objects (see next page). The same similarity runs through other
parts of speech.

This linguistic affinity might suggest that the Iteso and Toposa had a
contemporary origin. The Toposa split peacefully from the Jie after the
latter moved to their present habitat near Kotido; the movement brought
them to their present country about 150 years ago.[3] Superficial language
similarities are not good evidence of tribal origins, but what other little
evidence is available also supports the theory of origin in central Karamoja

[1] Wright, 1942.   [2] Turpin, 1916.
[3] Gulliver, 1952 (i).

English	Toposa[1]	Ateso
man	(n)akile	ekiliokit
woman	(n)aberu	aberu
tongue	(n)angadyep	angajep
breast	(n)akisim	ikisina
bull	(n)emong	emong
goat	(ny)akine	akinei
elephant	(ny)atome	etom
leopard	(ny)eris	eris
milk	(ny)akile	akile
meat	(ny)akiring	akiring
grass	(ng)anya	anya
water	akipi	akipi
smoke	(ny)apurru	apuru
fire	(ny)akim	akim
sun	(ny)akolong	akolong
moon	(ny)elap	elap

near modern Jie country about 150 to 250 years ago. Gulliver, however, suggests a slightly earlier origin in the Suk Hills 250 to 350 years ago, before the Jie broke off from the Karamojong. Both Karamojong and Jie have the tradition that a division of the Teso tribe, the Iseera, moved westwards with the Lango from whom they parted at Mount Otukwi.[2] These may have formed the second group of colonizers, referred to on page 8, who settled on Mount Napak and Mount Akisim.

4. *The first migration*

The term 'first migration' must not mislead. It is used to describe a long and continuing process lasting perhaps a hundred or more years, consisting of successive waves of settlement. The first migration was still in process in comparatively recent times. Oleumo, who is still living at Magoro and is believed to be approaching his centenary, claims that his father brought him as a small boy to Magoro from Karamoja. Okolimong, the soothsayer of Usuku, whose influence was so considerable at the time British administration was first extended to Usuku in 1909, was born at 'Aarapamu beyond Angisa in Karamoja'.

If the Iteso and Toposa obtained their separate entity after most of the other tribes of the cluster, the date when the first migration started cannot be early in the history of Hamitic expansion which, according to Westermann, began about the beginning of the sixteenth century. On the other hand, it is known from genealogical trees of the modern Iteso that the tribe was already established in Usuku 120 years ago.

In the latter half of the seventeenth century pressure from Hamitic invaders and a severe drought and famine caused a southward movement of the Lwo peoples, which eventually brought the Jaluo to their present home in the Nyanza Province of Kenya.[3] There is no tradition of wars

[1] P. de Roebeck, Sudan Political Service, personal communication.
[2] Gulliver, 1953 (ii).   [3] Driberg, 1923.

between the Jaluo and the Iteso. Yet the Jaluo must have passed through Teso district to reach Budama and Kavirondo. If the Iteso were by then established in Usuku, some contact would have been likely even if the Jaluo hugged the shores of Lake Kyoga and the Mpologoma river. It is likely therefore that the Iteso had not yet arrived in Usuku at the time of the Lwo migration. By the end of the eighteenth century, when the Lango again started moving to the south and west, the Iteso and the Kumam had already begun their outward expansion from Usuku.[1]

It is, therefore, probable that the first migration of the Iteso, which eventually took the tribe from Karamoja to the shores of Lake Salisbury in Usuku, began with the emigration of a few families at the end of the seventeenth or beginning of the eighteenth century. Thereafter more and more emigrants followed the early colonists until at the beginning of the nineteenth century the tribe was established in Usuku and its numbers had risen to such an extent that a second migration to new lands became necessary. The first migration may therefore be dated approximately between 1700 and 1800.

There is complete absence of tradition as to why the Iteso migrated from Karamoja. That the reasons were economic may safely be assumed but the incident which gave rise to the break is not remembered. The derivation of the word *Karamojong* from *aikar* 'to stay behind' and *imojong* 'the old men', and of *Ikokolemu* from *akoko* and *alem* has already been mentioned. Neither of these stories is widely enough held to be of any historical value.

While the Iteso have no traditions on this subject the Karamojong claim that the Iworopom (Iteso) were driven from Karamoja by force of arms. Turpin's informants[2] stated that about 1830 their grandfathers organized a powerful raid and completely broke up the Iworopom tribe. Some Iworopom were captured and absorbed by the Karamojong, but others fled along the northern base of Mount Elgon towards Teso district and others along the eastern side of the mountain to Wamia, the country of the Kenya Iteso. In 1894 rinderpest destroyed the cattle of the Karamojong, locusts ate up their meagre crops, and in 1896 the rains failed and disease carried off large numbers of their small stock. In the ensuing famine it is alleged that two-thirds of the Karamojong tribe perished or were scattered. 'Fully twenty per cent of the eastern Kumama . . . are of Karimojo, Jie and Dodosi origin.' The Karamojong did, and still do, refer to the Iteso as Kumam. 'About half the Bokora section of Karimojo emigrated to Kumama but many died of hunger or were killed by the Kumama.' That skirmishes and fights between the Karamojong and Iworopom or Iteso took place over water or grazing in their former lands in south-east Karamoja is probable and is implied in Teso traditions; these fights may have culminated in the large-scale battle to which Turpin's informants refer. It is, however, certain that by 1830 the

[1] Driberg, 1923.   [2] Turpin, 1916.

Iteso were already established in Usuku and that the movement of Iworo-pom or Iteso from their Karamoja habitat had started many years before, prompted by pressure from their eastern neighbours.

One significant fact is the relative population of the Iteso and their parent Jie or Karamojong. The population table in the 1913 Handbook of the Uganda Protectorate gives the African population of Teso district as 250,141 compared with an approximate 50,000 in Karamoja and Lobor together. Although environment may be responsible for a rapid increase and famine may have resulted in a considerable fall in the population of Karamoja, it is inconceivable that the Iteso were ever so numerically inferior to the Jie or Karamojong that they could have been driven out by them. It must be assumed that the movement was a peaceful one prompted by economic necessity. The country round Kotido and in south Karamoja is semi-arid and badly watered and there is no reason to believe it was otherwise 250 years ago. It is reasonable also to suppose that the economy of the inhabitants at that time approximated to the economy of their present-day descendants, for little development has yet taken place in the area. The ancestors of the Iteso were nomadic pastoralists. They placed reliance more on their flocks and herds than on agriculture, but cultivated sorghum and perhaps finger millet. Though they lived in stockaded home-steads in the rainy season, they had to roam far afield in the dry season in search of water and grass for their stock on which they almost wholly depended. Any serious drought or any substantial increase in livestock or population caused economic distress which could only be remedied by the migration of some of the people.

It was probably a drought or famine which set the Iteso on their first migration; perhaps it was the same drought or famine which started the Luo migrations southwards. The numbers of families migrating may have been few at first but when the news of the new, rich land was spread, the numbers increased rapidly until the migratory stream reached the barrier of Lake Salisbury.

There the Iteso halted, for they had no knowledge of canoes. They settled, and their numbers multiplied by the arrival of new immigrants until further expansion was inevitable and the second migration started. To this day it is the inhabitants of Usuku who are properly known as Iteso whereas other members of the tribe are called by their territorial group names, Ingoratok or Iseera.

The focal point seems to have been Magoro. The population to the square mile is markedly higher in Magoro and Toroma than in any other part of Usuku although there are no differences in climate or soil fertility.

The second migration outwards from Usuku began only in the last 150 years. The great grandfathers of many of the modern generation were still living in Usuku approximately 120 years ago, though in one or two cases the second migration had started and the great-grandfathers had moved to Gweri or elsewhere. Thus in Bukedea, out of 56 persons questioned as to the place where their *ekek* (extended family) founder lived (usually the great grandfather), 22 answered Magoro and 19 Usuku, which was a vaguer answer which would include Magoro; 11 answered Kokorio, and 1 Tisai: both places are close to Magoro but on the route of the second migration; 3 answered Turkana, and, if their answer is to be believed, it might indicate that the first migration was still in process when the outward expansion from Usuku, the second migration, had begun.

The route taken during the first migration must remain a matter of conjecture. After the break from their parent tribe the Iteso, or Iworopom as they were then called, moved southwards towards Mount Moroto. From the few traditions that exist it is probable that they journeyed much farther south to the country between Mount Kadam and the Suk hills and entered what is now Teso district from the east near Angisa and perhaps also through the gap between Mount Akisim and Mount Napak. The most likely route would be along the watercourse known as Kiriki, Greek, or Kelim which drains into Lake Salisbury near Angisa. The recurrence of the same names for geographical features along the route southwards from Jie and in Teso district itself is interesting. Kapel occurs as the name of a rock in three places between Kotido and Nabilatuk in Karamoja and again in Teso where it appears on maps as Kapiri. Ngora and Komolo also appear along the route in Karamoja and in Teso. This recurrence is not, however, of real historical value, since many of the features are named after their shape (e.g. Moruita 'pointed rock') or after trees (e.g. Okoboi, 'Terminalia spekei'). Karamojong informants still point to the small hills between Nabilatuk and the Teso border, Moruaturkan, Thakale, and others, and claim that they remember the day when Iteso used to live on those hills.[1]

5. *The second migration*

Usuku is well watered and fertile compared with the semi-arid country round Kotido. Flocks and herds multiplied, and all the time there was the increasing flood of immigrants from Karamoja which was by the beginning of the twentieth century to swell the population to more than double the present-day population of all Karamoja. The new immigrants turned more to cultivation and homesteads became more fixed; the area under cultivation grew and uncultivated land in Magoro began to be scarce; all around were vast unoccupied areas.

The process of the second migration was a gradual one like that of the first migration. The first families to move out from the Magoro focus probably did so about 1800 while families were still arriving from Karamoja. The process continued throughout the century and the advance guards had already crossed the waters of the Lwere river and the Mpologoma, into Pallisa county of Bukedi district and into Busoga, when further expansion

[1] J. M. Watson (personal communication).

was blocked by the extension of British administration in the first decade of the twentieth century.

As the country is well watered and there were no hostile tribes, the new migrations were not confined to one particular route. All accounts agree that there were three main thrusts outwards from the focus at Magoro.[1] The first, a smaller movement than the other two, was northwards to Ngariam and Katakwi. The second was westwards by way of Kapujan in Toroma and Gweri to Soroti and thence fanwise to Serere and Amuria and the shores of Lake Kyoga. The third was southwards across the ford at Ochomai into Kapiri and thence fanwise through Ngora and Kumi counties to Bukedea and Pallisa. The second and third migratory streams met again along the waters of the Agu channel, which separates Serere and Ngora counties. The first and the second migratory streams met in western Amuria. All three movements were taking place at the same time.

Those who crossed the ford at Ochomai were the forefathers of the modern Ingoratok, and those who migrated north or west founded the Iseera. These two groups of the tribe, called after the places where they settled, Ngora and Serere, have differences in dialect, which is why the groups are called *ineresinei* (from *einer* 'to speak'), and in age-set ceremonies. The people of Bukedea are often classed as Ingoratok but by tradition are really a separate small group, the Ikidea, who migrated eastwards (*kide*) from the Ngora and Kanyum areas. Those who stayed in Usuku retained the name Iteso.

The spread of Iteso in the second migration had important economic effects on the tribe. The Jopaluo bartered iron hoes with the Lango and the Lango in their turn would retail their surplus hoes to the Kumam amongst whom they would exchange the hoes for cattle, three hoes—such was their scarcity—being the equivalent of one heifer.[2] Previous to this, the Iteso had used only wooden hoes. The Bantu tribes also carried on a lively trade with the Iteso on the Lake Kyoga littoral. Banyoro ironwork was exchanged for hides, skins, goats, and ivory. Bark cloth and beads were much welcomed trade goods, and the Kumam even in the early part of the twentieth century wore barkcloth strips. But the most notable imports were the sweet potato and the groundnut, both of which crops were previously unknown. Oleumo of Magoro, who is mentioned above, claims to recall the day when the Iteso had no knowledge of these crops. The fertility of the soil and the plentiful rainfall and consequent increased crop yields made the change from pastoralism to agriculture complete. This in turn had an effect on the size and construction of the family homestead. Homesteads became permanent, for there was ample land in the vicinity of the homestead even for shifting cultivation. The population began to increase rapidly.

The extension of trade with neighbouring tribes also brought the Iteso into contact with other foreigners. Among the wars recorded with the

[1] Wright, 1942.   [2] Driberg, 1923.

Lango is one between the Iteso of Katakwi and the Lango of Moroto county. The Iteso had killed Obwa Witum's brother when he came to sell ivory to one of the Arab or Abyssinian buyers.[1] There are stories of Arab slavers,

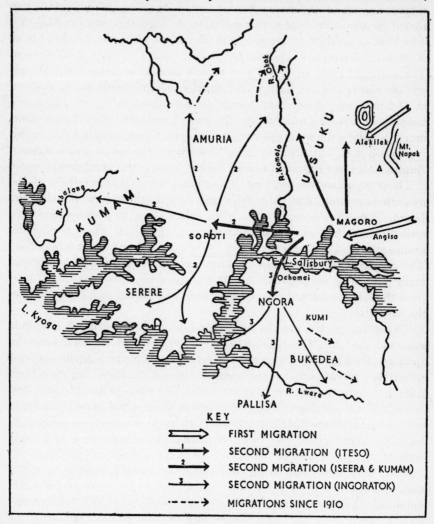

FIG. I. The migrations of the Teso tribe

who were greatly feared, who brought slaves across Lake Kyoga and were not averse to picking up more on the way. In 1897 the campaign against Kabarega and the Sudanese mutineers brought expeditions of Baganda. The Iteso and Kumam were looted and pillaged by both sides. They were also constantly at war among themselves until Semei Kakunguru brought a semblance of peace and order to the district.

[1] Tarantino, 1949 (ii).

6. *The Kumam in the second migration*

The Kumam traditions date back only to the time when they were living in the original Teso focus at Magoro. There is the story of a poor man named Aman who lived on the shores of Lake Salisbury. He moved to Soroti and became prosperous and the advance parties of his group pushed on to Kamuda and Lale without opposition.[1]

Evidence from an elderly Chopi informant indicates that the Kumam first came in contact with the Chopi at a time when the informant's great-grandfathers were alive, which would presumably be about 1840; the Kumam, who were known to the Chopi as Lango while the people now known as Lango were called Miro, had come from the direction of Kamuda and Lale and spoke a language which was foreign to the Nilotic-speaking Chopi.[2] Other traditions show that the ancestors of the Kumam came by way of Soroti, Lale, and Kamuda from Angodingod in Toroma.[2]

On this evidence it would appear that the break between the Teso and Kumam tribes is recent and dates only from the time of the second migration. Or if the Kumam migrated from Karamoja at approximately the same time as the Iteso and became a separate entity they must have followed the same migratory route and have been very friendly with the Iteso.

The former theory is the more likely. Driberg believes that the change in language among the Kumam took place within the period 1870–1920. It was not uncommon in his day to find old men in the Kumam villages who spoke nothing but their original Teso mother-tongue. Lango tradition, too, confirms that when the Lango first contacted the Kumam four days to the south-east (which would place them approximately near Magoro) they spoke a language unlike Lango but more like that of the Langudyang (Karamojong).[3] Kumam dances, ornaments, marriage customs, and agricultural methods are identical with the Teso ones. There is, moreover, an unbroken tradition of peace with the Iteso, and the Kumam and Iteso frequently intermarry.

Relations between the Lango and Kumam were also friendly before they came in close contact with each other and economic differences arose. In the beginning of the nineteenth century the second migration brought the Kumam up to the banks of the Omunyal river and the shores of Lake Kyoga in the modern Kaberamaido county without meeting any opposition. But when they advanced farther towards the Abalang river they met the Lango, who were migrating southwards and who had reached Ochero. This contact resulted in a breach of the friendly relations which had hitherto existed. In the ensuing fight the Kumam were routed by the Lango and driven back across the Omunyal river.[3]

[1] Wright, 1942.
[2] Walshe, 1947.
[3] Driberg, 1923.

Thereafter the initiative passed to the Lango, who continually raided the Kumam and penetrated as far as Katine near Soroti. The Kumam never again advanced beyond the Omunyal river until Semei Kakunguru with his army of Baganda took up their cause and established them on the line of the Abalang river.

CHAPTER II

KAKUNGURU'S EMPIRE, 1896–1904

1. *Semei Kakunguru*, 1895–9

SEMEI LWAKILENZI KAKUNGURU was already a tried general and important political figure in Buganda when he paid what was probably his first visit to Lango and Teso in 1895. He was married to a sister of the Kabaka Mwanga and after the Bunyoro campaign of 1893 had been allotted the chieftainship of part of the captured lands, the modern Bugerere county.

In 1895 Kakunguru joined William Grant's column with a force of some 400 Baganda. An attack was made on Kabarega's position opposite Mruli, which, although successful, failed to secure the capture of Kabarega. Forty Baganda were killed in action and Kakunguru withdrew to Bugerere. There followed a dispute with Apolo Kagwa, the Katikiro, which resulted in a court case at Mengo in which Kakunguru was severely fined. He thereupon resigned his office of *Kimbugwe*, withdrew from Buganda politics to his home in Bugerere, and thereafter turned his attention to Lango and Teso.

Captain Sitwell, in the course of a patrol of northern Buganda in February 1896, visited Kakunguru at his home in Bugerere and discussed means of coming to terms with the *Bakedi*, the naked tribesmen from the far side of Lake Kyoga, who were thought to be in league with Kabarega, and who periodically raided on the southern side of Lake Kyoga. With them Kakunguru was already gaining touch, laying the foundations of the influence which played so great a part in his subsequent career; and in September 1896 he brought a deputation of Kumam and Teso chiefs to Mengo to ask for protection against the Lango.[1]

It was in that year that he established his first fort in Teso on Kaweri island in Lake Kyoga with an expedition of fifty rifles under A. Gwantamu. Posts were also established on the two rocky islets in the vicinity. The remains of this occupation can be seen in the stone foundations of granaries, the mill-stones, and numerous nsambya trees. Kirkpatrick recorded that in 1898 'Kakunguru has a fort on Kaweri Island and says he is their chief. He says there are about 200 men on the island'.[2]

In the following year Kakunguru was fully occupied in campaigning against the mutineers, but in 1898 he accompanied Captain Kirkpatrick of the MacDonald expedition on a reconnaissance of Lake Kyoga. The following year with 440 Baganda auxiliaries he joined Lt.-Col. Evatt's 'Wakeddi Field Force' at Chiawanti in Lango. The force was ferried across Lake Kwania to the Namasale peninsula and in April 1899 surprised and

---

[1] Thomas, 1939.   [2] Kirkpatrick, 1899.

captured both Kabarega and Mwanga at Kangai. 'It is generally agreed that Kakunguru's influence enabled him to induce the Lango to reveal the enemy's movements; it is even claimed that he personally extracted Kabarega from the swamp in which he had taken refuge.'[1]

The acting Commissioner, Colonel Ternan, then placed Kakunguru in charge of the area to the north of Lake Kyoga 'to bring the unruly tribesmen under control and keep the region free of mutineer fugitives'.[1] He was given a number of guns but no subsidy and made his headquarters at Kagaa.

2. *Kakunguru's subjugation of Teso*

The fascinating story of how Kakunguru completed the subjugation of Teso and Mbale districts within the space of five years is told in a lengthy manuscript by one of his lieutenants, Simoni Waswa.[2] The pattern of occupation was everywhere the same; first an armed expedition would be made from an established fort to a new area; the pretexts were often obscure, sometimes a request for help from a warring faction or sometimes a threat of attack by local inhabitants; after skirmishes or pitched battles a new fort would be established and a garrison of armed Baganda installed. This garrison would then extend its influence over the surrounding countryside by establishing armed posts or minor forts. When local opposition had been overcome the region would be proclaimed a *saza*[3] and the smaller areas controlled by the outlying posts would be defined as *gombololas*. Baganda chiefs were appointed down to *muluka* level.

At the time of the capture of Mwanga and Kabarega in April 1899 Kakunguru's only fort was on Kaweri island. He immediately set to work to establish a base on the mainland in the heart of the area he was to administer. The fort at Kagaa in Lango close to the Teso border took only three weeks to build; its massive ramparts, which can be seen to this day, must have required the labour of many hundreds of unwilling workers. The Lango did not attack in force until after the fort was completed and they were then repulsed. Kakunguru at this time could command some 500 rifles, but they were not concentrated at Kagaa. Subsidiary posts had already been opened at Kangai, Ekwera, Dokolo, Akabo, Chakwara, and Aputi. Lango attacks continued, and within three months twenty-five Baganda had been killed in action. Nevertheless, in October 1899 Kakunguru felt he could leave Kagaa and journey to Serere peninsula by canoe, where he established a fort at Sambwe on the lake shore, which he left

---

[1] Thomas, 1939. [2] Waswa, 1950.

[3] *Saza* (more correctly *ssaza*) is the Luganda word for one of the administrative units into which Buganda was then and still is divided. Each *saza* is divided into a number of divisions known (in the singular) as *gombolola* (*ggombolola*) and each *gombolola* is in turn divided into a number of *miruka* (singular *muluka*). This Ganda system of administrative divisions was eventually adopted throughout Uganda. The equivalent English terminology, used elsewhere in this book, is 'county' for *saza*, 'sub-county' for *gombolola*, and 'parish' for *muluka*.

under the command of Maraki Magongo with ninety rifles. A new *saza*
was proclaimed, the first in Teso, organized on the Buganda model with
a hierarchy of Baganda chiefs. Occupation of the Serere peninsula involved
fighting and bloodshed, but contact had been established for some years
from Kaweri island and opposition was slight. Next month reinforcements
of 150 rifles arrived at Kagaa from Buganda and Kakunguru immediately
took the field against his principal enemy, the Lango. In a pitched battle
at Dokolo Baganda rifles triumphed over the bravery of the Lango;
casualties were heavy on both sides. The *saza* of Dokolo was then proclaimed. In eight months Kakunguru had lost seventy-three men in the
fighting and many more by disease. Early in 1900 he moved his headquarters from Kagaa fort to Bululu, which was made the headquarters of
a new *saza* of Kumam under Reuben Bitege.

Kakunguru's fame had spread as far as Usuku, for Omiat of Komolo came
to Bululu to beg his assistance against his neighbours. But Kakunguru had
now received a wider commission. Sir Harry Johnston had arrived in
Uganda to draw up the Buganda Agreement. There was no place in
Buganda for Kakunguru. He had quarrelled openly with Apolo Kagwa
and there was no room in Buganda for two such personalities as theirs.
Sir Harry Johnston was, however, so impressed by the capable manner in
which Kakunguru had set about his task of subjugating the Lango that he
proposed that he should be graded as a sort of Assistant District Commissioner; he told him 'to extend his influence eastwards through the Teso
country where scattered mutineers, Baganda rebels and Arab slave dealers
were harassing the country'.[1] In 1900 Kakunguru accordingly moved his
main force of 300 rifles through the Serere peninsula to Pallisa. He was
never again to be based in Teso, but he continued to direct operations from
his new headquarters in Bukedi and Bugishu districts.

The same technique was followed. He first assembled a field force at his
new headquarters in Bugwere by calling in some of the Serere and Kumam
garrisons and then presented a demand to the Teso chiefs to allow a fort
to be built at Bukedea. The field force of 350 rifles crossed the Lwere river
and routed the Iteso at Kidongole without difficulty. The Baganda found
Bukedea itself deserted. Scouting expeditions ranged as far as Mkongoro
and Agule, but on this occasion no forts were established. Kakunguru had
already become involved in his Bugishu campaigns, which demanded his
personal leadership. Nevertheless, at the end of 1900 he sent a force of
250 rifles from Pallisa to subjugate Ngora. A fort was established at Pege
in spite of vigorous opposition from the Iteso of Ngora and Kumi and, in
the following year, Ngora was proclaimed a *saza* under Jafari Mayanja.
On the way back to Pallisa the column built Mkongoro fort, the remains
of which can still be seen, and left a garrison of fifty rifles in it. The
Baganda did not have it all their own way, for an attempt to establish a fort
at Kumi was foiled by the Iteso of Nyero.

[1] Thomas, 1939.

These spectacular successes had lured large numbers of Baganda to Kakunguru's standard by promise of the quick rewards of a freebooter's life. He was unable or unwilling to check the excesses of these followers, who extorted and plundered without hindrance. Eventually complaints

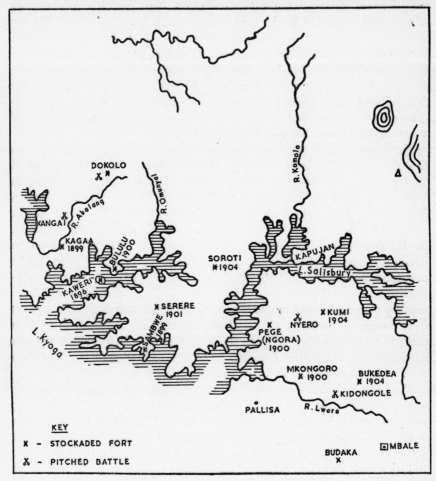

FIG. 2. Kakunguru's conquest of Teso, 1899–1904

filtered through to the British authorities and an administrative officer was sent to investigate. He found that the complaints were indeed justified; the country was desolated; food reserves and livestock were seized by the Baganda, and houses and crops destroyed. It was therefore decided that the British administration should assume direct control of the region.

Kakunguru was at Budaka surrounded by his satellite horde of armed Baganda. W. R. Walker, an administrative officer, with forty police was given the task of relieving him of his commission; he had to persuade Kakunguru to haul down the Union Jack he flew and to settle at Mbale without any executive authority. The negotiations were long and stormy, but Walker was at last successful. It was his followers, not Kakunguru himself, who had pillaged the country, and all these men had to be removed once Kakunguru had agreed to resign from the head of affairs. While Walker kept watch at Budaka, William Grant, the Provincial Commissioner, toured the Teso forts. At Bululu he left Musabira, a Munyoro, in charge with a Banyoro garrison. The Baganda were withdrawn from the outposts and concentrated at the new centre at Mbale. The same action was taken at Serere, where the *saza* fort had been built when Sambwe was abandoned, at Ngora and at Mkongoro; in these three centres Grant left parties of Uganda Government Police. Kakunguru's 5,000 minions congregated round him at Mbale and planted their gardens and trees. Apart from these garrisons at four centres in Teso there was no governmental control for the next two years, by which time an administrative centre had been opened in Mbale.

It was the first wish of the new administration that Kakunguru should complete his great work in Teso and in 1904 he was sent by the District Commissioner, Mbale, to establish posts at various places in Serere and at Soroti and Gweri, which had hitherto been unadministered. On this expedition forts were built at Kumi, which became the headquarters of a new *saza* including the old Ngora *saza*, and at Bukedea; outposts were established at Kapiri, Mukura, and Aturitur. Many of his Baganda followers were taken onto the government pay-roll and posted back to the outposts held before the withdrawal two years earlier. In the same year Soroti was constituted a *saza* under Reuben Bitege, who had formerly ruled Kumam, and Bukedea was placed under Luka Lukanda.

Kakunguru then disappeared from the Teso scene to engage in varied activities in Mbale and Busoga districts and to die, a bitter and fanatical old man, twenty-five years later.

3. *Kakunguru's legacy to Teso*

Teso's first experience of civilised ideas of government was brought by Semei Kakunguru, the able Muganda chief, who first reduced the district to order, cut the roads, and began to direct the local chiefs. The way in which he handled the country is a good illustration of the rare capacity of the Baganda for organisation and government, and also of their rapacity and overbearing tone towards all whom they consider beneath them. Order was indeed established, but rather after the method of making desolation and calling it peace; Kakunguru and his dependants accumulated cattle in large numbers, and many seem to have regarded the country as a sort of Eldorado, to which resort might be had in times of failure or disgrace at home.[1]

Although the excesses of his followers eventually brought about Kakunguru's downfall, his brief rule resulted in lasting benefits to the district.

[1] Kitching, 1912.

When he started his great work at Kagaa in 1899 he found warfare and anarchy; when he left Teso in 1904 the district was peaceful with an ordered government on the Buganda model, with a hierarchy of officials owing allegiance to a central power. It was organized into five counties under Baganda county chiefs, based on the forts at Bukedea, Kumi, Soroti, Serere, and Bululu. Any organization which might run contrary to his system he suppressed. The age-set ceremonies were rigidly forbidden by his followers either because they interfered with road making and other communal duties or because they were the basis of a military organization. So successful was this suppression that, in spite of the importance of these ceremonies in the social life of the people until that time, the structure of the ceremonies is today virtually forgotten. The organization of his government was so firmly established that it was accepted by the Iteso without opposition and it is even believed by some of the modern generation that the present system is indigenous.

His occupation affected the vocabulary of the country. It is to be expected that Luganda words would be adopted for objects with no Ateso equivalent such as *ekitabo* (book) and *emudu* (gun); Luganda borrowed many of these words from Kiswahili. But the influence of Luganda went much further and even common words have been replaced by Luganda equivalents such as *imisirin* (from the Luganda *emisiri* 'gardens') instead of the Ateso word *imanikoria*. Other examples are *egudo* (road), *amucalat* (lady), *emukopit* (peasant), *emusago* (court case), and *elukumit* (one thousand). In all these instances the Luganda form has been accepted into the Ateso language in preference to a vernacular word.

Of visible works his greatest achievement was his road system, which has formed the basis of the modern road network of the district. Although some of his roads have since been abandoned, their direction can still be seen by the lines of imported nsambya or mvule trees, which he caused to be planted at the roadsides. The roads, bridges, houses, and forts required a continual supply of local labour, which Kakunguru ensured was always forthcoming. When he built his station at Bululu he commanded labour from places as far afield as Asuret, Arapai, Soroti, Lale, Kamuda, and Katine. His forts soon fell into disrepair for they were not required. The work of subjugation had been quickly and efficiently done and there was little recourse to further fighting.

CHAPTER III

FIFTY YEARS OF BRITISH
ADMINISTRATION, 1904–54

1. *Teso administered from Mbale*, 1904–09

The distant administrators of Mbale could exercise but scant control over the vast expanses of Mbale and Teso districts. Intelligence reports as late as 1908 show that Teso was then unmapped and largely unexplored. The Baganda at the various outposts could but rarely be visited and unadministered tribes on the northern and eastern marches caused continual trouble. The collector at Mbale was informed by W. D. M. (Karamoja) Bell in 1906 of armed raids on the Iteso by 'Greeks and a Somali'.

Musabira, who had been left by Grant in charge of Kumam county at Bululu in 1902, was shortly afterwards killed by the Lango while on a punitive expedition in their country. His death was, however, unlucky for the Lango. His relative, Kazana, who succeeded him, was an able general and inflicted several crushing defeats on the Lango. Under his protection the Kumam moved up to the Abalang river never to leave that country again. 'Unassisted by Government, he extended his influence over the whole Kumam area. This very considerable influence Kazana placed unreservedly at the disposal of Government, when in 1907 British administration was commenced at Bululu.'[1] His influence was indeed considerable. It is recorded in the 1908 intelligence report that 'there is a stream six feet deep and eight feet wide running between Terrerie and Papaye, which divides Kazana's country from the Mbale district'.[2] Driberg ranks Kazana in his day as the most potent enemy with whom the Lango have had to deal.[3] Kazana followed Kakunguru's policy of alliance with the Kumam against the Lango. 'In spite of vigorous resistance the Lango were forced back almost to the line of the Abalang, with the exceptions of Agaya (now known as Kagaa or Ochero) and their outposts on the Namasale peninsula, and Kazana introduced among the Akum, who were now fast spreading westwards, a system of administration planned on the Baganda model. This system he organized and developed, including within its scope the Lango settlements at Agaya and Awelo.'[3] Kazana was recognized as chief of the Kumam country when British administration was extended to that part of Uganda, and he continued in office until his retirement in 1918. With the opening of the first administrative station in Teso at Bululu in 1907 responsibility for the Kumam area passed from Mbale. More than thirty years were to elapse before it was again included in Teso district.

[1] Uganda Protectorate, 1913.
[2] Ibid., 1908 (ii).
[3] Driberg, 1923.

Bululu was soon abandoned in favour of Nabieso and little remains today to mark the site of the station except the well-tended graves of the two officers who died there.

There were troubles on the eastern border. Kakunguru had never seriously attempted to administer Usuku. Some Baganda had settled at Kokorio on the north shore of Lake Salisbury in 1901 but an administrative post was not established there until 1905 when posts were added also at Kapujan, Amusia, and Magoro. This invasion from across the lake was resented and in 1907 it was necessary for the District Commissioner, Mbale, to take a force of police to arrest the ringleaders of the opposition at Toroma. Meanwhile, an attempt was made to open the way to Usuku across the Komolo swamp, and Reuben Kagwa led an expedition to found an outpost at Abela Rock. There was a pitched battle with the Iteso, who were worsted, but when the Baganda tried to establish a post at Katakwi, they were driven back to their base. In 1908 Enosi Kagwa Rujumba advanced again to the Komolo and established a fort; in the following year, with Baganda reinforcements from various places in Teso and from Mbale, he succeeded in making forts at Abela and Usuku which became the headquarters of a new *saza* under his rule. Attempts to extend his influence to Ngariam were repulsed. Affairs in the new county were at that time dominated by Okolimong, whose position was strengthened by his allegedly magic powers. He had foretold the coming of the Baganda 'wearing clothes which look like butterflies'. Fortunately his attitude was friendly and his influence ensured that the new county quickly became settled.

From the outset the British administration confirmed the position of local Iteso leaders. Outstanding among these was Oumo of Kumi, whose influence extended over a large part of Kumi county and over the lake to Magoro. He was a man of considerable wealth 'whose home at Kabata covered an area of half a square mile and whose children formed two football teams'. At Ngora Ijala commanded equal prestige. Ijala had quarrelled with his father, who had forced him to leave home and take refuge with friends in Busoga. There he acquired a knowledge of Luganda. When Kakunguru set up his headquarters in Pallisa, Ijala joined him and returned to Ngora in 1901 with the Baganda column to take his revenge. He soon persuaded his Baganda overlords to kill his father and to put him in his place. Under Baganda protection he extended his influence over the whole of the Ngora county. His rule was precarious in its early stages and his houses were fortified and continually guarded. Both Oumo and Ijala remained in power after the administrative station was established at Kumi in 1909. Ijala was, however, soon in trouble for cutting off a man's ears for committing adultery with one of his wives. He survived this misdemeanour, although the District Commissioner, Kumi, fined him twenty head of cattle.

Except in the outlying parts of Usuku there was little trouble in the district and by 1908 the country was settled enough for the first missionary,

Rev. A. L. Kitching of the C.M.S., to build his house at Ngora. In the 1908 Intelligence Report it is recorded that 'there are Hindi shops at Bululu, Serere, Angorla, Kangoro, Kumi, Makurrah, Kapiri, Seroti and Kararki'.[1] In 1909 a sub-station of the Mbale collectorate was established at Kumi.

2. *The introduction of cotton*

The opening of Kumi administrative station marked the start of an economic revolution in Teso. Credit for the introduction of cotton into the district probably belongs to the C.M.S. It is recorded that in the 1908/9 season 4,056 lb. of seed cotton were obtained from Kumi district. Government followed up this modest beginning with an all out effort with spectacular results. In 1909 a cotton instructor was appointed and a year later a ploughing instructor started a ploughing school at Kumi; and in the following year the first cotton experimental station was founded at Kadungulu. Within a year the cotton crop had jumped from 4,656 lb. to 500 tons, which was one-eighth of Uganda's total crop. Thereafter it rose rapidly to 8,836 tons in 1913/14, which was one-third of the Protectorate crop. This rapid increase was not achieved without much patient experimental work by the District Agricultural Officer, R. G. Harper, who spent some fourteen years of his service in Teso. It was Harper who evolved N.32 seed to replace the Allen and Sunflower, thereby improving the yield and bringing increased wealth to the district. In the first year of the new seed the crop rose from 2,424 to 11,803 tons, although the acreage cultivated rose only from 47,000 to 84,000. His N.17 seed was even more successful and was still in use in very recent times. Harper stayed in Teso long enough to witness the closing in 1916 of the Kadungulu Experimental Station, where he had begun his work, in favour of a site at Simsa near Soroti and, in 1920, the removal from Simsa to the present site of the experimental station at Serere.

An equally important innovation was the plough, which made the planting of increased acreages of cotton possible. Progress was, however, slow to begin with. In the ploughing school's first year sixteen oxen were provided by chiefs for training and 20 acres were ploughed at Ngora. Soon chiefs began to buy their own ploughs. Nevertheless, in spite of a second ploughing school at Kadungulu, there were only about 200 ploughs in use in the district by 1920. It had been difficult to obtain ploughs during the war years and prices had risen, but in that year supplies began to be more plentiful and prices began to drop. Thereafter the number of ploughs in the district rose in a spectacular manner to some 40,000 at the present day.

The rapid increase in the cotton crop produced an equally rapid expansion in communications. The seed cotton had at first to be transported to Kampala or to Kenya for ginning. There were no carts in the district—the

[1] Uganda Protectorate, 1908 (ii).

first ox-cart to be seen in Teso was brought by the ploughing instructor who opened the Kumi ploughing school in 1910—and the roads were in any case unfit for such traffic. The whole cotton crop had to be carried by head-loads to the lake ports. In two months in 1914 no less than 38,000 porters had to be found by the administration for this purpose and 5,000 tons of cotton were moved in this way. Meanwhile efforts were being made to find better means of transport and by 1917 it was recorded that 'porter transport of cotton is now, it is hoped, a thing of the past.'[1]

Donkeys and camels were tried without success, but it was on a canal for marine transport from Lake Kyoga to Lake Salisbury that the administration pinned its early hopes. The scheme was never successful but it was not finally abandoned until 1918 after considerable expenditure and effort. In 1913 some 900 men were employed on weed cutting in the channel from Sambwe to Agu. The cost of extending the canal to Lake Salisbury was then estimated at only £2,125.

The passage if made successfully would be the most important development scheme accomplished in the district. It would open up the rich country north of Lake Salisbury and bring it and the as yet unadministered country on its borders within a few days of Jinja and along its whole length the canal would serve the richest cotton growing area in the Protectorate.[2]

Grave difficulties were soon apparent. Mechanical weed-cutters were not available and cutting by hand was unpopular and slow. Although a channel was cleared as far as Agu, it quickly became blocked again and additional labour had to be found to secure the sides of the canal with stakes. After survey a fear was expressed that an extension of the canal to Lake Salisbury might lower the level of water in that lake. Nevertheless, by 1914 steamers of the Busoga Railway Marine were plying regularly at Bugondo, and two new ports were opened at Sambwe and Lale. A lighter worked between Agu and Sambwe 'handling about 30 tons of cargo a month, a fraction of the amount of cargo available for export from this port'.[3] The inland waterways of the district were put to good use. Fleets of canoes owned by the missions or by the native administration ferried cotton across Lake Salisbury and from Meroki to Lake Kyoga. As late as 1918 'the half-pressed bales from the Kumi and Toroma ginneries of the Uganda Company are transported to Gweri by Lukiko canoes across Lake Salisbury. They are then carted over the earth road to Soroti for pressing and the bales are finally shipped at Lale'.[4] The outbreak of war reduced the funds available for weed cutting and a startling drop in the water level in 1917 and 1918 eventually killed all hopes of steamers using Agu port; even at Lale the steamer had to stand well out in the lake.

The need for a port at Agu in any case no longer existed. After the establishment of two ginneries at Bugondo by the B.E.A. Corporation and

[1] Teso District Annual Report, 1916/17.
[2] Ibid., 1912/13.
[3] Ibid., 1913/14.   [4] Ibid., 1917/18.

the Bukedi (Uganda) Cotton Trading Company in 1912, the number of ginneries in Teso rose rapidly. Two years later there were five, and five years later ten, ginneries working. By 1920 the number had risen to twenty; this number proved uneconomic and within a few years some ginneries fell silent.

A steady effort had meanwhile been made to improve road transport. In 1913 work was begun on the metalling and culverting of main roads, and some commercial firms began to use ox-carts. Their experiments were sometimes premature, for earth roads did not stand up to this traffic. By 1915 the road from Bugondo to Serere had been metalled and a steel bridge constructed at Kyere, while on the southern side of the water a metalled road ran from Kumi to the ferry at Agu. The road from Soroti to Lale port was by then strong enough to carry the steam tractor and trucks of the Bombay Uganda Syndicate. Shortly after the war the roads had been improved to such an extent that motor transport became possible and by 1929 the railway had reached Soroti.

3. *Teso administered from Kumi*, 1909-14

The rapid expansion of communications for the needs of the cotton industry was only one of many problems which faced the early administrators in Teso. The many urgent tasks which this expansion entailed necessitated the establishment of a full administrative post within the area. Teso district was formally constituted by proclamation of 11 July 1912. Previously the area administered from Kumi had been part of Bukedi district administered from Mbale, although for all practical purposes it had been a separate district since the station was first opened at Kumi in 1909. Kakunguru's administrative arrangement, whereby the whole area was divided into five counties of Bukedea, Kumi, Serere, Soroti, and Usuku, was retained in the new district. The boundaries of the new district were approximately the same as they are today except that the modern Kaberamaido county formed part of Lango district; northern Amuria and the country round Omoro was included in the district but was unadministered.

This unadministered territory to the north and north-east caused immediate difficulties.

The general state of native affairs in that part of Usuku county bordering on the Koromojan unadministered territory was far from satisfactory throughout the year. The chiefs and people in this county are very backward and it will be some years before agents can be removed with safety. Lawless behaviour was frequent and several murders were committed, the people taking refuge in Koromoja in anticipation of enquiry and proceedings as they also do on the approach of tax-collectors. In January serious disturbances occurred. The natives of the Nariam and Adachal centres under Headman Jotum murdered Chief Amuge and 17 of his people and carried off a number of cattle. They fled into Koromoja with their cattle on the approach of the district officers. . . .[1]

[1] Teso District Annual Report, 1913/14.

In the north the Lango living in the unadministered part of the district continually raided their more peaceful neighbours near Orungo. In 1914 punitive measures were undertaken by the District Commissioner with a patrol of the King's African Rifles. The raiding Lango were effectively punished and stolen cattle restored, but no immediate effort was made to extend administration beyond Orungo. The patrol then proceeded successfully to avenge the murder of Chief Amuge. Jotum himself was shot while resisting arrest and the stolen cattle were recovered.

Raids by the Lango continued until in 1915 permission was obtained to establish a post at Omoro in the heart of the unadministered country. The post was under a Muganda agent and visited monthly by administrative officers. Although it was resented by some local headmen, against whom strong action had to be taken, there was no further need to resort to armed force. Within two years the Lango in the area were planting cotton and paying tax. Omoro was shortly afterwards constituted as a separate county, which was ceded to Lango district a few years after the war in the administrative reorganization, which also transferred Bukedea county to Bugwere district.

4. *The First World War*

The administrative centre at Kumi had been sited as a sub-station of Mbale and, although the population is heaviest in the neighbourhood of Kumi, it was soon found that the station was inconveniently placed as the headquarters of the new Teso district. The decision to move to Soroti 'for administrative reasons' was taken shortly after the formal constitution of the district in 1912. Soon after his appointment as Governor, Sir Frederick Jackson toured across Lake Salisbury to Soroti. His diary for 11th August 1911 reads, 'Stayed at Seroti and climbed hill to get a view of the country. Could see no better place for a station.' The move took place shortly before the outbreak of war two years later. The new station had an unlucky start. Within four months the District Commissioner and another officer had died of blackwater fever. The only permanent buildings on the new site were two houses and the district office and strong-room. The war effectively stopped all further development, so that living and working conditions for the government staff were far from satisfactory. At the end of the war the District Commissioner recorded somewhat peevishly that 'in spite of the heavy influx of European officials into the district, attention was being given to building of an experimental laboratory at Serere in preference to much needed housing in Soroti'.[1] The opening of Bugondo as a port and the erection there of two ginneries in 1912 had made it the trade centre of the district. Plans and surveys were made in anticipation of Bugondo developing as the largest town in the district. The traders were at first slow to move to the new headquarters at Soroti. Transport and mail facilities

[1] Teso District Annual Report, 1920.

were better at Bugondo and even as late as 1919 all telegrams from Soroti had to be sent to Bugondo post office by runner. Nevertheless, in spite of restrictions caused by the war, the new township at Soroti continued to grow. By 1917 'building of permanent shops at Soroti has proceeded in spite of the war. . . . Bugondo is now stagnant and has little trade except what is brought by the two ginneries.'[1] When to commemorate peace in 1919 the District Commissioner planted the avenue of jacaranda trees, which is still a feature of the town, Soroti had taken on its present form and layout. It was not the last time that there was talk of moving the district headquarters. The site near the rock was hot and malarial, whereas on the watershed at Arapai less than 7 miles away the climate was noticeably cooler and fresher. When the railway survey showed that the railway station was to be sited at Arapai there was an added reason for moving the town. But while the pros and cons were discussed, more buildings went up and the chances of removal grew more remote. The idea was not, however, formally abandoned until the end of the Second World War.

Teso's considerable manpower was used in the early years of the war on the increased production of cotton and on the road works and porterage tasks necessary to move the crop. Efforts to recruit for the Carrier Corps for service in German East Africa began in 1917, but out of nearly 18,000 men collected over 14,000 were rejected on medical grounds and the attempt was abandoned. Nevertheless, operations by the King's African Rifles against the Turkana necessitated the employment of large numbers of porters to carry the supplies of the expedition from the base at Lale port to Moroto in Karamoja. In 1918 the number so employed from Soroti and Usuku counties was over 32,000, and much of the time and effort of chiefs and administrative officers was spent in raising and controlling this army of carriers. The number of Iteso who served in the German East African campaign was not great. Many of these were absorbed at the close of hostilities into the force of chiefs' police, which was first formed in 1919 to guard the communal food reserves necessitated by the recent famine.

Hitherto the effort of the British administration had been directed mainly towards the establishment of law and order and the encouragement of cotton planting. The district and the people had other needs. The end of the war enabled the Uganda Government to recruit the necessary staff and devote funds to much-needed social and economic development in Teso.

5. *Economic and social development*

Although Harper's work at the experimental farm at Kadungulu was concentrated on the improvement of cotton strains, food crops were not neglected. 'Experiments with new food crops have been made at Kadungulu but it is doubtful whether the natives, who are no less conservative than Europeans in the matter of diet, will take to any new foodstuffs for some

[1] Teso District Annual Report, 1916/17.

time to come or alter appreciably their methods of cultivation.'[1] This forty-year-old prophecy has proved true in spite of the improvements achieved.

The drought, which in 1918 caused lake levels to drop to such an extent that the steamer was forced to anchor some miles out at Lale, while canoes could no longer ply on Lake Salisbury, caused widespread famine throughout the district in the following year. The now familiar system of compulsory grain storage at chiefs' headquarters, which later gave way in Teso to compulsory storage at the family home, was started as a result of this famine; communal plots of millet were grown under supervision in every village area. Nevertheless, in 1927 it was recorded that 'famine is at hand due to the negligence of the native. It is to be regretted that despite the large agricultural staff in Teso, no improvements in agriculture can be chronicled beyond a slight increase in the number of ploughs (2941) in use and the inauguration by the administration of acre plots at each gombolola.'[2]

This stricture was not deserved. The agricultural experimental station had been moved during the war years to Simsa, near Soroti, and in 1920 to Serere. In the early years of this new station the farm on the hillside quickly lost its fertility through soil erosion. As a result of this discovery considerable experimental work on measures to combat soil erosion was undertaken, and Teso district reaped the early benefit of this work. Strip-cropping and bunding are now such features of the countryside that it is apt to be forgotten that they were introduced so recently.

Famine relief had to be undertaken on a large scale in 1928, and many of the roads in Teso were constructed at this time in return for food for the labourers and their families. Perhaps as a result of this famine attempts were made to increase food production by opening up estates both by private enterprise and by direct government action. The idea was not new. In 1920 a representative of the London Produce Company had visited Teso and submitted a scheme to the newly formed Uganda Development Commission for clearing and planting a cotton estate of 8,000 acres. The scheme was not accepted, but the Bombay Uganda Company obtained land for a small estate at Achuna, and in 1929 a start was made by Government on stumping and ploughing large areas of land near the new railway station at Soroti and at Tira for use by Iteso cultivators. Further areas were chosen at Ngora, but the economies in staff and funds caused by the world slump curtailed and eventually stopped the scheme when little more than 100 acres had been cleared.

In 1931 'all agricultural activity was considerably influenced by the locust infestation. The major part of the wimbi, maize and mtama crop was completely destroyed. . . .'[3]

The heavy pressure on the land in south Teso and the consequent inevitable deterioration of the soil posed a problem to the administration, which has yet to be solved. In the north-eastern parts of the district there

---

[1] Teso District Annual Report, 1912/13.
[2] Ibid., 1927.
[3] Ibid., 1931.

was still land in abundance, but the bush was thick, water was scarce, and communications did not exist. It was believed that the prevailing north-east winds would spread the desert conditions of Karamoja westwards into Teso and thereby reduce the fertility of the land. The Teso Informal Committee, the forerunner of the district team, came into being in the 1930's to consider ways and means of tackling these problems.[1] The Teso Resettlement Scheme, which was the outcome of its deliberations, was never fully implemented and no organized removal of families from south Teso took place. But it resulted in the establishment of a Crown Forest Reserve on the Karamoja border and, in recent years, in the construction of communications and water supplies which have encouraged voluntary resettlement.

The Iteso did not have to rely entirely on the products of the soil in times of famine. The district supports a large cattle population, which, as a result of patient government endeavour, now represents a considerable source of wealth. Before the advent of the British administration disease took heavy toll of the cattle population every year. The disastrous rinderpest outbreak of 1890 is still remembered as the first real date in Teso history. A stock census taken in 1912 recorded only 115,991 head of cattle in an area approximating in size to the present-day district, without Kaberamaido county, with its 632,000. A European stock inspector was posted to the district from 1913 onwards, and veterinary officers visited as occasion demanded until a permanent posting was made immediately after the First World War. Their task was formidable and was probably accomplished so successfully only because continuity of staff was in those days deemed essential. H. A. Strauss, the first stock inspector, served in Teso nine years and W. S. Aitken, the first veterinary officer, for as long.

The export trade was quickly organized, although it was frequently interrupted by outbreaks of disease. 'There is considerable trade in cattle both among natives themselves and also with outsiders. Many cattle are sent annually to Mbale and Jinja for slaughter and some have also been exported to East Africa (Kenya). Immune cattle are very scarce on account of the shortage of staff of the veterinary division.'[2] This shortage of staff was remedied soon after the war, when an all out attack on cattle disease was launched. The veterinary staff in Teso in 1921 totalled eight Europeans. By 1926 at least one of the major scourges, pleuro-pneumonia, had been brought under control. 'With the exception of Usuku county there is little fear for there being a spread of pleuro-pneumonia . . .';[3] and two years later: 'Pleuro-pneumonia has now practically been stamped out in Teso.'[4] But rinderpest outbreaks continued to dislocate trade, involving heavy calls on staff. In 1928 seven veterinary officers and five stock inspectors were working on rinderpest control in Teso and the disease has remained a potential source of danger to the present day. But the organization in the

[1] Uganda Protectorate, 1937.   [2] Teso District Annual Report, 1916/17.
[3] Ibid., 1926.   [4] Ibid., 1928.

1930's of special export markets and inoculation of all cattle within the areas bordering on Karamoja have considerably reduced the danger.

The patient teaching of Roman Catholic and Protestant missionaries began even before the establishment of an administrative station in the district, when the Rev. A. L. Kitching of the C.M.S. founded the mission station at Ngora in 1908 and was followed soon afterwards by the fathers of the Mill Hill Mission.

It is to these missionaries that the Iteso owe the advances in education which have enabled them to progress with such rapidity. The administration relied entirely on the mission schools for the supply of Iteso chiefs to replace the Baganda agents. Not the least of the early difficulties in the educational field centred on the choice of language.

Luganda is becoming more widely spoken and tends to increase in use while education is in the hands of Luganda-speaking missionaries. . . . Seeing the difficulty of the Teso tongue, the small area of the Protectorate in which it is spoken, and the unlikelihood of any distrct officer, always subject to sudden transfer, ever acquiring the native language to a degree sufficient for carrying on business, the change is not unwelcome. Like other outlandish dialects (such as Welsh and Erse) its disuse might well be encouraged in favour of the language of the largest and most intelligent portion of the country of which it forms part.[1]

The Ateso language had wide differences of dialect due to the early migrations of the tribe already described. The early missionaries at Ngora, who first reduced the language to writing, naturally took the dialect of Ngora as the norm. Unfortunately, Roman Catholic and Protestant endeavour in this field was not welded together in the early days, and divergences in meaning and orthography were perpetuated. Luganda remained for many years the language of officialdom and even the medium of instruction in schools. 'Luganda is becoming widely spoken among the chiefs and headmen owing largely to mission influence and to that of the many Baganda in the district and it would now be possible to make the speaking of this language a qualification for Government employment.'[2] But one of the first decisions of the District Education Board which was set up in 1925 was to introduce Ateso as the medium of instruction in elementary schools. There was still need of a lingua franca. Within a year or two Kiswahili was officially adopted in place of Luganda but never prospered, because of mission opposition, and has in recent years been discarded in favour of English.

The Church, like the Government, relied on Baganda workers for its early effort. A Muganda missionary, Andereya Batulabude, had begun evangelical work in Teso some years before Rev. A. L. Kitching's arrival. The first African candidates for ordination were Baganda, but training of Iteso church workers went rapidly ahead. The Native Anglican Church quickly expanded until in 1926 Rev. A. L. Kitching was consecrated the first bishop of the newly created Upper Nile diocese. His cathedral was at Ngora where he had started his work twenty years earlier.

[1] Teso District Annual Report, 1912/13.   [2] Ibid., 1914/15.

The work of the Christian missions was not confined to religion and education. The C.M.S. undertook pioneer work on the control of leprosy. Dr. C. A. Wiggins, after retirement from the post of Director of Medical Services in Uganda shortly after the First World War, devoted himself to this work. He joined the staff of the Freda Carr C.M.S. hospital, recently founded under the direction of Dr. E. V. Hunter, where he started a leper ward. In 1928, in co-operation with Government, he established several leprosy clinics in the district. While attendance was compulsory much useful work was done, but within a year attendance was made voluntary and the clinics ceased to justify the effort. Dr. Wiggins then started a hospital for leper children at Kumi and an adult centre at Kapiri. Shortly before the adult centre was moved to its present site at Ongino a few years later, this valuable work passed to other hands; it has continued to expand and some 800 lepers not only from Teso but also from the neighbouring districts are now under treatment at this leper mission.

The early efforts of the Government Medical Department were devoted to the control of plague and small-pox, which took heavy toll of life each year. The early Baganda conquerors of Teso suffered over 1,500 casualties from disease, mainly small-pox and plague. The Indian medical officer at Kumi himself perished while combating an outbreak of plague in Usuku. In the early days, little could be done beyond isolating affected persons and burning the houses in which the cases occurred. By 1917 a medical officer had been appointed and vaccination and inoculation were started; nevertheless, in that year there were 827 deaths from plague and 1,729 from small-pox. It was some time before the district was free. In 1929 'work in Mkongoro and Kanyum was at a standstill from June owing to plague. Plague also interfered with trade in Soroti from August to December.'[1] The eradication of these two diseases owes much to the work of the early health inspectors and above all to R. C. D. Hooper, who served for many years in the district. The Iteso have given him a lasting testimonial by coining the word *ehupa* into the language to mean a health inspector.

6. *Native administration*, 1909–37

The British administration, when it took over Kakunguru's organization, found it necessary and convenient to use Baganda executive staff. But from the beginning a consistent policy was adopted of replacing Baganda by native officials. This was no easy task, for the local population was uneducated and untrained. It says much for the honest application of this policy that its logical conclusion was achieved within such a short period of time. By 1913 the organization of native administration in the district was complete. Iteso chiefs had been appointed to all sub-counties and a county council had been established in each county, consisting of the local chiefs under the presidency of one of their number. These councils were

[1] Teso District Annual Report, 1929.

deliberative and judicial bodies, but had no executive functions. Baganda agents were retained to assist and to instruct most of these sub-county chiefs and it was these agents who held the real executive power. But the reduction in their numbers was so rapid as to give local administrators some cause for alarm.

In regard to the Government agents who have been so largely responsible for the training and organization of the native government and to whom has been ascribed the rapid progress of the district and its present day peacefulness and prosperity, a radical change of policy has been introduced from headquarters. These agents were placed in charge of the chiefs to instruct them in proper methods of conduct and control of their people and they have been withdrawn from such charges as and when their chiefs have proved themselves fit to rule alone. Last year five chiefs were in accordance with this policy declared independent and the agents withdrawn from their countries. This year a further six were emancipated. During the year, however, instructions were received that the establishment of agents was to be substantially reduced and at the close of the year eighteen had to be withdrawn. This has involved the making independent of fourteen more chiefs, some of whom were indeed ready for emancipation; but others were not ready and some anxiety is felt as to the effects of this acceleration. . . .[1]

In spite of the outbreak of war the policy was steadily carried out. The training of local chiefs owes much to W. G. Adams who was District Commissioner throughout most of the war years. When he left Teso in 1919 the process was almost complete and only the county agents remained. There were no longer anxieties concerning the speed at which the policy was implemented, only doubt that the agents themselves had been adequately recompensed by the Government for the valuable services they had rendered. When the Native Law Ordinance came into force the following year, the District Native Council was formed to consider alterations to customary law.

The institution of this Council is a good forward step making the time closer when the district will be sufficiently advanced to govern its own people without the help of Baganda agents. These agents have done, and continue to do, extremely good work, but . . . the policy to be followed is the ultimate total retrenchment of these agents when the Lukiko and the chiefs are in a sufficiently advanced stage to govern by themselves, rather than their permanent retention on the score that 'we get on very well as we are'.[2]

Up to 1919 each county was regarded as a watertight compartment and only a native of a county could become a chief in it. A wider view of district administration demanded that the best use should be made of the talent in the whole district. 'They are all Teso and under Soroti as headquarters of the district.'[3] So began the idea of a local government service. The talent at that time was to be found in Kumi county. 'Kumi on account of its

---

[1] Teso District Annual Report, 1912/13.
[2] Ibid., 1919/20.   [3] Ibid., 1920.

supremacy in intellect produced by the two Ngora schools has been for some time the exemplary county of the district. During the last few months many changes have been made throughout the district in respect of gombolola chiefdoms, and Kumi has been extensively drawn from to fill vacancies.'[1] These appointments of Ingoratok chiefs in other parts of the district were to be the cause of resentment in later years.

The final stage of retrenchment of Baganda was begun the next year with the appointment of the first Etesot county chief, Nasanaeri Iporiket, to Kumi county. This experiment was quickly followed by installing Enoka Epaku, Eria Ochom, and Isaka Onaba as the first county chiefs of Soroti, Usuku, and Serere counties. This arrangement suffered an initial set-back by the death of one of these men and of his successor within a year. Talent was so scarce that this loss was serious. But this fact alone did not explain the failure of the experiment. The doubts of the early administrators regarding the pace at which the policy should be implemented were perhaps well founded, for by 1926 affairs were far from satisfactory:

> The total revenues accruing to chiefs from licit and illicit sources is excessive for their needs and quite disproportionate to their responsibilities and public services in general. A principal difficulty with which the Government has to contend is the very small difference in intelligence, mentality or character between the most retrograde peasant and the best of the chiefs. There has been no ruling class in the country in the past and the majority of the chiefs approximate in reality more nearly to petty officials of a clerkly type than to real chiefs or leaders of the people, who could by precept and example ensure any proper progress of the race. Stability of character, whether good or bad, is in the present phase conspicuously weaker than is found in the average African race. This is probably due to the suppression of their natural tribal characteristics by importation of Baganda ideas, which have not been either complete or very suitable to the natural genius of the tribe. . . .[2]

Two county chiefs were publicly dismissed the following year and deported from the district, one of whom was the same Enoka Epaku who had so hopefully been appointed at the beginning of the experiment only seven years before. The remaining county chiefs were given smaller areas to control by splitting all the counties into two and thereby forming the new counties of Amuria, Napak, Kasilo, and Ngora in addition to the former counties of Soroti, Usuku, Serere, and Kumi. Baganda agents were again introduced, not as executive heads of counties, but as advisers to a group of counties. Timuteo Mukasa supervised Kumi, Ngora, Usuku, and Napak, and Eria Gyagenda the remainder.

This time there was no retrogression and by 1937 the time had come to take another step forward. The spread of education had resulted in a class of educated or semi-educated men, who wished to share in the administration of local affairs, but who were often feared and repressed by the chiefs,

---

[1] Teso District Annual Report, 1920.　　　　[2] Ibid., 1926.

many of whom were of inferior education. It was to counteract the obvious
dangers of this situation that the District Commissioner, F. R. Kennedy,
worked out the system of councils in Teso, which with local variations was
later introduced in all other districts of the Protectorate. The council of
chiefs had, of course, been in existence for many years, but its function
was judicial or advisory and its composition exclusively chiefly. Under
Kennedy's scheme this autocratic body had to give way to representative
councils of peasants, traders, and schoolmasters. Such a novel conception
would hardly have achieved the success it did, had not the District Commissioner ensured that it contained a strong element of appeal to local
sentiment. In the surge of national enthusiasm at this time the Luganda
words for units of administration, such as *saza* and *gombolola*, were discarded in favour of the Ateso *ebuku* and *etem*. Kennedy organized his new
councils on these convenient units of administration, which had been
imposed by Kakunguru and accepted by the Iteso; at the same time he
tried to build on the Teso political organization, which had existed before
the Baganda conquest. But the only political organization of the Iteso was
the age-set system, which had been destroyed by Kakunguru's command.
The inclusion in the new councils of clan leaders (*apolok ka atekerin*)
proved a happy alternative. This move ensured popular support for the
councils, although clans have no political significance in Teso and clan
leaders are in effect petty chieftains.

The bulk of elected members were recruited from the ranks of the so-called
'clan' or 'kinship group' leaders, who for the most part inherit their positions.
There is thus a nucleus on the councils of men accustomed to command respect
and brought up with a sense of duty to the community. It seems worthy of note
that the authority of these clan leaders, . . . whose existence and potentialities
had for years been ignored, has now been sufficiently revived to enable them once
again to become a vital force in the tribe. The restoration of their prestige and
authority was at first obstructed by the chiefs who, having themselves no
hereditary claims, feared rivalry from these men who have. Their fears have,
however, been put to rest by the whole-hearted manner in which the clan leaders
have co-operated with them in the work of administration.[1]

Kennedy's experiment was the start of local government in Teso.

7. *The Second World War and after*

The institution of the council system was as much a political revolution as
the introduction of cotton was an economic one; it began the inevitable
curtailment of the legislative, advisory, and policy-making powers of a
powerful, small group of bureaucratic chiefs, and substituted a democratic
system of local government. At first no violent changes were apparent;
chiefs became the chairmen of the new councils and no attempt was made
to define their relationship and responsibility to the councils; neither was

[1] Teso District Annual Report, 1937.

there any attempt at a statutory definition of the functions of the new councils.

The years immediately preceding the Second World War saw substantial progress in many directions. Through the perseverance of the Veterinary Officer, H. Cronly, the antipathy which the Iteso had formerly shown to selling their cattle was at length overcome, and stock markets, now an accepted and usual feature of Teso's economy, were established and a regular cattle export trade begun. The efforts of M. G. de Courcy Ireland and other agricultural officers resulted in the acceptance by the Iteso of those soil conservation methods, particularly strip-cropping and bunding, which make the district a model in this respect today. Mixed farms were started at each county prison to produce food for the prisoners, which they still do with great success, and to provide enforced agricultural education for the large numbers of Iteso who pass through them. The native administration embarked on an ambitious programme of building in permanent materials and by 1940 had completed all prisons and county headquarters in Teso and all sub-county buildings in Kumi and Ngora. A start was made to provide much-needed water-supplies by drilling; the Iteso have recorded their gratitude to the pioneer driller, S. Gill, by coining the word *egilon* to mean a borehole. The Teso Informal Committee[1] went ahead with plans for resettling families from the crowded areas in south Teso and chose Kateta in Serere as a possible reception area.

Although the outstanding political advance during these years was the institution of the council system and the start of democratic local government, the transfer to Teso of the Kumam counties of Kalaki and Kaberamaido from Lango district in 1939 and the return of Bukedea county from Bugwere district a year later probably gave more general satisfaction at the time.

After the outbreak of war the rate of progress lost impetus and ground to a halt. The efforts of a depleted government staff were concentrated on tasks of war concern such as recruitment of Teso's 6,000 men for the armed forces, the campaign for increased food production, collections for war charities, and controls over essential supplies. There were local problems caused by the siting of a large camp for civilian internees near Soroti and by the location at Soroti of a detachment of the R.A.F. and of an army transport unit; for, when sinkings at sea made overland communication with West and North Africa essential, Soroti became a rail-head base for lorry convoys to the Sudan.

The resettlement schemes were abandoned. Shortages of essential supplies stopped further building. As the world food shortage grew more stringent, there was a steady change from economic to food crop production; by 1945 cattle sales were worth more as an item in the district economy than the cotton trade, and the average yield had fallen to the distressing figure of 81 lb. an acre.[1] Yet in spite of war needs, production slackened,

[1] Uganda Protectorate, 1937.   [2] Ibid., 1949.

for there were no consumer goods to buy in the shops and consequently no economic stimulus. The district was not even able to feed its own inhabitants, for in 1944, after failure of the rains, there occurred a famine necessitating the import of considerable quantities of food for relief.

During these war years only one political advance was attempted. This was the reorganization in 1942 of the ten counties of Teso into four divisions each under a divisional chief with a deputy. The primary object of this policy was to give the men in charge of these large areas greater responsibility and better training in the sphere of administration.[1] At the same time a new post of Secretary-General was created, to act as a co-ordinator of divisional chiefs and the channel for administrative dealings between them and the District Commissioner. By 1945 'it had become evident that no contemporary African chief had the necessary ability to administer efficiently units of this size and complication'.[1] The fault did not lie wholly in this direction. The units proved unwieldy; the divisional chief of Kumi, for instance, was responsible for some 40,000 taxpayers and for the supervision of fourteen sub-counties; it was inevitable that court work and routine administrative matters fell hopelessly into arrears. Moreover, the amalgamation was never popular. Loyalty to the smaller units persisted and the decision to revert to the county system in 1946 was universally popular. Only seven of the ten counties were re-constituted, Kasilo, Kalaki, and Ngora being absorbed into the neighbouring counties; of these seven counties, six approximated each other in population, but the seventh, Kumi, was nearly twice the size of any other. This anomaly was finally corrected in 1951 by its division into two counties of Kumi and Ngora, thus giving the eight counties which today (1954) exist.

The soldiers returned to civilian life without disturbance. Soon, however, new wants and needs among the people were felt and voiced. More schools were demanded and more hospitals, more roads, more permanent buildings, and more water-supplies; more enthusiasm than formerly was shown in trading; but, above all, there was a quickening interest in political matters, a desire to have more control over local affairs.

It was in part to meet this demand that important political advances were planned very soon after the end of the war, initiated by F. R. Kennedy, by then Provincial Commissioner of the Province. In 1947 two new appointments of Treasurer and Chief Judge of the District Native Court were created. These two officers, with the Secretary-General, became the central executive of the native administration on financial, judicial, and administrative matters respectively and are now usually known as 'the senior officials'. They were appointed, as were the chiefs, by the Governor, but for a set term of years, and the District Council was given the specific right to vote for candidates. At the same time the District Commissioner formally relinquished his chairmanship of the council, which was given the right to choose its own chairman, although choice was restricted to the county

[1] Uganda Protectorate, 1949.

chiefs and senior officials. It was Kennedy's intention that the chairman should not only preside at council meetings but should deal with all council business; but this arrangement did not prove practicable; the chairman had his normal official duties and often lived at some distance from the district headquarters at Soroti, and responsibility for council business has consequently devolved on the Secretary-General. At the same time the District Council was given the formal right to vote upon candidates for senior chieftainships, although the actual appointments continued to be made by the Governor. Junior chiefs were to be elected by secret ballot of the taxpayers of the area subject only to the veto of the District Commissioner. Although the latter system was carefully nurtured it was never popular and was abandoned at the request of the District Council after two years.

The reorganization of world economy and release of manpower after the war enabled the Government and the Teso African Local Government to expand their staff and activities and to take up with increased energy the programme of economic development abandoned in 1939. The years since 1947 have seen as spectacular changes in the economic as in the political scene. New areas have been opened up to settlement in Amuria by planned construction of new roads and water-supplies. New techniques have boosted production, in particular the breeding of a new variety of cotton seed and the chemical treatment of cotton seed against black-arm disease. Acreages, crop yields, and cash returns have risen accordingly, and signs of increased material prosperity throughout the district are not lacking. More meat is consumed locally than ever before; a bicycle is now considered a necessity of life for women as well as for men; more cigarettes are consumed in Teso than in any other district of East Africa. Signs of trade expansion have nowhere been more apparent than in Soroti itself. The little line of low shops sheltering behind the mango trees from the dust of the murram road has since 1948 grown into a sizeable town more than three times its pre-war size which is still increasing rapidly.

The political changes of 1947 were the first of many which have taken place since the war. An attempt to reorganize financial and taxation procedure to give local governments in Uganda more financial responsibility was followed by the enactment of the African Local Governments Ordinance of 1949, which gave statutory definition to the councils which had existed in Teso since 1937. The constitution of these councils was not materially altered by the new ordinance, although the opportunity was taken when the new councils came into being to introduce a system of proportional representation according to population. Hitherto county councils had been formed by the election of a fixed number of members from each sub-county in the area regardless of the size of the sub-county. Similarly sub-county councils had been formed by the election of an invariable number of representatives from each parish council. In addition county, sub-county, and parish councils had seats reserved for ministers or schoolmasters of the Muslim, Roman Catholic, and Protestant missions, and for a number of clan leaders. Special representation of religious missions and of clan leaders was abandoned in the new county and sub-county councils, and the number of persons elected to the higher council was made to depend on the taxpaying population of the electoral unit. By the same ordinance the district councils were given the statutory right to alter native customary law, a power hitherto exercised by the council of chiefs, and to pass by-laws on all matters on which chiefs were formerly empowered to issue orders under the Native Authority Ordinance. But the pace of change was so fast that this new ordinance was not destined to have a long life. Even at the time of its enactment the need for a full inquiry into local government in Uganda was recognized and was carried out in 1952.[1] The recommendations of this inquiry are to be given effect in a new ordinance entitled the District Administration (District Councils) Ordinance.

8. *Conclusion*

The Iteso themselves have advanced a long way since the first families moved out from Karamoja with their flocks and herds to look for pasture in new lands. When the early European observers knew them, 'the Teso though quick-tempered and revengeful were a cheerful and simple race. The peasants were still a naked people and even prominent chiefs were to be seen in their own villages as naked as when they were born.'[2] Their path has not always been easy. Their freedom to indulge in profitable raids on neighbours and to enjoy the lengthy festivities of age-set ceremonies was wrested from them by the conquering Baganda, who provided instead the drab substitute of forced labour on public works. The British administration, so far from restoring this former freedom, introduced a new obligation, poll-tax, and, by forcibly encouraging the planting of cotton, ensured that there was no excuse for failure to pay it. Compulsory labour was still required to till the lands of the chiefs in the days before luwalo commutation was allowed, and to move the cotton crop and the loads of military expeditions. The teaching of the mission schools and of the Government has been quickly assimilated and the wealth from cotton has brought about a startling rise in living standards. The early story was one of gifts by outsiders to the Iteso; peace and a pattern of administration from Kakunguru; Christianity and education from the missionaries; communications and trade from the activities of the early European and Indian traders; and economic, social, and political improvement from the British administration. The future story will be one of achievement by the Teso people themselves.

---

[1] *Report of an Inquiry into African Local Government in the Protectorate of Uganda*, by C. A. G. Wallis. Government Printer, Uganda, 1953.
[2] Teso District Annual Report, 1913/14.

CHRONOLOGICAL TABLE

1700   Approximate start of the first migration, which brought the Iteso from Karamoja to the north shore of Lake Salisbury in Usuku county.

1800   Approximate start of the second migration, which brought the Iteso west and south from Usuku over the whole of Teso district and the north of Bukedi and Busoga districts; the approximate start of contact and friction between the Lango and the Kumam.

1890   Disastrous rinderpest epidemic.

1896   Fort established on Kaweri island by S. Kakunguru. Baganda garrison of fifty rifles installed. Deputation of Teso chiefs taken to Mengo to see Kabaka Mwanga.

1898   Survey of Lake Kyoga shores by Captain Kirkpatrick accompanied by S. Kakunguru.

1899   Capture of Kabaka Mwanga at Kangai on the Lango/Teso border. Kakunguru authorized to subjugate area north of Lake Kyoga. Forts established at Kagaa in Kaberamaido, at Sambwe in Serere county, and at Dokolo in Lango district. Serere *saza* proclaimed.

1900   Bululu fort built. *Saza* of Kumam proclaimed. Kakunguru authorized by Sir Harry Johnston to subjugate Bukedi. Fort established at Pege near Ngora.

1901   Ngora *saza* proclaimed. Fort built at Mkongoro.

1902   Kakunguru relieved of his command and settled at Mbale. Baganda garrisons removed from the Teso forts. Banyoro garrison under Musabira left at Bululu and Uganda police posts at Serere, Ngora, and Mkongoro.

1904   Kakunguru sent by the Collector (D.C.), Mbale, to establish *saza* headquarters at Soroti, Kumi, and Bukedea.

1907   Administrative headquarters established at Bululu to control Kumam and Lango country. Punitive expedition by the Collector, Mbale, in Usuku.

1908   Mission station established at Ngora by Rev. A. L. Kitching. Indian traders reported at most centres in Teso district. First cotton crop recorded (4,056 lb.).

1909   Headquarters of Lango district moved from Bululu to Nabieso. Administrative headquarters established at Kumi as a sub-station of the Mbale collectorate.

1910   A ploughing school opened at Kumi.

1911   An agricultural experimental station opened at Kadungulu.

1912   Teso constituted as a separate district. B.E.A. Corporation and Bukedi (Uganda) Cotton Trading Company built the first two ginneries in Teso at Bugondo. Mission station founded at Ngora by the Mill Hill Mission. Retrenchment of Baganda agents begun.

1914　District headquarters moved from Kumi to Soroti. Punitive expedition with military forces in Amuria and Usuku counties.

1915　Administration extended to Omoro county.

1916　Agricultural experimental station moved from Kadungulu to Simsa near Soroti.

1919　Start of a native administration service. Chiefs appointed for the first time outside local areas. Famine. System of compulsory grain storage started.

1920　Appointment of the first Teso county chief, N. Iporiket, to Kumi county. Formation of the Teso District Council of Chiefs. The agricultural experimental station moved from Simsa to Serere.

1923　Bukedea county transferred to Bukedi district, which was split into the three districts of Bugwere, Bugishu, and Budama.

1924　Statutory recognition of the District Native Council of Chiefs under the Native Law Ordinance of 1919.

1926　Dismissal and deportation of county chief, E. Epaku, and the re-employment of Baganda agents. Counties reduced in size by the formation of Amuria, Napak, Kasilo, and Ngora counties.

1928　Famine.

1929　The railway reached Soroti.

1930　Locust infestation followed by famine. Leprosy centres started by Dr. Wiggins at Kumi and Kapiri.

1937　Introduction of the council system: councils established at district, county, sub-county, and parish levels.

1938　Famine.

1939　Transfer back to Teso of Kumam county from Lango district and Bukedea county from Bugwere district.

1941　Panel of lay members first appointed to native courts in Teso.

1942　Amalgamation of counties into the four divisions of Kaberamaido, Serere, Amuria, and Kumi.

1944　Famine.

1946　The divisional system abolished and the district reorganized into seven counties: Kaberamaido, Amuria, Usuku, Soroti, Serere, Kumi, and Bukedea.

1947　The District Commissioner withdrew from chairmanship of the District Council. A central organization of the native administration formed by the appointment of a Treasurer and a Chief Judge, who with the Secretary-General appointed earlier are the executives of the District Council.

1950　System of election to councils according to occupation abandoned in favour of a system of proportional representation.

1951　Ngora county re-constituted.

PRESENT-DAY POLITICAL ORGANIZA-TION OF TESO DISTRICT

The changes in the political organization of the district, which have taken place in the last eight years, have been so varied and so rapid that some account of the resulting structure is essential. Changes are still taking place with the same rapidity and any such account will soon be out of date. It is, therefore, important to remember that the following description of the political organization of Teso takes 1 July 1955 as its date line, the day on which the District Administration (District Councils) Ordinance came into effect.

The administrative district of Teso is the northernmost of the five districts of the Eastern Province of Uganda. The total land area of the district is 4,649 square miles and its population in 1948 was 405,189; the average annual increase since then is estimated at $1\frac{1}{2}$ to 2 per cent.

The District Commissioner is 'the principal executive officer of the Government personally and directly responsible to the Provincial Commissioner of the province for the peace and good order of the district and for the efficient conduct of all public business in it'.[1] This responsibility for peace and good order is ultimate rather than direct, for the senior officer of the Uganda Police in Teso is responsible for executive control of the police and the District Commissioner has been freed from many of his judicial duties by the appointment of a resident magistrate. The District Commissioner's duties as the licensing and revenue officer of the district have also lately been lightened by the appointment of a treasury officer with full responsibilities.

For effective administration the district is divided into eight counties, each having an approximately equal population, of which the senior executive officer is the county chief. Each county is divided into five or six sub-counties, administered by a sub-county chief. Both these grades of chief have a staff of clerks and police and are responsible for judicial and financial as well as normal administrative duties. There are also two lower divisions known as parish and village. There are, on an average, three parishes in every sub-county and two or three villages in every parish. The parish and village chiefs are really agents of the sub-county chief. They have no staff, no offices, and no judicial powers.

Officers of the various technical departments of the Central Government stationed in Soroti have individual responsibility for the work of their department within the district and collective responsibility as members of the District Team, which meets under the chairmanship of the District Commissioner, for the progress and co-ordination of all governmental activities in Teso. The District Team consists of the senior officers of each government department working in the district and some representatives of the Teso African Local Government. It has no statutory basis, but of recent years has taken an increasing part in the formation and interpretation of government policy at district level. In 1954 the

[1] Uganda Protectorate: Administrative Instructions 1 (2).

Medical, Veterinary and Animal Industry, Agriculture, Forests, Co-operative Development, Education, Public Works, Labour, and Geological Survey (rural water-supplies) departments were represented on the District Team.

Many of the affairs of the district which concern Africans only are, however, administered not by central government agencies but by the Teso African Local Government, whose territorial jurisdiction is co-terminous with the district boundaries but whose personal jurisdiction is limited to Africans.

The Teso District Council, which is the legislative and policy making body of the Local Government, consists of some ninety councillors. Eleven of these, senior officials or chiefs, are members of the council by virtue of their office. The elected members, who form the majority of the council, are chosen by an indirect system of election by which each county council in Teso elects from among its own elected members one member for every 1,500 taxpayers in the county council area; the elected members of the county council are in turn chosen by the sub-county council from its own elected members on the basis of one member for every 750 taxpayers in the sub-county council area, and so on down to the lowest administrative unit where members are chosen by a show of hands by all taxpayers in the area. In addition to the *ex-officio* members and the elected members there are up to twenty-nine nominated members of the council. Nineteen of these are chosen by the elected members and *ex-officio* members together, and of these nine must be senior clan leaders. The remaining ten are nominated by the District Commissioner. This system of nomination exists partly to ensure that all sections of the community can be represented, when desirable, and partly to ensure that the council is not deprived of the services of valuable men through electoral vagaries. The chairman of the council is elected, but choice is limited to one of the *ex-officio* members who as a senior chief or official has invariably had long and valuable experience as chairman of lower councils or of committees and who is accustomed to lead.

Much of the work of the council is necessarily performed by committees. The District Commissioner may 'appoint such financial, standing or advisory committees as he thinks fit for the proper administration of the District and may decide the membership of them'.[1] In practice only two such committees are appointed apart from the Education Committee which will be described later, one for financial matters and one for all other purposes, and the District Commissioner usually appoints without question the persons chosen by the council to sit on them. The District Commissioner must, however, sit as the chairman of both committees[1] and can thus exert influence and guidance on council matters, although he takes no part in council meetings apart from addressing the council at the beginning of the session and conveying the Central Government's comments on council resolutions where necessary.

The responsibilities of the African Local Government *vis-à-vis* those of the Central Government are at present somewhat ill-defined. There is, of course, financial control exercised by the Central Government through approval of the annual budget by the Provincial Commissioner and through audit and other safeguards. The only services for which the African Local Government can at present be said to have full responsibility are those concerning the provision and maintenance of roads and bridges, other than trunk roads, and those concerning the erection and maintenance of all buildings required by the Local Government,

[1] African Local Governments Ordinance, 1949.

such as staff houses, offices, or stores. For these services it employs its own public works staff. The African Local Government is also responsible for the administration of local government prisons and native courts, but the ultimate responsibility for supervision of the courts is specifically laid on the District Commissioner in his magisterial capacity.

The Teso District Council is the Local Education Authority for the district with responsibility for primary education. Much of the money required for this service is, however, contributed from central funds and the administration of the service is therefore entrusted to an Educational Committee of the council, appointed by the Provincial Commissioner, of which the District Commissioner is chairman and which contains a number of representatives of the religious missions responsible for the running of the schools.

In most other services there is a considerable and complicated division of responsibility. Thus, to take medical services as an example, the African Local Government is responsible for erecting, maintaining, and furnishing rural hospitals and dispensaries, but the Central Government accepts responsibility for equipping these units with medical equipment. The salaries of trained senior staff are paid by the Central Government, but of untrained staff by the Local Government, and all staff are controlled by a central government officer, the District Medical Officer. Drugs and dressings are supplied by the Central Government, but when quantities prove inadequate the Local Government makes supplementary provision. Food for the patients in rural hospitals and dispensaries is provided by the Local Government. The Central Government provides one ambulance at district headquarters while the Local Government provides others and so on.

For the purpose of carrying out its functions the District Council is empowered to levy certain fees and taxes. The 1954–5 local government estimates show total revenue of £313,006 of which £164,820 are derived from taxes, £9,500 from court fees or fines, £50,900 from a subvention from the Central Government for primary education, £15,700 from a grant from the Central Government towards the cost of law and order services maintained by the Local Government, £6,070 from a grant from the Central Government towards the upkeep of certain roads, and £53,021 are transferred from the Development Fund, which is fed from an annual bonus paid by the Central Government on cotton production in the district. Expenditure in the same year was estimated at £236,914 on recurrent services and £115,121 on capital works, the difference between revenue and expenditure being met from surplus funds, which were still estimated to be £259,499 at the end of the year. Of the recurrent expenditure, education accounted for £107,483, administration, courts, police and prisons £61,423, and public works £44,436. Of the capital expenditure by far the greater part went on new buildings, which included new sub-county offices, staff houses, two new maternity wards at mission hospitals, part of a new secondary school, as well as many lesser items. £17,000 were, however, devoted to rural water-supplies, mainly boreholes.

The District Council is also given power to legislate on native customary law and on certain other specified subjects. The council of chiefs formed in the 1920's was given the right under the Native Law Ordinance to amend native law. This function was inherited by the elected councils formed in 1937 and many resolutions having the force of law were passed in the years following, which covered not only matters of customary law such as marriage and adultery, but also such matters as soil conservation and public health. Since these legislative powers were formalized by the African Local Governments Ordinance of 1949 they have been little used and only four by-laws have been passed; they concern beer drinking, control of ferries, education tax, and diseased cassava.

The executive work of the African Local Government is carried out by the three senior officials and by chiefs under the general supervision of the District Commissioner. The only technical staff employed by the Local Government in 1954, apart from the public works staff already mentioned, was a prisons inspector and a number of forest rangers. Of the senior officials, the Chief Judge is responsible for all judicial matters, the Treasurer for all financial matters, and the Secretary-General for all administrative matters.

The title 'chief' is to some extent a misnomer. Chiefs have no traditional or hereditary authority. They are 'officers of the African Local Government recognized by the Protectorate Government as Chiefs'[1] and are thus both local government officials and civil servants, responsible to the Governor. This compromise in function is reflected in the method of their appointment whereby the District Council votes on candidates for the post of county or sub-county chief and lower councils for parish or village chiefs. The appointment is, however, made on behalf of the Governor by the Provincial Commissioner in the case of county and sub-county chiefs and by the District Commissioner in other cases after taking into account the voting of the council.

The district organization is largely reduplicated at county level and, to a lesser extent, at sub-county level. County teams, consisting of field officers of government departments stationed in the counties under the chairmanship of the county chief, aim at co-ordinating the activities of central government departments at county level. County councils, under the chairmanship of the county chief, discuss all matters of concern to the county; these councils do not, however, have any financial or legislative powers and are mainly consultative bodies and electoral colleges.

The judicial system of the district allows for the administration of two separate systems of law. Offences by persons of any race against the statutory law of the Protectorate and civil actions involving non-Africans are triable in the District Court of Teso, a subordinate court of the High Court of Uganda. Offences by Africans against native customary law or against district council by-laws and civil disputes between Africans are triable in the native courts, which are established at district, county, and sub-county levels. The powers of these courts and their jurisdiction in civil matters vary between the three levels. The organization and procedure of native courts is described in detail on pp. 269–71. It should be added that the division between the two types of court according to the systems of law administered by them is in some respects more apparent than real. Native courts are specifically empowered to administer certain statutory laws and do in fact administer many others. Offences against the Penal Code are in most instances offences also against native customary law. In effect the district court tends to hear only those cases which involve non-Africans or those which, owing to their seriousness or complexity, come to the notice of the Uganda police. Thus in an average year the total cases heard in the district court number about 750 while those in the native courts number about 9,000.

[1] African Local Governments Ordinance, 1949.

Lastly, it should be emphasized once again that this brief outline describes conditions in June 1955 which will be considerably altered when the District Administration (District Councils) Ordinance of 1955 becomes operative. This ordinance provides the machinery for putting into effect the recommendations of the Inquiry into African Local Government, which took place in 1952. The judicial system is also likely to be varied in the near future in pursuance of a policy which seeks to integrate the African court system into the judicial framework of the Protectorate.

PART II

SOCIAL ORGANIZATION

CHAPTER I

KINSHIP GROUPINGS

1. *Introduction*

THERE are three distinct social groupings in Teso society. The first of these is a grouping through kinship; it contains the family, extended family, and clan. The second grouping has a territorial basis; it contains the *etem* and *einere*; neither word is easily translatable and their meaning will be explained in Chapter II below. The third grouping, which is now virtually extinct, has a basis of common initiation into an age-set.

The kinship grouping is of supreme importance in matters of childbirth, marriage, death, inheritance, bride-price, and blood-money. The important pursuits of war, hunting, age-set initiation, and rain-making were carried out by the territorial grouping; but with limitations on war and hunting and suppression of age-set initiation, the territorial grouping nowadays has only a limited social significance. The age-grouping formerly had political and, to some extent, religious functions, but is no longer a factor in Teso social organization.

2. *Family and extended family*

The lowest and smallest kinship unit is the family, which occupies a homestead (*ere*, pl. *ireria*). It consists of the father of the family with his wives and unmarried or occasionally married children, and such other relatives as are dependent on him.

The Iteso use the word *ekek* both for this unit and for the larger kinship unit, the extended family. *Ekek* (pl. *ikekia*) means 'door' and the members of the extended family are those who come from one door. I have used the word 'extended family' to mean all those relatives of the householder in the homestead who spring from a common ancestor about three or four generations back. The average Etesot is unable to trace his lineage further back than this. The extended family normally lives in one particular area even though members may temporarily move to other parts of the district in the course of their work. It is a strictly exogamous group.

Each extended family has a recognized head (*loepolokit*) elected by the adult male members of the extended family; he is normally the senior member of the family in possession of his full faculties. This family head has important duties to perform in the division of deceased persons' estates and in the allocation of land (see pp. 228–233 and 241–256). The extended family is responsible for receiving and for paying both blood-money and bride-price (see pp. 257–8 and 202–7).

The Iteso themselves do not recognize any distinction, except in the division of personal property, between family and extended family. The ties of relationship are as close in the latter as in the former. This feeling of close kinship is illustrated by the words used for relationship. To the Iteso all members of the extended family, who are of the same generation, are brothers or sisters. All who are of the previous generation are fathers or mothers. They are not merely called by these terms of close relationship; they are treated as though the relationship was as close. The following list of relationships within the extended family illustrates this unity. The same terms are used for relatives on the mother's as on the father's side of the family.

1.	Father	*Papa*
2.	Mother	*Toto*
3.	Father's father	*Papaa*
4.	Father's mother	*Tata*
5.	Father's wife	*Toto* or *aberu ka papa*
6.	Father's wife's son	*Onac*
7.	Father's wife's daughter	*Inac*
8.	Mother's father	*Papaa*
9.	Mother's mother	*Tata*
10.	Father's brother	*Papa*
11.	Father's brother's wife	*Toto*
12.	Father's brother's son	*Onac*
13.	Father's brother's son's son	*Okoku*
14.	Father's brother's son's daughter	*Akoku*
15.	Father's brother's daughter	*Inac*
16.	Father's brother's daughter's daughter	*Akoku*
17.	Father's brother's daughter's son	*Okoku*
18.	Mother's brother	*Mamai*
19.	Mother's co-wife's brother	*Amuran*
20.	Mother's brother's family	*Ateker kaluka mamai*
21.	Mother's brother's wife	*Aberu naka mamai*
22.	Mother's brother's son	*Onac*
23.	Mother's brother's daughter	*Inac*
24.	Father's sister	*Ijaa, Toto* (if eldest)
25.	Father's sister's husband	*Papa*
26.	Father's sister's son	*Onac*
27.	Father's sister's daughter	*Inac*
28.	Mother's sister	*Ijaa, Toto* (if eldest)
29.	Mother's sister's son	*Onac*
30.	Mother's sister's husband	*Papa*
31.	Mother's sister's daughter	*Inac*
32.	Son	*Okoku*
33.	Son's wife	*Aberu ka okoku, Akoku*
34.	Son's son	*Etatait, Okoku*

35.	Son's wife's parents	*Amurak*
36.	Daughter	*Akoku*
37.	Daughter's husband	*Omuran, Okoku*
38.	Daughter's son	*Etatait, Okoku*
39.	Daughter's (or son's) daughter	*Atatait, Akoku*
40.	Brother	*Onac*
41.	Brother's wife	*Aberu ka onac*
42.	Brother's son	*Okoku, Okoku ka onac*
43.	Brother's daughter	*Akoku, Akoku ka onac*
44.	Sister	*Inac*
45.	Sister's husband	*Amuran, Okilen inac*
46.	Sister's son	*Ocan*
47.	Sister's daughter	*Acen*
48.	Husband	*Okilen*
49.	Wife	*Aberu*
50.	Husband's father	*Papa*
51.	Husband's father's brother	*Papa*
52.	Husband's father's sister	*Toto*
53.	Husband's mother	*Toto*
54.	Husband's brother	*Onac ka okilen*
55.	Husband's sister	*Inac ka okilen, Amwika*
56.	Husband's brother's wife	*Akain*
57.	Husband's brother's son	*Okoku*
58.	Husband's brother's daughter	*Akoku*
59.	Husband's sister's husband	*Amuran*
60.	Husband's sister's son	*Okoku ka amwika, Okoku*
61.	Husband's sister's daughter	*Akoku ka amwika, Akoku*
62.	Co-wife	*Akain*
63.	Co-wife's relations	*Amurak*
64.	Co-wife's son	*Okoku*
65.	Co-wife's daughter	*Akoku*
66.	Wife's father	*Omuran, Papa ka aberu*
67.	Wife's mother	*Amuran, Toto ka aberu*
68.	Wife's brother	*Omuran, Onac ka aberu*
69.	Wife's sister	*Amuran, Inac ka aberu*
70.	Wife's brother's wife	*Amuran*
71.	Wife's brother's son	*Okoku ka omuran, Okoku*
72.	Wife's brother's daughter	*Akoku ka omuran, Akoku*
73.	Wife's sister's husband	*Okilen ka amuran*
74.	Wife's sister's son	*Okoku ka amuran, Okoku*
75.	Wife's sister's daughter	*Akoku ka amuran, Akoku*
76.	Husband's family	*Itunga ka okilen*
77.	Wife's family	*Itunga ka aberu, Amurak*
78.	Relations (generally)	*Ipajan*

The two tables which follow show these relationships in diagrammatic form. The symbol △ represents a male and ○ a female, while ▲ is the person from whose point of view the table is made up.

TABLE 1

Consanguinal kinsfolk (ipajan)

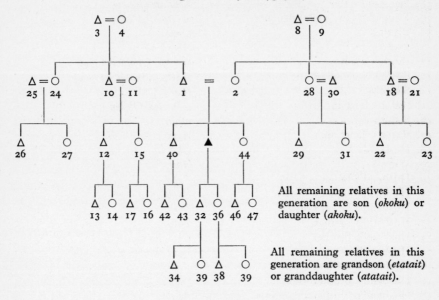

All remaining relatives in this generation are son (*okoku*) or daughter (*akoku*).

All remaining relatives in this generation are grandson (*etatait*) or granddaughter (*atatait*).

TABLE 2

Affinal kinsfolk (amurak)

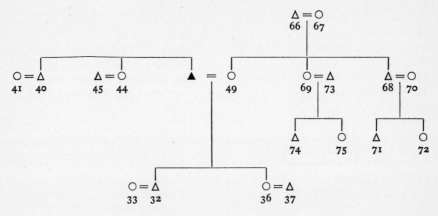

3. *The clan—introduction*

The word 'clan' is used throughout this book to translate the Ateso word *ateker*, which means a division of society consisting of several extended families. It must, however, be emphasized that the clan in Teso has few, if any, of the features associated with clans in neighbouring Bantu or

Nilotic tribes. Thus the members of any one clan in Teso do not claim descent from a common ancestor; nor do they possess a common totem; the Teso clan is in no sense a political unit; nor is it an exogamous unit; members of any one clan appear to have no obligations on a clan-wide basis. Not only are these classic features absent from the Teso clan, but there is also one feature present which is wholly alien to the recognized concept of a clan. This is the feature whereby a woman changes her clan taboos on marriage and again on re-marriage to those of her husband.

The translation is also unsatisfactory because the word *ateker* is not always used in the same sense. The Iteso, in common with many other Nilo-Hamitic peoples, had no idea of tribal unity and no word in their vocabulary to express it. The word *ateker* is therefore coined nowadays to translate 'tribe' or 'nation'. The word is also loosely used when *ekek* or extended family is really meant. Thus in the court record quoted on page 231 (Kumi County 17/50) the word *ateker* was used to refer to clan relatives, whereas the persons concerned in the distribution of the deceased's estate were the extended family relatives.

These difficulties have been recognized and other translations of *ateker* suggested, such as 'kindred group', 'kinship group', or 'sept'. Nevertheless, the word 'clan' has been used by many writers on the Nilo-Hamitic peoples[1] to describe the social grouping known as *ateker*, and for the sake of uniformity the same word has been adopted here. Provided it is remembered that there are many features of the *ateker* system which differ radically from those of the normal clan system, the name is unimportant. These features will be discussed under three headings: clan names and origins; clan taboos; and clan functions.

4. *Clan names and origins*

The social division referred to as a clan is known as *ateker* or *ateger* (pl. *atekerin*, *ategerin*) among the Iteso, Lango, Kumam, Karamojong, Jie, Dodoth, Turkana, and Toposa. The word means by derivation a state of amity or alliance.[2]

Not only is the word describing this social grouping identical among these tribes, but several of the *ateker* names are held in common. Thus among the Lango Driberg records Inomo (Inomu), Ararak (Irarak), Agorya (Igoria), Atengoro (Itengor), Akarawok (Ikarebwok), and Atekit (Atekit). The modern spelling of the Teso clan is shown in brackets. He notes that the names Atengoro, Ararak, and Agorya correspond to the Turkana, Nitigor, Erarak, and Ogorok.[2] In Karamoja there are other names which correspond: Ng'katekok (Atekok), Ng'ioropom (Iworopom), Ng'itengor (Itengor), Ng'imiroo (Imiroo).[3] Ngikariwok (Ikarebwok), and Ngikatap (Iatapi) appear among the Jie, Karamojong, and Turkana.[4]

The total number of clans in Teso is not known. It was claimed forty

[1] Huntingford, 1953; Gulliver, 1953 (ii); Driberg, 1923.
[2] Driberg, 1923.   [3] Clark, 1950.   [4] Gulliver, 1953 (ii).

years ago that among the Wamia, the Iteso of Tororo and Kenya, there were only twenty-five.[1] Among the Turkana at the present day there are only twenty.[2] But in 1921 130 were listed without any claim to finality,[3] and even this total was scoffed at as inadequate: 'names of the different *atekerin* . . . would fill a decent-sized Directory, so numerous are they'.[4] The occasion of the council elections in 1950 provided an opportunity of obtaining a representative cross-section of clans in the district. Two hundred and twelve men and five women were elected or appointed as county councillors. Of these, ten belonged to foreign tribes, Bakenyi, Baganda, Acholi, and others. The remaining 207 Iteso and Kumam belonged to the following clans:

Clan	Usuku	Amuria	Soroti	Serere	Kabera-maido	Bukedea	Kumi and Ngora
Atekok	4	5	2	9	—	4	11
Ikarebwok	6	6	8	12	3	7	14
Irarak	5	8	11	6	6	5	12
Ikomolo	2	2	—	1	—	2	3
Inomu	—	—	—	—	—	—	3
Igoria	1	—	3	—	—	—	—
Ibasere	1	—	—	—	1	—	1
Ilogiri	1	1	—	—	—	—	—
Itikokin	2	—	—	—	—	—	—
Ikocila	1	—	—	—	—	—	—
Imenakolia	1	—	—	—	—	—	—
Ipalama	1	—	1	—	—	—	—
Imugenya	1	—	—	—	—	—	—
Ilale	—	—	1	—	—	—	—
Igurotok	—	—	1	—	1	—	—
Ikeritok	—	1	—	—	—	—	—
Idudi	—	1	—	—	—	—	—
Ikelim	—	1	—	—	—	—	—
Icoolo	—	1	—	—	—	—	—
Ipokor	—	1	—	—	—	—	—
Ikatele	—	—	—	—	6	—	—
Itengor	—	—	—	—	1	—	—
Iyepas	—	—	—	—	1	—	—
Imadira	—	—	—	—	1	—	—
Isimara	—	—	—	—	1	—	—
Ipasanga	—	—	—	—	1	—	—
Ipasama	—	—	—	1	—	—	3
Iganitok	—	—	—	—	1	—	—
Inyakoi	—	—	—	—	—	3	—
Itisa	—	—	—	—	—	1	—
Ateria	—	—	—	—	—	1	—
Itepes	—	—	—	—	—	1	—
Iworopom	—	—	—	—	—	1	—
Ikabwongo	—	—	—	—	—	1	—
Icaka	—	—	—	—	—	—	1

Though this survey covered the whole of Teso, the numbers concerned were so few that the results do little more than indicate that clan names are indeed numerous and that the total number may be far in excess of the 130 recorded in 1921. Little useful purpose would, however, be achieved

[1] Dundas, 1913. [2] Gulliver, 1953 (ii). [3] Lukyn-Williams, 1936. [4] Kennedy, 1937.

in attempting to make a comprehensive list. The list also indicates the wide distribution of clan names throughout Teso.

The distribution of clans is very widespread within smaller areas as well as within the district. The following list of clan leaders in Usuku county shows a typical distribution of the major clans within a county area:

Clan	Toroma sub-county	Katakwi sub-county	Magoro sub-county	Ngariam sub-county	Usuku sub-county
Atekok	I	I	I	I	I
Ikarebwok . . .	I	I	I	I	I
Irarak	I	I	I	I	I
Ikomolo	I	I	I	I	I
Inomu	I	I	I	I	—
Igoria	I	I	I	—	I
Iworopom . . .	I	—	I	I	I
Imiroo	I	I	—	I	I
Isore	—	—	—	I	I
Ilogiri	I	I	—	I	—
Ibasere	—	I	I	I	—
Ikocila	—	—	—	I	I
Itikokin	I	—	—	I	I
Icaka	I	—	—	—	—
Imoruduko . . .	I	—	—	—	—
Imorio	I	—	—	—	—
Ibekuna	I	—	—	—	—
Ileuban	I	—	—	—	—
Igetoma	—	—	—	—	I
Isureta	—	—	—	—	I
Iatapi	—	—	—	—	I
Irieta	—	—	—	—	I
Isuguro	—	—	—	—	I
Ikiriwo	—	—	—	—	I
Ijokoparan . . .	—	—	—	—	I

As an example of clan distribution within a very small area the following table shows all the clans represented in the village areas of Wila in Amuria, Opuyo in Soroti, and Kasilang in Serere county. The total of adult males in each clan is also shown. The figures are from agricultural surveys undertaken in 1937 (1953 in the case of Kasilang):

Wila		Opuyo		Kasilang	
Atekok . . .	20	Atekok. . .	54	Atekok . . .	18
Ikarebwok . .	84	Ikarebwok . .	54	Ikarebwok . .	67
Irarak . . .	46	Irarak . . .	28	Irarak . . .	69
Ikomolo . . .	5	Ikomolo . .	6	Ikomolo . . .	11
Igoria . . .	7	Inomu. . .	1	Igoria . . .	2
Ilogiri . . .	3	Igoria . . .	18	Imugenya . .	2
(incomplete)		Itengor . .	18	Irieta . . .	2
		Isore . . .	30	Icatok . . .	2
		Ininika . .	6	Arengak . . .	1
				Imalei . . .	1
				Imatenga. . .	1
				Imito . . .	1
Total adult males: approximately . 200		Total adult males: . 215		Total adult males: . 177	

The distribution can be carried even lower. Within Kasilang village the main clans were distributed among nine settlement sites as follows:[1]

Settlement site	Irarak	Atekok	Igoria	Ikarebwok	Ikomolo
Kasilang and Omugenya .	17	6	1	5	0
Akoboi and Okolong . .	3	0	0	8	11
Okwii	9	0	0	20	0
Obiit.	16	3	0	2	0
Aasi	19	9	0	15	0
Okaalen and Okimai . .	5	0	1	17	0

It will be observed from these examples that four clans are represented in nearly all of the localities mentioned. They are the Atekok, Ikarebwok, Irarak, and Ikomolo clans. The first three are also noticeably larger than any other clans. Informants at Kumi stated that there were really only four clans in Teso: Atekok, Ikarebwok, Irarak, and Ikomolo, and that all other clan names denote subdivisions of these four. This idea is supported by a group of Iteso (Amootoi ka Etesot) which studied Teso origins. This group named six, not four, major clans: Atekok, Ikarebwok, Irarak, Ikomolo, Igoria, and Inomu. It is claimed that all other clans broke off from these six.

Watson believed that the modern ateker was a fraction of a larger clan, which had in the past split and become a separate unit. The new ateker took the name of the parent unit at the time of partition, but as time passed the connecting links between these new clans and their parent unit gradually broke down, while the bond of common parentage failed to unite the new clans with each other.[2] This theory explains why the Irarak of, say, Serere profess no affinity with the Irarak of, say, Ngora, and why the taboos which characterize the clans vary from one clan to another with no apparent connexion between clans having a common name.

Driberg has described the process by which new clans were formed in this manner among the Lango, and it is not unreasonable to suppose that a similar process occurred in Teso.

It will be observed that clans show a tendency to sub-divide, some of the sub-divisions (as comparison will show) having lost all trace of the original prohibitions. This process was largely facilitated by the fact that clans separated considerably owing to war and migrations, and that the members of a clan are not all settled together. These sub-divisions are treated as separate clans and intermarriage is accordingly possible. They are formed in two ways, distinguishable by the appellation of the clan. The commonest is due to the branching off of sub-divisions of a clan in ancient days, owing possibly to a quarrel between the sons of the head of the clan. This is shown by the addition of me tung (of the branch) followed by the name of the ancestor from whom the sub-division traces its descent. The clan Jo Akarawok, for instance, has many such sub-divisions, one (for example) being Jo Akarawok me tung Enyang, or that branch of the Akarawok clan which is descended from Enyang.

New clans, or sub-divisions of old clans, may be formed by a founder coalescing

[1] Wilson, 1953.   [2] Watson, 1937.

two clans together. A clan so formed may intermarry with either of the original clans. Thus for example a man of the Akarawok clan elects to leave his friends and settles among the Jo Oki. Finally he marries a girl of the latter clan and breeds a family. Normally he retains his old clan customs and hands them down to his children; but it would appear that sometimes his children, being at a distance from the other members of the old clan, and not holding communications with them, elect to form a new clan, which would be called Jo Akarawok me Jo Oki. Customs and tabus from both clans may be included and additions may be made, even to the extent of eliminating all traces of their old clan except the name. Some old clans are now extinct, and the only record of their existence remains in the names of such amalgamated clans.[1]

These extra names denoting origin are not found in Teso, but it may be that the extra name has survived and the original one has been lost, or, alternatively, that the original has survived, as Watson believes, and the extra one has been lost.

This process of clan formation by fragmentation is possibly still continuing. In Bukedea each of fifty-five men questioned was asked to state his clan (*ateker*) name, his sub-clan or extended family (*ekek*) name, his extended family founder, his clan taboos (*italia*), and the place of origin of his extended family. Fifteen of those questioned belonged to the Atekok clan, seventeen to the Ikarebwok clan, and four to the Irarak clan, and eleven other clans were represented. A sample taken from this recording shows the following extended families and extended family heads.

Clan (Ateker)	Sub-division or extended family (Ekek)	Extended family founder (Papa ekek)
Atekok	Isengoria	Onyesetor
Atekok	Ikwabukwi	Akol
Atekok	Ilekai	Elekata
Atekok	Iwonga	Palekor
Ikarebwok	Ikapelio	Odewa
Ikarebwok	Isoromatok	Igenya
Ikarebwok	Ibwino	Oruja
Ikarebwok	Ikwabukwi	Okoboi
Irarak	Idoti	Orengetum
Ikomolo	Idetima	Ogala
Inyakoi	Ingaana	Mayangor
Imesura	Iunyai	Ekijim
Iworopom	Ibitin	Igira

Of all the extended families listed only one, Ikwabukwi, occurred in more than one clan.

It is possible that these subdivisions gradually expand until a new clan is formed. This new clan may be known by the original *ateker* name or by the name of the subdivision or extended family.

How the clans or extended families first obtained their name is not

[1] Driberg, 1923.

known. The name of the *ekek* founder rarely bears any resemblance to the
ekek name. In the above sample only Elekata resembles Ilekai. Some of the
names are translatable: thus Isengoria is said to mean 'chosers of good
women' (from *aseun* 'to choose' and *angor* 'women'). Iwojamorokin are the
'owners of long-hafted spears'. Ijokoparan is presumably derived from *jok*
(good) and *aparan* (day). The Karamojong clans are believed to have been
named after the tribes overrun by the Karamojong;[1] it is possible that some
of these names were perpetuated after the Iteso broke away from the
Karamojong.

5. *Clan taboos*

No serious attempt has been made to compile a comprehensive list of the
taboos or observances (*etal*, pl. *italia*) which form the basis of the clan
system. These taboos or observances are far more numerous even than the
clans and vary not only according to clan but also according to locality.
Nevertheless, the following constant features emerge.

Taboos, or things which must not be done, are far more numerous than
observances, or things which must be done; in fact, the only observance
recorded by me is the obligation for women, especially pregnant women,
to kick the soil off mole-hills.

Taboos are observed for the most part only by women and, to a far lesser
extent, by children. Nevertheless, some taboos have been listed which are
observed also by men. In Kasilang all members of the Ikomolo clan were
forbidden to touch *esimat* (Solanum nodiflorum). Porters on a safari on
Mount Napak refused to eat the meat of kob on the grounds that it was
taboo to their clan. Members of the Igoria clan are not allowed to hunt
wild animals.[2]

The association of taboos with childbirth or child welfare is very noticeable. Thus many of the taboos are observable only during pregnancy or
until the birth of a woman's first child. Failure to observe taboos is held
to result in abortion, sterility, or disease in children, particularly sores on
the head.

A child always adopts the taboos of its father's clan unless it is illegitimate,
in which case it adopts the taboos of its mother's clan. A woman changes
her clan taboos on marriage to those of her husband's clan; on re-marriage
she again changes her taboos to those of her new husband's clan.

Most taboos concern animals, particularly the duiker (*amor*) and kob
(*etil*). The same association with animals exists among the Lango. 'Taboos
connected with the duiker are observed by 55 different clans; the waterbuck
is associated with 27 clans; and the plant *adyebepar* is prohibited to 19
clans, the majority of which have no genealogical connexion.'[3] Roscoe
states that Teso clans were totemic but gives no evidence.[4] Driberg
believes in a totemic origin for Lango clans.[3] There is no indication that

[1] Clark, 1950.   [2] Wilson, 1953.   [3] Driberg, 1923.   [4] Roscoe, 1915.

Teso clans were originally named after an animal, plant, or other natural object, in the same way as the Jo Akwaich or Jo Ayom clans in Lango. Nor is there any evidence that clan members believed in some mystical ancestral relation with any particular animal or natural object.

The variety in taboos even among taboos involving the same animal in the same clan is considerable. The following list shows the taboos connected with the duiker in the Ikarebwok clan.

1. men may not eat;
2. women may not eat;
3. men and women may not eat;
4. men and women may not look at it;
5. men and women may not touch the skin;
6. women and girls may not eat or sit on skin;
7. women and children may not eat or sit on skin;
8. women and children may not touch the skin;
9. women may not look at it and children may not eat it;
10. women may not touch it;
11. women may not sit on the skin;
12. women may not look at it.[1]

The variation between taboos within the same clan but in different localities is very wide. Lukyn-Williams has listed more than sixty different taboos for the Ikarebwok clan.[1]

The following list of taboos will illustrate many of the points just mentioned: the preponderance of taboos over observances; the fact that taboos are observed mainly by women; the association between taboos and childbirth; the preponderance of animal taboos and the considerable variety.

(1) *Kasilang (Serere county)*[2]

Irarak

(i) Women forbidden to shave their head until the birth of their first child.
(ii) Women forbidden to look at an oribi until the birth of their first child.
(iii) Women forbidden to deck their head with Panicum maximum grass until the birth of their first child.
(iv) Women forbidden to touch roots or to use tree roots for making fire until the birth of their first child.
(v) Women forbidden to enter the compound through a gap in the hedge until the birth of their first child.

Atekok

(i) Women forbidden to shave until the birth of their first child.
(ii) Women forbidden to sit on the foundations of stores until the birth of their first child.

[1] Lukyn-Williams, 1936. [2] Watson, 1937.

(iii) Women forbidden to cross the path of ants (Megaponera foetens) until the birth of their first child.

(iv) Women forbidden to touch *esimat* and *ecuga* until the birth of their first child.

Ikarebwok

(i) Women forbidden to look at an oribi until the birth of their first child.

(ii) Women forbidden to fetch fire until the birth of their first child.

(iii) Women forbidden to sit in the shade of the store when the sun is sinking until the birth of their first child.

(iv) Women forbidden to enter the compound through a gap in the hedge until the birth of their first child.

(v) Women forbidden to shave their head until the birth of their first child.

Ikomolo

(i) Women forbidden to touch skins of oribi until the birth of their first child.

(ii) Women forbidden to light a fire in the evening or carry fire about until the birth of their first child.

(iii) All members of the clan forbidden to touch *esimat* (Solanum nodiflorum).

(iv) Women forbidden to sit on the gate poles of the compound or climb over them until the birth of their first child.

Igoria

(i) Women forbidden to touch *esimat* or pass over it until the birth of their first child.

(ii) Women forbidden to light a fire at night or carry it about until the birth of their first child.

(iii) Women forbidden to look at oribi until the birth of their first child.

(iv) Women forbidden to eat the flesh of oribi.

Itengor

(i) Women forbidden to eat the intestines of any animal until the birth of their first child.

(ii) Women forbidden to sit on skins of oribi until the birth of their first child.

(iii) Women forbidden to light a fire at night or carry it about until the birth of their first child.

(iv) Women forbidden to enter the compound through a gap in the hedge until the birth of their first child.

(v) Women forbidden to shave their head until the birth of their first child.

(2) *Orungo (Amuria county)*

Ikarebwok. No woman should sit on the skin of a duiker or eat its flesh. A child may not sit on the skin of a kob; if it does the child will get sores.

Ikarebwok. A child should not sit on goat skin lest it get sores on its head. Pregnant women must not pass over a mole-hill; they must kick the soil from the mole-hill, otherwise an abortion will follow. Pregnant women must not sit on the skin of a duiker. Pregnant women may not eat duiker meat.

Irarak. Pregnant women do not eat goat on pain of abortion. No woman eats the flesh of duiker. A pregnant woman must not step over ants.

Irarak. Pregnant women may eat duiker but other women may not for fear of sterility. Child and mother may not sit on skins of duiker. Women and children may not sit on skins of kob. Women may not pass over a root (*atagowit*). Women drinking water from a pot into which rainwater has fallen become sterile.

Igoria. Women and children must not eat duiker or touch its skin. Women must not shave their hair when pregnant.

Atekok. Men and women may not eat mushroom (*eswei*). If a man eats it, even unknowingly, his wife will catch disease if he has sexual intercourse with her. Women become sterile if they eat it. A small child must not go near *eswei* being cooked on pain of death. Pregnant women may not eat duiker. Women must not touch skins of duiker. Women must not walk over ants (*amuriat*); if the woman is pregnant she aborts, if not pregnant she becomes sterile.

Atekok. Women must not sit on skins of duiker or kob and pregnant women must not eat the flesh of these two animals. Pregnant women must not pass over a mole-hill. Women must not walk over ants.

Atekok. Women must not sit on skins of duiker. *Ekurakei* firewood must not be used. Moles (*enukunyuk*) must not be burnt on pain of blindness.

Atekok. Women must not sit on skins of duiker nor eat its meat. Pregnant women must not look at moles on pain of aborting. If they see moles women must kick the ground. Pregnant women must not pass over mole-hills.

Atekok. Women and children must not sit on skins of duiker. Pregnant women and young women must not eat oribi; old women may. Pregnant women must not chase moles.

Ibobolia. Pregnant women must not tie *edinyot* (a swamp grass) round their heads. Small children must not touch *emolotikei* (a plant), otherwise their hair falls out and sores appear. Pregnant women may not eat stomach contents. Pregnant women may not pass over a mole-hill.

Igetoma. Small children must not look at a monkey (*emabwor*) on pain of blindness.

Igetoma. Women must not sit on skins of duiker. Young women must not eat duiker meat. Pregnant women must kick the soil from mole-hills on pain of abortion.

It is not claimed that either of these lists is exhaustive and probably, with more careful inquiry, many of the apparent anomalies would disappear. For instance, the fact that certain taboos are observed 'until the birth of the first child' or 'while pregnant' may be due to variation in stating the same thing. A detailed investigation might even produce evidence of similarity in taboos, whereby the course of clan fragmentation could be traced, but no such investigation has yet been undertaken.[1]

It is probable that the variations in taboos are due to the process of clan formation described in the previous section. If a man settles among a new clan he will usually retain his own clan taboos, but his children might elect to preserve their entity by forming a new clan, taking some taboos from their father's clan and some from the clan among which they live. This process has been recorded among the Lango.[2] The variations may also be due to the continual breaking down of clans into smaller clans without assumption of a different name. Thus Driberg lists the taboos of the Jo Akarawok; jo Akarawok me Jo Oki; Jo Akarawok me Jo Amor; Jo Akara-wok me tung Burutok; Jo Akarawok me tung Enyang; Jo Akarawok me tung Okelo; Jo Akarawok me Jo Awili; and Jo Akarawok me tung Achola. The duiker is taboo to all these ten clans, but they have many other taboos which differ from clan to clan. The duiker is not reserved to these clans either; the Jo Atekit clan and the thirteen subdivisions of the Jo Atekit also have prohibitions regarding duiker. But despite the breaking up of these clans into smaller ones the prohibitions on the animal totem has persisted although other prohibitions vary.[2]

The function of taboos would appear to be one of cohesion, binding in closer unity the individuals of the clan. 'Today taboos are still observed to a limited extent, but as little economic gain arises from the furtherance of the clan, the taboos are becoming functionless and in all probability will rapidly disappear.'[3] It is my impression that clan taboos are still rigidly and extensively observed. A questionnaire to teacher trainees at Soroti in 1950 showed that they all knew some or all of their clan taboos. If educated young men still know their clan taboos, the probability is that their con-servative and less educated women folk still know and observe them. In a follow-up survey in Kasilang in 1953 it is recorded: 'The period between

[1] I was not able to devote time to the detailed and lengthy inquiries which would be necessary to produce an authoritative study of clan taboos. E. P. Engulu (1937) states that the most important and general taboos are the following: not to touch the skins of duiker, kob, oribi, roan antelope, bushbuck, baboon, ground squirrel, goat, sheep, or calf; not to touch the plant *esimat*; and not to pass through or over mole-hills, black ants, cattle kraal gates, spear hafts, or fences of compounds.

[2] Driberg, 1923.　　　　　　　　　　　　　　　[3] Watson, 1937.

the two surveys 1937 to 1953 has not been followed by any appreciable decline in the observance of clan taboos. Public opinion still demands that the majority of the taboos be observed, but an increasing number of people doubt their effectiveness.'[1]

6. *Clan attributes and functions*

From the discussion in the preceding pages the following main features of the clan system emerge:

(i) The name *ateker* is common to other tribes of the Karamojong cluster.

(ii) Several clan names are common to other tribes of the Karamojong cluster.

(iii) Clan names are very numerous and distributed all over Teso, even within the smallest locality.

(iv) Four or six clans are larger than the others and may be the founder clans of the tribe, though there is no strong tradition to support this theory.

(v) New clans are probably formed by a continuing process of fragmentation in which the new clan retains the old clan name but varies the taboos, or in which the sub-clan or extended family name is adopted and the old name disappears.

(vi) The basis of the system is a number of taboos.

(vii) Taboos are associated with childbirth and observable mainly by women.

(viii) Children belong to the clan of their father and observe their father's clan taboos. Women change taboos on marriage and again on re-marriage to those of their husband's clan.

(ix) Most taboos concern animals, especially duiker and kob.

(x) There is considerable variety in taboos of the same clan according to locality.

The functions of the clan in modern Teso society are not easy to assess. One of the original and main functions of the system was presumably to guard against in-breeding. Clans certainly were exogamous units. Many informants claim they still are. But they often tend to use the word *ateker* loosely, meaning either an extended family or a social unit having a common clan name with other units but a different set of taboos. Thus a man of, say, the Ikarebwok clan having a certain set of taboos cannot under any circumstances marry a girl of the Ikarebwok clan having the same set of taboos, even if no close relationship can be traced and even if the families come from different localities. But marriages between two members of, say, the Ikarebwok clan having different sets of taboos, though rare, are not unknown.

[1] Wilson, 1953.

Clans appear to have no significance regarding property. Cattle are owned on an individual basis and there is no evidence that ownership on a clan basis was ever the rule. Nevertheless, each clan used to possess its own cattle brand, which often differed between male and female beasts. There is, however, no evidence that children's hair styles were modelled on these brands as in Karamoja.[1] In the process of land settlement movement was by groups of different clans moving out from one *etem* area.[2] A particular clan did not therefore lay claim to a tract of country. Several families of different clans owned land in close proximity to each other and subsequent allocation has been on an extended family basis. The conception of clan lands, as generally understood, did not exist in Teso.

A very few clans have specific functions associated with them. Inomu are healers or witch-doctors,[3] although other informants say that Imokolya are the witch-doctors and that entry into this clan is achieved not by birth but by initiation of individuals showing a likely aptitude for the trade. Igumenya are said to be renowned as rain-makers.[3]

The Isureta are the ritual cursers. Any man who breaks an agreement or denies a debt may be taken before an individual or a group of Isureta for a trial by ordeal. The curse (*aigat*) is put upon the debtor in a ceremony at an ant-hill. A white animal, usually a hen, is slaughtered or burnt alive while the curse 'let him die' is uttered. The Isureta then stop the holes of the ant-hill with special leaves or herbs such as *ikero* or *itulel*. No person must look behind him when leaving the ant-hill. If the debtor was lying, he will begin to die within a few days and any relatives, who went through the ceremony with him, will also fall sick. The curse can be removed by payment of the debt or obligation and payment of a cow to the Isureta, who will then unblock the holes of the ant-hill. The effect of this curse is believed to be infallible all over Teso, but it appears to be practised nowadays only in Usuku.

The main function of the system appears to be purely ritualistic. The innumerable customs of birth and marriage are governed by clan ritual and vary from clan to clan. Whereas it is the smaller unit, the extended family, which governs such vital matters as bride-price and blood-money payments and questions of property and inheritance, it is the ritual of the larger unit, the clan, which is followed in all social ceremonies. Thus clan ritual determines the method of disposal of the placenta at birth, the presents received by the new mother, the procedure at twin ceremonies, the gifts bestowed at marriage, and marriage ceremony procedure; the very ceremony of clan initiation of women (*ainyonyo*) varies in detail from clan to clan. These customs and ceremonies are described in greater detail in Part III below.

Belief in the efficacy of clan ritual and clan taboos is still real. Any woman who fails to follow the rules and taboos of her clan will fall sick and

---

[1] Clark, 1950.
[2] Wright, 1942. See p. 68 below.
[3] Kennedy, 1937.

begin to waste away; she may never conceive a child, or if she does conceive, she may abort; her children will get sores on their heads or their
eyelashes will fall out.[1]

7. *Clan leaders*

The title *apolon ka ateker* is translated as 'clan leader'. Each clan having
separate clan taboos had its recognized leader, whose position was to some
extent hereditary although dependent on the assent of the clan members.
The members of, say, the Ikarebwok clan in Ngora, would not recognize
the clan leader of the Ikarebwok clan in Amuria as their own clan leader.
Clan leaders had a local authority confined to those clan members of one
locality, who observed identical taboos. Inasmuch as the clan functions
were mainly ritualistic the clan leader's functions were centred round the
observance of ritual, though he probably exercised control over domestic
disputes within the clan which were not settled on an extended family basis.

The modern clan leader has assumed entirely different functions, partly
as a result of the conscious recognition by Government of clan leaders'
authority in 1937. He is now an unpaid agent of Government, a fifth grade
chief, a sort of justice of the peace. He is appointed by the chiefs to help the
chiefs from among the more prominent or wealthy members of the community. To that extent his position is hereditary, for wealth is inherited.
There is no fixed establishment of clan leaders, which depends on the
numbers and strength of the various clans in the area. A typical establishment of clan leaders within one county, Usuku, is shown on p. 57. The
position is popular, for it carries respect and rewards, as is shown by the
slang name for a clan leader, *omusalotwo*, which means 'his wages are in
the beer gourd'. A clan leader is not elected by the members of his clan.
His modern duties and powers of arrest are defined on pp. 268 and 270
below.

[1] Engulu, 1937.

CHAPTER II

TERRITORIAL GROUPINGS

1. Etem[1]

THE word *etem* (pl. *itemwan*) means the fire-place situated outside in the courtyard, where on special ceremonial occasions a beast might be roasted. This original meaning has been extended to describe the ceremonial meeting-place of the people of one locality, where important matters concerning their relationship with each other and with people of neighbouring localities were discussed. Hence the word came to mean the locality served by the meeting-place and, collectively, the people belonging to that locality.

This territorial grouping was of considerable importance in Teso society. A man might be born, marry, and die in his *etem* area. Except for occasional visits to distant hunting grounds or expeditions to attack other *itemwan*, he would seldom leave his *etem* area. The men of one *etem* hunted together and fought together and were initiated into their age-sets together. They had a common unity and loyalty in their *etem* name.

The size of an *etem* area in pre-administration days corresponded roughly with the modern parish (*eitela*), which is usually an area of land clearly defined by natural swamp or valley boundaries. Thus in Toroma sub-county in Usuku there were four *itemwan* of Kokorio, Amusia, Kapujan, and Toroma. The number of parish areas in modern Teso is in the region of 150.

Within any one *etem* area there were several clans settled, whose leaders met at the *etem* meeting-place to discuss *etem* affairs. The distribution of clans within a typical village area, which is roughly half the size of an old *etem* area, has been described in the last chapter. In the process of settlement of the country by the Iteso, new *itemwan* were formed by groups of men of one or two age-sets moving out to new land. Thus the new *itemwan* from the start would contain members of several different clans. In the diagram on the facing page three neighbouring *itemwan* are established at

---

[1] I have not attempted to provide an English translation of the word *etem* because I know of no word which will convey the social implications of the *etem* grouping, which are considerable, while also indicating the association with a particular locality. Gulliver uses the word 'settlement' in writing of the Jie. 'Homesteads are arranged into settlements consisting of from one to eight clan-hamlets. Each settlement occupies a specific area but does not own it as a group. . . . Nearly all settlements are named groups; primarily they are distinguished by the possession of a ritual grove at which the ritual of the constituent clans takes place, but with the support and co-operation of all the members of the total group (or usually, all initiated male members). There is also a common ritual for rain-making, warding off disease and disaster, and so on . . .' (P. H. Gulliver, *The Family Herds*, London, 1955).

A, *B*, and *C*, with clearly defined, contiguous boundaries. Within each of these three *itemwan* there are a number of different clans settled on the land as shown by the numerals.[1] In due course, owing to pressure on the land or other causes, a group of families consisting of the men of one age-

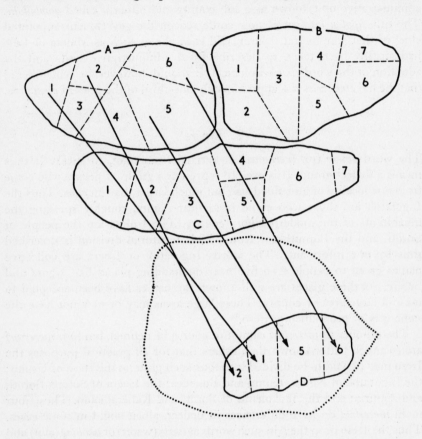

set with their wives and children move out from *etem A* to settle new land. They pass through *etem C* to empty land beyond, find a suitable area, and there settle. The group contains members from clans 1, 2, 5, and 6, but not from clans 3 and 4. At first the new *etem D* may not have contiguous boundaries with *C*, but as time passes and the new *etem's* population grows these common boundaries will become established as shown by the dotted lines.

The *etem* meeting-place was usually a prominent rock, tree, or grove. Such trees or groves are still reverenced and carefully preserved. The *etem* community had a recognized head, *apolon ka etem*, whose position was hereditary and whose functions were largely ceremonial. Desecration of the *etem* grove required compensation to the *etem* chief of a bull. His functions

---

[1] Gulliver calls these clan areas 'clan hamlets'.

did not include leadership in war or in hunting, for which there were different leaders, the *apolon ka ajore* or the *apolon ka eriga*.

When in the wave of nationalism in the 1930's it was decided to replace Luganda terminology with Ateso, the word *etem* was coined to describe the administrative unit known as a sub-county and hitherto called *gombolola*. The title *apolon ka etem* is now conferred on the government-appointed chief of that administrative unit. Old *etem* names such as Malera or Lale had already been taken to describe these administrative units and the adoption of the word *etem* was logical. It should, however, be remembered that the old *etem* area was approximately one-third of the present *etem* area.

2. *Einere*[1]

The word *einere* (pl. *ineresinei*) is derived from *einer*, to speak. It thus means a dialect group. It is used to represent a group of people who come from one locality of undefined size but much larger than an *etem*. Thus the Ingoratok are those who come from near Ngora, roughly speaking the inhabitants of the modern Ngora county. The Isolota are the people of Soroti, and the Ikumitok of Kumi. This territorial division is described thus by one informant: 'The words Ingoratok or Iseera are collective names given to people who live near outstanding places like Ngora and Serere. As these places are well-known the names have been accepted to mean a large area or county. These large areas may or may not have the same way of pronouncing Ateso.'

The number of *ineresinei* cannot of course be defined, but four *ineresinei* are so much better known than others that for all practical purposes the Iteso may be said to be divided into four such groups: the Iteso of Usuku; the Ingoratok of Ngora, Kumi, and Bukedea; the Iseera of Serere, Soroti, and Amuria; and the Ikokolemu of Soroti and Kaberamaido. These four main *ineresinei* do have differences in dialect, albeit slight in some cases. Thus the Iteso drop the *k* in such words as *akipi* (water) or *akolong* (sun) and pronounce them *aipi* and *aolong*. The Iseera use *g* for *b* and refer to *Ikaregwok* instead of *Ikarebwok*. The Ingoratok dialect has been taken as standard Ateso. The Ikokolemu have radical differences and speak a language that is akin to Lango and no longer intelligible to the Iteso. Nevertheless, many words denoting relationship, numerals, and animals are identical.

The reasons for these differences of dialect are presumably historical. The Iteso are the original inhabitants of Usuku from the first migration. The Ingoratok are the descendants of those who in the second migration passed south over Kapiri ford. The Iseera spring from those who in the

[1] I have not attempted to provide an English translation of *einere* other than 'division' of the tribe. This is the term used by Driberg whereas Gulliver uses the purely territorial term 'district', which fails to indicate the social significance of the grouping, slight though it is, and is liable to misinterpretation inasmuch as the word is nowadays inevitably associated with the administrative division of the province known as 'district'.

second migration moved westwards and northwards. The Ikokolemu adopted the Nilotic language of the Lango with whom they came in close contact.

The *ineresinei* have thus a linguistic, territorial, and historical significance. In very modern times they have also attained a political significance. The groups, especially the two larger groups of Ingoratok and Iseera, openly vie for political appointments. The same informant records: 'these names, Ingoratok and Iseera, do not mean a different clan or people. It is only of very recent years, through political agitators and ambitious and envious people, that these words have been wrongly and deliberately mis-interpreted to mean different parties with party interests.'

The importance of the *ineresinei* in the social structure of the Iteso is slight and except in political matters the *ineresinei* command no real loyalties. That this large grouping did have some social significance is suggested by the fact that similar large groupings appear among other Nilo-Hamitic peoples. Thus the Lango tribe was divided into the Jo Kide, Jo Aber, Jo Burutok, and Jo Moita.[1] The Karamojong recognize three such groups: the Ngi-Pian, Ngi-Bokora, and Ngi-Matheniko. Among the Turkana and Toposa there are two.[2] Some social cohesion is discernible within these large groupings by reason of identity in age-system ritual, which often differs from that practised in neighbouring *ineresinei*. In the next chapter it will be seen that the ritual of the age-system practised among the Iseera differs radically from that practised by the Iteso and slightly from that practised by the Ingoratok.

[1] Driberg, 1923.   [2] Gulliver, 1953 (ii).

CHAPTER III

AGE-SYSTEM GROUPINGS

1. *Introduction*

WHEREAS the extended family, clan, *etem*, and *einere* all play some part in the modern social or political organization of the Iteso, the age-set system belongs to the past; the details of the age-set ceremonies and the songs which were sung at them are now largely forgotten. The suppression of these ceremonies by the Baganda was so drastic and lasting that early European observers saw no trace of the age-system; neither Roscoe, Kitching, Kruyer, nor Schut makes any mention of the subject; there is no reference to it in official documents until the 1930's; although unpublished recordings were made in 1921 and 1937, the first published account of the system did not appear till 1942.[1] The ceremonies were abolished in 1900 so that there are now very few persons in Teso who have themselves been initiated into an age-set or who have seen an age-set ceremony. Information is therefore difficult to assemble.

The word 'age-set' is used to translate the Ateso word *aturi* (pl. *aturio*) meaning a group of men having a common identity through ritual initiation with other men of approximately the same age. Once a man has been initiated into his age-set he remains in it for the rest of his life. He will, during his life, pass through several age-stages, which must not be confused with age-sets:

imukeru	a baby, until the age of 2, when it is weaned.
ikoku	a child, until the age of 6.
etelepat	a boy, until the age of fourteen, when puberty occurs.
etumunan	a youth, until the age of 18.
esapat	a young man, until the age of 26.
ekiliokit	a full grown man, until the age of 42.
apolon	an elder, until the age of 66.
emojong	an old man, until death.

This division of society into sets according to age is a feature of all the Nilo-Hamitic peoples.

Nilo-Hamitic societies have no chief or any centralised machinery of state control. Kinship, lineage, and clan have practically no political importance. It is the age-system that provides the framework of the political structure. Not that the age-system is to be identified with the political system, but in societies such as the Nilo-Hamitic every corporate activity, of which political activity is the form par-excellence, is organized on the structural basis of the age-system.[2]

[1] Wright, 1942.   [2] Bernardi, 1952.

2. *Age-set functions*

It is not easy to assess the functions of the age-set system in Teso society fifty years after its demise.

It is popularly believed that the Baganda suppressed the age-set cere-monies because they interfered with road making and other forms of communal labour; it is even suggested that the Baganda feared the military organization which the system engendered. But there is no evidence that the system ever did produce a special warrior class dedicated to fighting for a certain period of its existence. On the contrary, all men could, and did, take part in raids according to their inclination.

If the system provided the framework of political structure among the Teso, by giving individuals or groups a recognized position in communal activities and deliberative councils, it presumably perished as rapidly as it did because the Baganda and, later, the British, substituted an alternative system of political control which was immediately acceptable. The implica-tion is that the system was already playing a diminishing part in the political life of the Iteso, perhaps through their contact with neighbouring Bantu tribes, and would ultimately have disappeared without the impetus given by the Baganda. There is no other way of explaining the rapid and complete disappearance of a system which has persisted in its entirety to the present day in Karamoja and other Nilo-Hamitic districts. The same disintegrating forces were presumably at work in Lango, where the system still existed in 1923[1] but is now defunct.

The age-set system did, however, play a vital part in the settlement of modern Teso district by the Iteso. New *etem* areas were formed and settled by immigrants, who moved out from a parent *etem* on a basis of age-groups instead of on a basis of kinship groups as in Nilotic or Bantu societies.

The age-system also provided a sort of religion. The whole sphere of natural existence was regarded as within the powers of one or other of the eight age-sets. This religious significance of the system will be elaborated later.[2]

3. *Structure of the age-set system (eigworone)*

The structure of the Teso age-set system consisted of a fixed number of age-sets which followed each other in rhythmical rotation. Entry to an age-set was by initiation, which took place about every three years. This

[1] Driberg, 1923.

[2] The account of the age-system among the Lango (*aworon*) shows that age-sets were closely associated with rain making. Rain-making festivals were said to belong to the dominant age-set. This association between the age-system and rain making is not apparent in Teso, but the following note by the late Father Kruyer is of interest: '*Elelekecha* (is a dance) for imploring rain; in some parts (Kokoryo in Usuku) it is a sort of puberty dance. . . .'

initiation was known as *eigworone* (from *aigwor* 'to cry'). The word refers not only to the initiation ceremony but also to the initiation or totem name adopted by the age-set at the ceremony. *Ewoe* (from *awoere* 'to sing') is an alternative word to describe the initiation or age-set name and may be used also in the meaning of age-set. *Adwaron* is the state of coming of age. It is derived from *adwaris* 'sourness'. Previously the initiates had the sweetness of childhood; now they take on the sourness of age. *Adwaron* is also used of the ceremony itself. Over most of Teso the *eigworone* ceremony prevailed, but there existed a separate ceremony known as *asapan* (from *esapat* 'youth') which was an initiation into man's estate performed on an individual basis. Whereas the two forms of ceremony could exist side by side without conflict, it appears that *asapan* was, and is, practised almost exclusively in Usuku, while *eigworone* was general elsewhere.

The number and the order of *eigworone* names appear to have been constant over all Teso. There were eight such names:—

Ikaalen	Floods	Iputiro	Warthogs
Ikosobwan	Buffaloes	Igolei	Hawks
Itomei	Elephants	Iderin	Bushbucks
Imoru	Rocks	Irisai	Leopards

(In South Teso, among the Ingoratok, Imosing (Rhinoceroses) replaces *Iderin* in the sequence.)

These age-set names followed each other in strict rotation, Bushbucks after Hawks; Leopards after Bushbucks; Floods after Leopards and so on. Since the period between initiations was about three years, the whole cycle took about twenty-four years. It was therefore not unusual to have two age-sets of the same name, a senior and a junior, in existence at the same time.

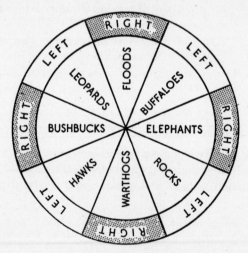

The age-sets belonged alternately to the right or to the left side according to the position of the set in the cattle kraal during the ceremony of initiation.

Initiation into an age-set was sponsored by the age-set next but one in seniority to the age-set of the initiates. The formal initiation was marked by a whipping contest between the two age-sets immediately senior to the initiates. Thus Hawks (left hand) contended with Bushbucks (right hand) in initiating Leopards (left hand). At the next initiation ceremony Bushbucks (right hand) contended with Leopards (left hand) in initiating Floods (right hand). Thus initiates always entered the same side (*ewai*) as their sponsors and the opposite side to the age-set immediately senior to them. According to other sources[1] age-sets changed sides according to whether they were the senior or junior age-set in the contest, the senior set always taking the right side. Thus Bushbucks (right hand) contended with Leopards (left hand) in initiating Floods (right hand). But in the next initiation ceremony Leopards (right hand) contended with Floods (left hand) in initiating Buffaloes (right hand). By this system initiates still entered the same side as their sponsors and the opposite side to the age-set immediately senior to them, but the side was always the right side, the side of the senior age-set participating in the whipping contest. It has also been suggested[2] that the sponsoring age-set was not necessarily the set next but one in seniority to the initiates, but the set which won the whipping contest in the previous year. Thus in the last six contests held at Asuret the following results obtained:

Date (approximate)	Contesting age-sets	Winning age-sets	Initiates' age-sets
1885	Floods / Rhinos	Floods	Buffaloes
1888	Floods / Buffaloes	Buffaloes	Elephants
1891	Buffaloes / Elephants	Elephants	Rocks
1894	Elephants / Rocks	Rocks	Warthogs
1897	Rocks / Warthogs	Rocks	Hawks
1900	Rocks / Hawks	Rocks	Rhinoceroses

The weight of evidence, however, appears to be in favour of the first explanation. Four of the eight age-sets in the cycle belonged to the right, and the other four to the left side. The side was as immutable as the name. Each age-set was initiated at a whipping contest between the two age-sets immediately preceding it, the senior of which acted as sponsors. The new age-set took the side of its sponsors.

The system just described resembles the age-set system of the Lango[3] in which the age-sets followed each other in strict rotational order at known

---

[1] Amootoi ka Etesot, 1946.
[2] Watson, 1937.   [3] Driberg, 1923.

intervals. The Teso system differed radically from that of the Karamojong, Toposa, and Jie, among whom age-sets did not follow in a fixed order and among whom a number of age-sets were grouped together to form an age-generation having a distinctive name and recognized political functions.

4. *Age-set ceremonies* (*eigworone*)

Eigworone initiation ceremonies were held every third year, although occasionally shorter or longer periods have been recorded. They normally took place in November or December about three months after the harvest. Osuban in the Teso calendar is the month of celebration, the equivalent of November.

The area served by one initiation ceremony was usually that of an *etem*; the boys of one *etem* would be initiated together. Occasionally, however, the area was larger and it is stated that one initiation ceremony for Orungo, Gweri, Wera, Kuju, Arapai, and Katine was held at Dakabela.

Most informants agree that boys were initiated shortly after puberty at the age of 14 to 16, but there is evidence that initiates were considerably older, 22 to 24 years old.[1] The oldest age-set encountered during inquiries in 1921 was the Buffaloes of 1885. This fact might support the view that initiates were more than 20 years old, in which case the Buffalo age-set members would be about 58 years old in 1921.

Each initiation year members of the sponsoring age-set, the set next but one above that of the initiates, agreed upon the date and chose the youths to be initiated, who then wore decorated aprons.[1] The ceremonies lasted three and sometimes four days and took place at a special cattle kraal (*aujo*) built for the purpose. On the first day the sponsoring age-set and their opponents, the set immediately junior to them, arrived armed with shields and plaited hide whips. The sponsors took their position on the appropriate side of the kraal or, according to some accounts, on the right side. The two sets then indulged in a whipping contest, which was often severe; occasionally an eye would be lost or an ear cut off. The initiates took no part in the contest. Their turn came the following year. After the contest dancing took place and special *eigworone* songs were sung. On the first and second day the initiates were given formal instruction by the sponsoring age-set, mainly in the art of fighting. There was more dancing on the second day. On the third day the ceremonial washing of the initiates took place at a nearby swamp or river, after which they had to return to the kraal without looking behind them. The last act in the ceremony was the slaughtering of a bull; the dung from the entrails was smeared on the initiates' faces, shoulders, arms, and chests, with prayers for prosperity of the age-set. 'We have taught you,' the sponsors cried, 'you are now alive.'

During the ceremonies the initiates wore bells on legs, arms, and necks and carried a thin stick. They did not sleep in the kraal at night, but were

[1] Amootoi ka Etesot, 1946.

allowed to return to nearby houses or to huts erected near the kraal. During the three days they were not allowed to feed themselves. It was the duty of unmarried girls to wash the initiates' faces and to place food in their mouths. Women were not initiated, although while boys received their instruction, unmarried girls were similarly instructed by women outside the kraal.[1] Initiates lived with the girls during the ceremonies but were strictly commanded not to commit fornication with them on pain of bringing death and disaster on the whole age-set.[2]

After the three-day ceremony at the kraal was over, initiates returned to their own villages where feasting continued for at least ten days and sometimes for a whole month.

Age-set ceremonies were not confined to initiation. During the period between initiations feasts were held, usually in April, at which preliminary instruction might be given to the next batch of initiates. Mention is also made of ritual feasts at which the Elephants (right) and Rocks (left) contributed millet, which was exchanged by the *apolon ka etem* for a bull. At the feast the Floods sat on the right and the Buffaloes on the left, while Elephants and Rocks respectively prepared and served the slaughtered beast. At a later date a similar feast was held for the remaining four age-sets. Bushbucks (right) served Warthogs, who sat on the right, and Leopards (left) served Hawks, who sat on the left.[2]

This account of the age-set ceremonies is based partly on verbal information, but mainly on recordings made in 1921 and on the account prepared by the Amootoi ka Etesot society; both these sources are based on *eigworone* customs in Soroti and Serere counties. Customs in Kumi, Ngora, and Bukedea did not differ greatly.

5. *Age-system in Usuku*

The *asapan* ceremony, which was and is the normal age-system ceremony in Usuku, involves more of an element of individual apprenticeship than of communal instruction. A youth, wishing to be raised to man's status, must find a sponsor, for whom he works for one or two months, performing menial tasks, living in his sponsor's house, and calling him father. The sponsor gives the youth instruction. At the end of the period of instruction the youth adopts a new 'bull' name either from the bull slaughtered on the occasion of his return home or by his own choice in the following manner: the boy squats under the udder of a cow and his sponsor calls out 'Ojakol, suck the milk'. If the youth does not wish to accept this name he shakes his head. The sponsor might then call out, 'Lemukol, suck the milk'. If this name pleases him, the youth sucks the cow's udder to signify assent. When the period of apprenticeship is over a feast is held at the youth's own home, to which he must return running. At the feast he is given a bull by his father or a heifer or goats.

[1] Lukyn-Williams, unpublished notes, 1921.   [2] Amootoi ka Etesot, 1946.

The proximity of Karamoja and the fact that Kakunguru never extended his control over Usuku perhaps explain why *asapan* is still practised in Usuku. There are indications that the popularity of the ceremony is declining. The sub-county council of Usuku recently debated the value of *asapan*:

The members who were in favour of *asapan* said that *asapan* used to be a Teso custom and that nobody was forced to *asapan*. That whenever a boy went to *asapan*, at the end he would be awarded a cow or five goats.

The members who were not in favour said that *asapan* hinders the development of a country, and that there is no profit in *asapan*. It is a waste to slaughter cows or goats or to brew beer at *asapan*; all this should be used to educate children. Women of those boys who have not been through *asapan* ceremony are not allowed to eat of the meat of the beast slaughtered at the burying ceremony of one of the boys who died before *asapan*. This is bad.

During *asapan* people were chased and beaten so much that in the end they might die. A youth who goes to *asapan* must act like a slave; i.e. carry water, grind millet, collect firewood, herd cattle, be smeared with butter like a woman; sometimes such a youth may be of the Christian faith. We would recommend that anybody who is caught performing *asapan* should be imprisoned for six months.

A further age system ceremony recorded from Usuku is that of *ailom otem* or *aijar iwore*.[1] This appears to be a form of entry into the dominant age-set through purchase. Until a man has entered the dominant age-set he is not supposed to drink beer or to shave the hair under his armpits. Entry is a lengthy process beginning with offerings by would-be initiates of fowls, *emuna* (groundnuts mixed with butter), and honey. Later each would-be entrant, who may be from 17 to 30 years of age, must produce a bull; boys not yet ready for entry, aged 12 to 17, must bring a he-goat. Negotiations then begin for the hand-over. When the members of the dominant age-set have accepted the bulls and goats and agreed to hand over, they choose a new age-set name for the new entrants. It appears that this ceremony only took place about every thirteen years; there was no fixed order of age-set names; the following names have been quoted: Ikosobwan (Buffaloes), Itomei (Elephants), Itukoi (Zebras), Irisai (Leopards), Iputiro (Warthogs). This system resembles the age-generation system of the Jie and Karamojong, but there is no indication that sub-sets were formed during the thirteen-year period. Unlike *asapan*, this ceremony appears to be defunct, although its decline may have been more recent than that of the *eigworone*.

6. *Religious significance of the age-system*

The religious significance of the age-set system has already been briefly mentioned. The whole sphere of natural existence was methodically

[1] Wright, 1942.

divided between the eight age-sets, so that each set had religious or ritual powers over a series of associated objects or activities. The division does not always appear logical and according to one legend gave rise to doubts and disputes. This legend concerns a dispute between Floods and Hawks in Osuguru in Serere consequent on Floods claiming control over hippopotami.

Hawks started the dispute by claiming control over hippopotami, because they graze on pasture land and only go into the water to sleep. Floods, however, contested this claim because, although hippopotami graze like cattle on pasture land, they spend most of their time in the water. The persons present at the dispute were unable to find the correct answer because both claims appeared to have equal validity, so it was decided that the two age-sets should fight it out. Hawks eventually won the fight and their powers over hippopotami were thus established.

The age-set powers and objects associated with those powers are shown in the following list, which is based largely on recordings made in 1921, on Mr. E. P. Engulu's list,[1] and on the findings of the Amootoi ka Etesot society. Many discrepancies occur in these accounts, all of which are based on experience in the Soroti and Serere areas only. Whereas many of the associated objects belong logically to the powers of the age-sets, animals, birds, and, to a lesser extent, crops, seem to be divided among the age-sets with no apparent logic. In most age-sets among the associated objects there occurs an animal name which appears to be the second or reserve totem name of the age-set, such as kobs (Floods), zebras (Buffaloes), lions (Rocks), hippopotami (Hawks), rhinoceroses (Bushbucks), and elands (Leopards); these secondary names occasionally appear as the name of an age-set.

Floods: The underlying notion is control over water and heavenly bodies, and logically associated objects include rain, hail, mosquitoes, fish, fish hooks, lightning, wind, rainbows, sun, moon, stars, daylight, darkness, and various animals or birds which frequent the water such as ducks, frogs, crocodiles, egrets, and the like. The inclusion of kobs is less easy to explain.

Buffaloes: This age-set had powers over seasons and division of the earth, and the list of associated objects includes many of the animals which live on the land: the monkey family, rabbits, lizards, chameleons, goats, sheep, donkeys, zebras, giraffes, elands, certain birds including the ground hornbill, rodents, and shields which are made from giraffe or buffalo hide.

Elephants: The idea surrounding this age-set was one of strength and size, and power over fire, iron, and wood. Hence the list of associated objects included trees, canoes, milk-pails, spears, hoes, axes, drums, mortars, and tables; a more modern slant is given by inclusion of European imported objects such as corrugated iron sheets, bicycles, motor-cars, and railways.[1] The most important powers concerned fire, grass, and houses.

[1] Wright, 1942.

The inclusion of bees is less logical. Giraffes, claimed also by Buffaloes, are said to be within the powers of this age-set.

Rocks: This age-set controlled supplies of food and beer and thus had powers over millet, sorghum, beans, and hyenas, which live in the rocks. But the list also includes lions, crows, grasshoppers, and guinea-fowls, perhaps because the last two eat food crops.

Warthogs: The essential idea is one of fertility and reduplication and the list of objects includes women, pigs, hens, pigeons, and bees, which are also claimed by the Elephants set. An added idea is control of healing and the age-set consequently has witch-doctors within its powers.

Hawks: The underlying idea is wealth, particularly in cattle. In fact it is stated by some informants that the real meaning of the word *Igolei* is 'cattle', a synonym for *ibaren*, wealth in cattle, and not 'hawks'. Thus the associated objects include women, who are also claimed by the Warthogs age-set, sheep (which are claimed by the Buffaloes), cattle, milk, butter, blood, cattle dung, and, less obviously, hippopotami, waterbucks, dogs, kites, pythons, and locusts.

Bushbucks: This age-set controlled soil and associated objects such as ant-hills, flying ants, termites, moles, sweet potatoes, cassava, pots, and, less obviously, rhinoceroses (an alternative name for the age-set), and hartebeests.

Leopards: The underlying idea is plunder or theft. Associated objects include the wild cat family, crested cranes, guinea-fowls (which are also claimed by Rocks). Less obvious inclusions are elands, groundnuts, simsim, and peas.

The songs sung by the different age-sets at the *eigworone* dances concerned the age-set totems or their associated objects. Most of the songs were about animals and the singers imitated the movements of the animals as they sang.

Thus, to take a few examples,[1] the Floods age-set sang:

(i) *Jelele! Jelele! Ilosi okido.*
     Jelele! Nat kelimun kodoi okido.

(Flowing, flowing! You move onto the island.
Flowing! Just when it has been said you move onto the island.)

(ii) *Toto, koinakinai aiyo, aiyo.*
      Toto, koinakinai aiyo.

(Mother, give me fish.)

Buffaloes age-set praised their totem thus:

(iii) *Kocoite inangi akoniluk; iriono, iriono ekosobwan, iriono.*

(Take care when you hit the wide-horned beast; black, black is the buffalo, black.)

---

[1] From recordings by F. Lukyn-Williams in 1921 (personal communication) and Amootoi ka Etesot, 1946.

Elephants age-set had many songs about their totem:

(iv)   *Eruo etome; eruo etome kayongo.*
         Eruo etome Logirokileng.
         Eruo etome kayongo; eruo etome dangadanga.

         (The elephant trumpets in a frightening manner.
         The elephant trumpets Logirokileng.
         The elephant trumpets in a frightening manner;
         The elephant trumpets roaringly.)

(v)   *Edakas itomei Kanyipa, Kanyipa. Kowo! Ijeja, ijeja!*
         (The elephants graze at Kanyipa. Sing, alas!)

and about their associated objects:

(vi)   *Anomo akai kowai ka je, akai. Koyautu akipi koarere akim.*
         (The house burns on yonder side. Bring water to quench the fire.)

One of the most popular themes of the Rocks age-set songs was the lion:

(vii)   *Engatuny eari kaibwa; engatuny eari kaibwa.*
         Eari ekori da dangadanga; engatuny eari kaibwa.
         Etukosi itiang; ekatiang lotingiro.
         Eari eloba da kaibwa; eari egwapet da kaibwa,
         etuko da kaibwa, eari ekori da kaibwa;
         eari ekosobwan da kaibwa;
         eari apoli da kaibwa lotisogoli.
         Kigwori isio dangadanga;
         kabwoikisi isio engatuny kecuma kakwara kaara.

         (The lion kills and keeps; the lion kills and keeps.
         He kills the giraffe and keeps; the lion kills and keeps.
         The animals gather; mine is the tawny one.
         He kills the hartebeest and keeps; he kills the eland and keeps,
         the zebra and keeps, the giraffe and keeps;
         he kills the buffalo;
         he kills the water buck the curved-horned animal.
         We sing his praises; let us stand and spear the lion
         with our spear and kill it.)

(viii)   *Oye! Kowo! Eigworone etiang, apolon engatuny, engatuny etiang, kadedengan*
         engatuny dangadanga kadedengan.
             Kiari isio imori.
         Oye! oye! Kigworo isio engolingiro, kowomo! kowomo!
         Oye! oye! Kigworo longiro ededeng orot,
             etiang loajokan elipunio.
         Eruo longiro korot, etiang loti apolon.
         Igworotoi, oye! Kigworo isio engatuny.

         (Oh! Sing! The lion is head of the age-set; the lion is fierce, terribly fierce.
             We killed the little duiker.
         Oh! We celebrate the tawny beast, owomo!

Oh! We celebrate the tawny one, fierce in the path, magnificent beast, smooth skinned.

The tawny beast roars in the path, the immense one.

He is celebrated, oye! We celebrate the lion.)

Songs of the Warthogs age-set included:

(ix) *Ingiolol eputir toto acoa guluteng ingiolol. Ouu! Iyaa!*
(The warthog with his teeth outside is the mother of wisdom.)

(x) *Toto, adwalakaar atap. Koyautu akiria kowai je kesidikoto.*
(Mother, the porridge is runny. Bring more flour from over there to make it stiff.)

(xi) *Ebangaana ekokor; emony ebai kokolorikoo ekositiang.*
(The cock is foolish; it crows cock-a-doodle at night, our animal.)

Hawks age-set songs included:

(xii) *Papa ya, papa komanyakinai aberu.*
Papa ya, papa, ejok aberu, papa ya.
(Father, father, pay bride-price for a woman for me.
Father, a woman is good, father.)

(xiii) *Oye! Ekokote ka aberu, ekokote ka angor kanukopolok.*
(Ah! The envy of a woman, the envy of old women.)

(xiv) *Abongos akile awaket, akile; kejukas idwe komata akile.*
(The milk has returned to the udder. Let us send our children to drink milk.)

(xv) *Aur akinyet kowai ka je, akinyet kowai je.*
Oo! ekawoe, aur akinyet.
(The ghee is smelling in the house over there.
Oh! my song, ghee is smelling.)

In the Bushbucks age-set many of the songs concerned the secondary totem of the age-set, the rhinoceros:

(xvi) *Etupete amosing, etupete amosing, kowo.*
Etupete amosing dangadanga, etupete amosing, kowo.
Etupete amosing angirotum, etupete amosing, kowo.
(They follow the rhino.)

(xvii) *Emani akware kiakia ekingok, ekingok ka imosingo.*
(He walks by night always, the dog of the rhinos.)

(xviii) *Ebangaana angerep, emini ebai, angerep emini ebai.*
Oo! ekawoe! ebangaana angerep emini ebai.
(The ant-hill is foolish, it produces white ants at night.
Oh! my song! the ant-hill is foolish.)

Leopards age-set songs included:

(xix)   *Aur enino kowai je, enino. Emamu nat ikanyum.*
(Cooked simsim smells in yonder house. There is no fresh simsim.)

(xx)   *Eramiramakin alaro, emaido ejok, ibore emaido, emaido.*
(The drying floor is beaten level. Groundnuts are good.)

PART III

SOCIAL CEREMONIES AND CUSTOMS

Note: Frequent reference is made throughout this Part to the considerable variation which exists between clans in the details of social ceremonies, particularly those concerning childbirth and clan initiation by smearing. I have tried to record the salient features of ceremonies which are common to all clans, but in some instances the details recorded may be applicable to one clan but not to another.

CHAPTER I

BIRTH

1. *Parturition*

T HERE is no custom of segregation before confinement and a pregnant woman goes about her daily tasks until the pains overtake her; but from that time until the third day after birth she should stay inside her own hut and not even her own husband should see her. Should persons of another clan see her at this time harm will be caused to the new-born child. In practice the woman does sometimes leave her hut, but the child must never be seen during this period of confinement.

A woman is usually assisted in parturition by her husband's mother (*toto*) or by another elderly woman of her husband's clan. I can find no support for Roscoe's contention that her own mother helps to deliver her. If this were true, the husband would see his mother-in-law; the ritual of mother-in-law avoidance is rigidly practised by the Iteso. There exists, however, a class of professional midwives who may help the husband's female relatives or act instead of them; they expect payment of money or of a goat for their services.

To deliver the child the expectant mother kneels with her thighs apart and her buttocks resting on her heels; her arms are stretched backwards and supported by a woman sitting behind her; her husband's mother or the midwife kneels or sits directly opposite her ready to receive the baby in her outstretched hands. According to early accounts the expectant mother did not kneel but sat and was not supported by an attendant woman behind her but by stones placed between her back and the wall of the hut. The new-born babe is washed with warm water, but it is alleged that formerly in some parts it was licked by its mother.[1]

The correct disposal of the placenta is most important. Customs differ slightly according to clan, but in all cases the placenta must be put out of the reach of enemies who could by possessing it cause the death of the child. The placenta is usually buried in the thicket by the woman who delivered the child during the three days of confinement or immediately after them. But according to other accounts it used to be buried inside the hut near the door.[2] The placenta of twins is put in a special pot (*adogoria*), which has two mouths, and left in a swamp or, in some clans, buried in a path. Different clans use either a hoe, or a knife, or a sharp wooden stick for burying the placenta, which should be buried between two sticks to ensure further fertility in the woman.[3]

The umbilical cord must be cut either by a knife or by a sharp piece of

[1] Kruyer (undated). [2] Roscoe, 1915. [3] Engulu, 1937.

grass according to clan ritual. Ritual also decides what material shall be used to tie the cord, banana fibre, or fibre of the *ebiong* (Ficus glumosa) or *ebirai* trees.[1]

The customs thus briefly described are still general throughout Teso although an ever increasing number of births take place in hospital. In 1953 there were 1,043 births in government hospitals and dispensaries and about half that number in mission hospitals out of an estimated total of 12,500 births in the district. It is noteworthy that those who come to hospital must, and readily do, consent to departure from clan ritual in the matter of disposal of the placenta and of cutting and tying the umbilical cord. Although ante-natal clinics are held at hospitals and at some dispensaries there is no system of ante-natal visiting by trained nurses or midwives. The effects of modern medical knowledge on childbirth are, in fact, still slight. It is therefore fortunate that abnormal births are rare. A child born feet first is unlucky and it is thought better that it die in infancy.[2]

2. *Birth ceremonies*

After the birth certain ceremonies are observed. After the third day the floor of the hut is smeared with cow dung. The woman's mother has been informed and sends pots of beer and some food. The food is then prepared and laid out on trays outside the hut of confinement. One calabash of mixed food is taken to the new mother by the midwife or woman who delivered her. When she has tasted it all the assembled women eat. The new mother then tastes the beer in the same way and the midwife dips her fingers in the beer and brings them to the infant's lips. The assembled women and the men, who have been waiting apart, are then invited into the hut to drink the beer. The woman's mother does not attend this ceremony, which is known as *aipuduno*, the ceremony of taking the baby out of the house. For subsequent births after the first the same ceremony is repeated but the woman's mother does not contribute beer.[3]

After the birth of her first child it is customary for the woman to visit her father-in-law's house and to receive certain presents; these generally consist, among other things, of dry beer, an earthenware pot and an instrument for stirring food. The presents vary from clan to clan. According to other sources the gifts come from the woman's own parents and not from her husband's family. They consist of millet, salt, simsim, groundnuts, stirring stick (*eipiret*), hides for a bed, cow peas, a gourd, a sling for carrying children, a wooden spoon for mixing porridge, beer, the stomach of a beast, flour, and a receptacle for butter for smearing the child. If the woman's parents live far away, the foodstuffs may be obtained from a local neighbour, provided he is of a different clan from the husband's.[4]

[1] Engulu, 1937.   [2] Roscoe, 1915.
[3] Schut (undated).   [4] Engulu, 1937.

3. *Birth of twins*

The birth of twins (*imwatok* or *ibangin*) is welcomed but is dangerous, for there are many superstitions connected with it and special ceremonies are necessary. For instance, failure to attend the twins' birth ceremony may result in a period of bad luck, failure of crops, and even blindness; should a twin, after being rebuked by its parents, crawl under a granary, evil will befall the family. Another belief is that the breath of twins can affect peoples' skins.

The method of informing the woman's parents of the event is strange. One of the husband's male relatives must go and take by stealth certain food from the granaries of the woman's parents. On his return journey he raises an alarm. The woman's relatives in turn will return and try to steal food back. Among certain clans the male relative may throw an arrow (*ekojo*) on to the roof of the woman's parents' house and they in turn must return to throw it on to the husband's house. This ritual is often disregarded nowadays, but the ritual of avoidance is still strong. The two families should never meet at this time.

The birth of twins must be celebrated by all neighbours. A special drum (*emidiri*), covered with lizard skin, is used together with two small drums (*ideteta*). Mock alarm is shown by the family and men folk run about with shield and spear adopting threatening attitudes. Separate ceremonies take place in each of the two families concerned. Food and beer are provided in large quantities. The beer must be drunk, initially at any rate, from a special pot (*adogoria*) having two mouths. The dance sometimes lasts several days until the woman is fully recovered, but is nowadays usually limited to one day and is not always observed. The father of the twins must provide a sheep or goat; two pieces of the skin of this animal must be preserved to serve as clothing for the twins. 'It is also usual for guests to bring presents; formerly pieces of iron were used, but nowadays cent pieces are a common gift.'[1] One is given to each twin and the woman's mother-in-law strings them. After the dancing and feasting are over, the mother-in-law makes little garments from the sheepskin and attaches the cents to them. The grain which is left over is made into beer and a quiet family party ensues without dancing.[1]

The period of avoidance between the families may last some time and is ended by a formal ceremony known as *eriyam* performed in both homes. Kitching records a ceremony known as *abwaturori*. After the birth of twins the parents are not permitted to pay a visit outside the village nor any outsider to enter their own village without first performing the ceremony of *abwaturori*. This is carried out beneath the log archway that spans the entrance to every Teso village. The father and his visitor, or host, as the case may be, kneel opposite to one another beneath this archway and between them is a bowl containing a paste of flour and water. The father of twins smears some of this paste

[1] Schut (undated).

over his face and breast, then over the breast and face of the other; after this has been duly carried out the visit can proceed with no fear of evil consequences. This ceremony is also necessary when a girl in her first pregnancy wishes to pay a visit to her father or her uncle, whom she would call father if her real father were dead.[1]

This ceremony is the *abwatun ore* ceremony, a part of *eriyam*, in which the members of the two families sprinkle or smear each other with water, cow dung, porridge, or any such substance. The *eriyam* ceremony is conducted with the same mock alarm and mock fighting. There is feasting, drinking, and dancing. The songs are usually scurrilous, mocking, or obscene, such as:

> *Opolot, papa ka idwe, ebur akwan; e e e! ebur akwan.*
> *Agwang, tataa ka idwe, idonyony; e e e! idonyony.*[2]

After this ceremony the two families may return to a normal relationship.

4. *Barrenness and infant mortality*

Barrenness and the early death of successive children bring great shame on a woman. It is never recognized that failure to bear children may be due to impotence of the husband and that barrenness and infant mortality may be due to some simply explained abnormality. Such misfortunes are attributed to an evil spirit and propitiatory ceremonies are essential. Recourse may be had to a witch-doctor (*emuron*) who prescribes medicine. The medicine may cause the woman to bear but great care is needed to ensure that the child does not perish quickly like the others.

A fresh doorway is cut in the side of the house for the use of the child; on no account must it be taken through the other, or allowed to use it when old enough to walk. A young white fowl is also selected and carefully kept; when the child grows up this fowl is killed and eaten by father and son together, the white feathers being stuck all round the child's special doorway. By this means it is thought that evil will be averted from the child so that it may not suffer the fate of its predecessors.[3]

Such a child is called *epeduno*.

At the ceremony to cure barrenness the witch-doctor may chant:

ijo ijoun	bring forth
iriamai okoku	may a child come true
iriamai esapat	may a boy come true

and, holding the woman round the waist:

kolomu kane	let it come forth here.

The woman herself may resort to spells, and if after the death of one child she fails to conceive any more, she may visit her dead child's grave

---

[1] Kitching, 1912. [2] Schut (undated). [3] Kitching, 1912.

and sprinkle it with water and take from it some of the clay. She then smears her whole body with the clay in the doorway of her house. Some go further and dig up the grave till they find the bones and take some of the earth which adheres to the bones for smearing their bodies in the doorway of their house.[1]

One of the most important ways of averting death in children is by bestowal of a derogatory name to propitiate the evil spirit.

5. *Naming a child*

A child is named at birth when its umbilical cord is cut. The eldest child should, subject to the exceptions mentioned below, always be given the name of his father's father if he is a boy, or of her father's mother if she is a girl. Subsequent children are usually named after their father's relatives but occasionally after their mother's relatives or even after a witch-doctor who has caused a woman to bear a strong child after several weak children have perished. The choice of name in such circumstances is largely a matter of chance.

But when several previous children have died, a name must be chosen which is ridiculous or derogatory in meaning. In this way the evil spirit may be appeased. Such names are Alupot or Olupot (dirt), Okurut (germ), Chuli (a type of weasel). Other names, the meanings of which are obscure, are given to such children: Opolot and Oryokot are the most general. Judging by the frequency of these names in Teso the fear of infant mortality must be continually in the mind of Teso women. The belief that this choice of a propitiatory name will save the child is believed even by the best-educated Iteso.

Certain names are invariable. For instance, all twins must be called Opio (Apio if a girl) and Ocen (or Acen). If the same woman bears twins for a second time the first should be named Odongo (or Adongo) though nowadays Odongo is used as a first twin's name regardless of this restriction. If she bears only one child after bearing twins it must be called Okello (or Akello).

Another name, taken from the Bible, is given at baptism and to add further confusion a nick-name is often bestowed well after birth and later accepted in place of the real name. There is a modern tendency to copy European ways of naming and to take the name of the father rather than the grandfather and to use more than one christian name.

Two examples will serve to illustrate these customs of naming children. The son of Oguti was called Cholobo after Oguti's father; he was also dubbed Okello in the family because he followed twins; in childhood he was called Cholobo or Okello; at baptism he took the names Christopher, Joseph, William and is now known as C. J. W. Okello. His son is called Oguti, but his father often calls him Onyege which was a nick-name given

---

[1] Schut (undated).

to the former Oguti. When baptized he will, in addition to his christian names, retain his father's name Okello, though he himself did not follow twins.

Outeke was the second son of Oputan, whose father was Ejiet, whose father was Opus. Outeke has twelve surviving daughters and one surviving son. The first daughter was named Adeke, to ward off evil, and Kemerapus after Outeke's sister. Later, when baptized, she added the name Lucy. Twins were called Apio and Odongo, but Odongo died. So did Outeke's next eldest son, called Oputan after Outeke's father, and the next son named Ejiet after Outeke's grandfather. The next son was taken through the wall of the hut and given a derogatory name, Okia (medicine). He has survived and when baptized will perhaps drop the name Okia and take as a surname his own father's name, Outeke.

CHAPTER II

MARRIAGE

1. *Bride-price*

THE payment of bride-price is the essential element of marriage. Without it a union can never be regarded as a marriage whether or not there has been a civil or religious ceremony under the Marriage Ordinance. The bride-price recompenses the girl's clan for the loss of a clan member. If later she returns to her relatives the bride-price must therefore be returned. The rules regarding the payment of bride-price are many and complicated and are described in full on pp. 202-7. The amount, method of payment, witnessing, and distribution are all matters of extreme importance. Although bride-price is controlled by law at five head of cattle (three for a woman who has previously been married), in fact it averages at the present time ten to fifteen head, and a prominent chief recently paid twenty-five head on his son's behalf. It is stated that after the rinderpest outbreak of 1890 bride-price fell as low as one head of cattle and thirty goats.

2. *Child betrothal*

In former times child betrothal (*aitar*) was common, but is now rare. A girl can be espoused at any age, in fact it used to be quite usual to betroth her before she was born in order to raise a loan or pay a debt.[1] The betrothed girl wears an iron band round her arm to denote her betrothal. The future husband and his father expect the girl as she grows up to help their family on certain occasions such as harvesting, or sowing crops, or beer parties. The bride-price for the girl is paid slowly by instalments to enable the girl to reach maturity. Both future husband and future bride may be tested by the elders of the other's family, the boy on field work and the girl on domestic work.

Formerly the girl was given no opportunity of refusal. If pressure from her family was insufficient she was beaten and if that did not suffice a hole was dug in an ant-hill into which she was put with only her head above ground so that her whole body was stung by soldier ants. She was then taken out and urine was rubbed into the wounds. This punishment invariably stopped further argument.[1]

Although children are nowadays very rarely betrothed in this way, there have been recent cases in Usuku of pledging very young girls for gambling debts. Only one case of marrying an immature girl has come to my notice—also in Usuku.

[1] Schut (undated); Amootoi ka Etesot, *c.* 1946.

3. *Marriage preliminaries*

Nowadays most marriages are arranged by the parties concerned, though some are still arranged by parents. When a boy and girl decide to get married they inform their parents and on a pre-arranged day the boy's relatives visit the girl's relatives to discuss bride-price. Beer is provided. In deciding bride-price pieces of wood are used; the father of the girl hands so many pieces and the boy's relative drops some until mutual agreement is reached. The girl is then engaged and may wear an iron ring on her arm.

On a pre-arranged day the girl's relatives come to see the cattle. They refuse to eat or drink until they have seen them. If agreement is reached beer is drunk and the boy is thereafter called *amuran*. A goat is provided by the boy's relatives and eaten. Finally, on a pre-arranged day the cattle, or some of them, are handed over in their kraal to the girl's relatives by the boy's relatives before witnesses. Beer is provided and a goat eaten.

It is not unusual for the future bride to be tested in domestic duties by the female relatives of her husband for a period of three days or more soon after the marriage has been arranged. According to other informants this period of test takes place after the bride has been escorted to her husband's village at the time of the wedding.[1]

4. *Marriage ceremony*

When the preliminaries are satisfactorily concluded, the marriage day is appointed, on which the bride is escorted with much noise and jubilation from her parents' to her future husband's home by her female relatives and by those of the bridegroom. After arrival at the husband's home the escorting bridesmaids may often refuse to allow the bridegroom to approach his bride until he has given them suitable presents. These used to consist of ornaments, cloth, chickens, or even goats, but nowadays settlement is usually made in cash. No special clothing or ornaments are worn for the marriage ceremony, although the bride is often smeared with butter. After giving presents to the bridesmaids the bridegroom may tell his sisters to bring the bride, but they are met with a mock show of refusal or with tears. The bridegroom must himself then pretend to drag her away by force. In very recent years this mock reluctance of the bride has taken the form of refusal to eat or refusal to sleep with her husband. The bridegroom must give her a present before she will agree to accede to his requests. The marriage is consummated that night and on the following day the escorting bridesmaids usually return to their village, though a few may stay to attend the bride for her first few days of married life. Although beer and food are provided for the wedding guests there is no ritual feast on the wedding day. Among some clans the smearing ceremony, which is described below, is an

---

[1] Driberg (1923) gives details of similar tests among the Lango (p. 156).

integral part of the marriage ceremony and may take place at the bride's home before departure or at her husband's home on arrival.

Shortly afterwards the father and relatives of the bride visit the husband very early in the morning and sit at a distance and light fires. When the husband opens his door and the chickens come out, the visitors grab them (*asut*).

Once the marriage ceremony is completed the husband and his mother-in-law should never see each other. Even an unintentional meeting would bring bad luck to both. This taboo is not universally respected nowadays, but is nevertheless strong.

Although mock seizure is an element of the marriage ceremony, marriage by seizure is not a Teso custom. There have, however, been instances of the custom in the district. In a recent court case the plaintiff, a Kumam, accused a Mukenyi of forcibly marrying his daughter. He won the case and was awarded 25s. compensation. The recorded evidence shows that the husband briefed three friends to help him abduct the girl while she was working in the fields; a canoe had been arranged to take her across an arm of Lake Kyoga to Kaberamaido county. The court asked the accused whether it was a Bakenyi custom if a man wished to marry a girl to take her by force; the answer was returned: 'Yes, it is our custom.'

The breaking of iron (*aibil aswat*) is a custom whereby a marriage is solemnized by husband and wife breaking a piece of iron in the house and each keeping his or her piece. Such an oath binds man and woman to be faithful to each other.[1] The custom is not much practised but still exists. One informant estimated that about one marriage a year was still solemnized in this way.

Modern marriages celebrated in church follow European custom. The bride wears a white dress and the bridegroom a suit. The marriage is followed by a reception. Modern superstition demands that the bride steps over money on the ground when entering her new home.

5. *The smearing ceremony*

A woman on marriage must be initiated into the clan taboos of her husband. This ceremony is known as the smearing ceremony (*ainyonyo*) and may take place at the time when the new bride is brought by her relatives to her husband's village on the marriage day. Customs vary, however, from clan to clan, and the ceremony is sometimes performed at the bride's own home in the doorway of her own mother's house or that of her nearest female relative. It may sometimes be delayed until after the birth of her first child. The ceremony is, however, a binding one and is seldom not observed. The girl to be initiated is seated at the door of her husband's house on the skin of an ox, which must have been slaughtered, with her legs stretched straight in front and holding a child in her arms. She is then smeared with

[1] Schut (undated).

ghee by her mother-in-law and the older women of her husband's family. In the ghee are mixed shavings of *esaas* sticks. *Esaas* sticks are usually rough at first but become smooth with constant use and shaving. They are believed to have magic properties and to bring bad luck or even death on children or others who touch them when not entitled to do so. Certain clans do not use special *esaas* wands but refer to the sticks used by the ordinary generic term *ebela* (pl. *ibelai*). Other women of her husband's family are smeared with her. The bride when smeared should sleep with her husband that night without first bathing (*atikokin akinyet*). But according to some informants a woman never sleeps with her husband when smeared but with the other women who are smeared with her, who must not sleep with their husbands until they have bathed.

This ceremony ensures fertility as well as initiating the bride into her new clan observances. It is therefore always performed when a new bride has, after a reasonable lapse of time, failed to show the symptoms of pregnancy.

A widow remarrying must go through this ceremony again to enter the clan of her new husband.

If the smearing ceremony is not performed owing to poverty or absence of relatives, a woman's children must not be seen by her relatives until she has been smeared or until they have grown up.[1]

6. *Status and duties of wives*

Polygamy is still common in Teso in spite of fifty years of missionary endeavour. Although the total of each married man's wives was recorded during the 1948 census, this information has not yet been extracted and made available, and there are therefore no actual figures to show the proportion of polygamous to monogamous marriages or to show whether polygamy is increasing or decreasing. There were 143,411 adult women and 120,434 adult men in Teso district in 1948. Women marry at a much earlier age than men and few if any remain unmarried; it follows that a much larger proportion of the 143,411 women would be married than of the men. The proportion of polygamous to monogamous marriages must therefore be fairly high, and this fact is certainly supported by a survey in a small village area where, out of 215 adult men, 47 were single, 118 had one wife, 34 had two wives, and 16 more than two wives.[2] This proportion of 42 polygamous to 100 monogamous marriages is possibly lower than the average for the whole district. In a survey in Amuria in 1937 of 113 families, it was shown that the average number of wives per husband was 1·89.

All marriages are invariably contracted according to native custom by the payment of bride-price. Nevertheless, many of the Iteso are Christians and their marriage to their first wife is usually performed in church under the provisions of the Marriage Ordinance. It follows that most of the men

[1] Engulu, 1937.   [2] Wilson, 1953.

who marry a second wife are, according to the law, liable to prosecution for bigamy for contracting a second marriage by native custom while the first marriage by Protectorate law is still valid.

A wife is expected to cook her husband's food, to brew his beer, to fetch water, and to keep house and compound clean. In house building she must fetch grass for thatching, and plaster with mud and cow dung; in Usuku she must also thatch. She must take her part in agriculture, mainly in weeding, harvesting, and carrying the crops home. In a polygamous household a wife has the right to expect a separate house of her own after her first harvest home. She has the sole charge of her own children.

Women obtained by capture in war were not married to their captors nor treated as concubines. Their status was that of daughters and they were given in marriage to others. They suffered no disability other than the absence of their own family relations to comfort them. Slaves were also obtained by purchase, mainly from Busoga district. This trade was particularly common at times of famine in Busoga, and some of the men thus bought as slaves are living in Teso to this day. Girls purchased in this way were married to suitors by their purchasers and suffered no restraints. The usual price was a bull for a male slave, and a heifer and five goats for a female slave.[1]

A husband should not have intercourse with his wife from the start of her pregnancy until after the weaning of her child, which may be from two to three years later. With an increase in monogamous marriages there are indications that this custom is not infrequently disregarded. It is, however, still considered normal, as the record in a recent District Native Court case shows:

> Kaladi: You were the village chief; did I not tell you that my wife was pregnant at the time I divorced her?
>
> Answer: You could not have been telling the truth because she still had an unweaned child with her and a woman cannot be pregnant at such a time.

Formerly extra-marital intercourse was severely censured and the penalties when pregnancy resulted were heavier than nowadays. Unless compensation was quickly paid the families concerned often resorted to fighting. It is commonly alleged that morals are nowadays looser and that extra-marital unions are more common than in the past. In monogamous marriages the custom of abstention from sexual intercourse during pregnancy and before weaning would certainly tend to lead to greater promiscuity. Formerly it was unknown for men and young women to drink beer together, whereas nowadays women and men often attend beer parties together and it is claimed that this mixture of the sexes at beer drinking encourages promiscuity. 'Venereal diseases were hardly known before the entry of the Baganda some twenty years ago, but are now common except in the far off parts near Lake Salisbury.'[1] These words were written about

---

[1] Kruyer (undated).

thirty-five years ago. The position is far more serious today. In 1951 36,567 cases were treated in government hospitals and dispensaries; others were no doubt treated in mission hospitals; others went to witch-doctors while others received no treatment at all. Even on the figure of those treated in government institutions nearly one person in ten in Teso suffered from venereal disease during the course of the year.

CHAPTER III

DEATH

1. *Disposal of corpses*

IN olden days the dead were buried either in the cattle kraal or in the house in which they lived, the house continuing to be occupied for some time after the interment. When huts containing graves were finally abandoned, they were never pulled down or destroyed, but left to decay.[1] These customs are no longer followed and the dead are now buried in the compound, the grave often being marked with a small mound of stones or a cement slab. It is not unusual, however, in the case of important persons, to erect a house over the grave.

The corpse used to be wrapped in the skin of an ox or in a goat-skin bag, but this custom has given way to the less expensive one of winding the corpse in *amerikani*.

Special funeral rites exist in certain cases. Dead twin children are put in earthenware pots and left in thickets near swamps to rot. Persons struck by lightning are also buried in swamps. At the death of an insane person a black bull is killed and the stomach contents poured on the deceased's body. Children who die very shortly after birth are buried in the hut, though among some clans the corpse is put out for vultures or hyenas. It is said that dead lepers too were put in the bush for hyenas to eat.

The usual burial position for a woman is on her left side and for a man on his right side. The knees and elbows are not bent. Roscoe, however, states that after the body was washed the left arm of a man or the right arm of a woman was bent so as to put it under the head.[2] According to Kitching corpses used to be buried in a sitting posture.[1]

2. *Burial ceremony*

The funeral ceremony is in two parts, *aipuduno* and *asuban. Aipuduno* is the ceremony of taking out the corpse from the house. The same word is used for the ceremony of taking out the new-born babe from the house. It lasts about three days.

On the first day after death burial takes place; mourners throw earth on the corpse before the grave is filled in but otherwise there is no ceremonial, though mourners used also to throw grain on the corpse.[2] Mourning is always exaggerated. It is suggested that 'a modicum of grief is magnified into wild despair by a desire to avoid any suspicion of having been concerned in the death of the person lamented, either by poison or some form of witchcraft. . . .'[1] It is customary to show grief by attempting to commit

[1] Kitching, 1912.   [2] Roscoe, 1915.

suicide. 'People have been known to impale themselves on stakes, to hurl themselves on spears, or dash their heads on a rock. Another may hang himself or rupture his larynx by a sharp blow upon the edge of an *eritei*, or winnowing tray.'[1] After the body had been committed to the grave mourners used to shave their heads.[2] Nowadays female mourners wear cloth round their heads but do not necessarily shave their heads.

Relatives take turns to guard the grave against ghouls or marauding animals. Sometimes the grave was so guarded for several weeks but nowadays the vigil rarely exceeds a week.

Although the burial ceremony is nowadays often performed according to Christian rites, the exaggerated mourning is an integral part of the ceremony.

On the second day of *aipuduno* the clan leaders make a count of property and call for debts. A bull is killed for the mourners by the heir. On the third day beer, contributed by the mourners, is drunk.

3. *Memorial ceremony*

Asuban is the ceremony of throwing away the ashes of the fire, which is kept alight near the grave. It marks the end of formal mourning. There is no fixed time between the burial ceremony and the memorial ceremony. 'Mourning for a rich man may last twelve months, and seldom less than six months even for a poor man.'[2] The interval between the two ceremonies is nowadays shorter. From the day of the funeral till the memorial ceremony close relatives should sleep by and guard the grave. Notice of the memorial ceremony is given by the heir of the deceased and all relatives within the extended family should attend it, for allocations of the deceased's property are made on this occasion. Roscoe asserts that the mourners after shaving their heads at the burial ceremony did not shave again or pare their nails until the memorial ceremony.[2] The ceremony ends with a feast at which the heir provides a bull, and beer is drunk.

[1] Kitching, 1912.   [2] Roscoe, 1915.

PART IV

MODE OF LIVING

CHAPTER I

THE PERSON

1. *Former male fashions*

THE earliest account of Teso clothing fashions states that:

the men are of good height, 5 feet 7 inches to 5 feet 10 inches, slightly built, and wiry. They wear as ornaments shells, beads, brass wire round the neck, and bracelets of brass wire and ivory. Most of them wear skins or a little bark cloth round the waist, but some are quite naked. They carry spears. The women wear a string of beads round the waist, and a little skin hanging down in front, besides the usual ornaments. As a race, they have not the thick lips or flat noses which mark the negroid type, and are, in fact, less like the typical negro than are the Waganda.[1]

Johnston records of the Iteso that they are 'singularly nude and do little to adorn their heads or bodies'.[2] His photo shows a group of naked men, some with shaved heads, others with a tuft of hair, wearing neck-rings and a string of beads round the waist, and anklets. The men were still naked when European administration started a decade later. 'The peasants are still a naked people and even prominent chiefs are to be seen in their own villages as naked as when they were born.'[3] But in 1912 Kitching referred to the 'all conquering march of calico and other Manchester goods. First come the calico trousers, cheapest to obtain and most serviceable to wear.'[4]

Driberg records the use by the Kumam of some covering even before the arrival of Europeans. 'Although young men went nude, the old men used to wear a fringe of banana leaves round the waist, or if this was unobtainable, a small skin apron. Now a small piece of cloth is worn suspended in front in place of the skin, and the young men always wear a strip of barkcloth or calico tied round the waist and drawn between the legs.'[5]

Though the men were formerly nude they affected some ornaments, 'a brass bracelet or two of great weight and anklets of the same material and equally cumbrous bulk. Occasionally the bracelets are of iron. . . .'[4] Metal waist belts were also worn and may very occasionally still be seen on the borders of Karamoja. Bands of coloured beads or cowrie shells were worn by men on the neck, upper arms, wrist, and loins. 'Beads are much in vogue, the fashions varying, small white and crimson being most in request at present. . . .'[4] On ceremonial occasions such as a dance these bead bands are still worn.

There were other ways of ornamenting the body. As among Nilotic

[1] Kirkpatrick, 1899.
[2] Johnston, 1902.
[3] Teso District Annual Report, 1913/14.
[4] Kitching, 1912.
[5] Driberg, 1923.

peoples the two front teeth of the lower jaw were removed both by men and women. The operation was performed at puberty by a practised dentist whose fee was a chicken or some millet. He knocked out the teeth with an axe struck against a piece of wood held behind the teeth or extracted them with a hooked iron implement designed for the purpose.[1]

Men had tattoo-marks on the forehead, chest, stomach, upper arms, and loins. These marks were made by applying the juice of the *emaido* twig, which left a scar.

It was usual to perforate the nostrils, ears, and lips with a thorn. The hole so made was slowly extended by inserting pieces of grass or wood.[1] The Karamojong fasten a heart-shaped metal plate from the hole in the nostrils and insert a metal or quartz plug in the hole in the lower lip. I can trace no record that the Iteso followed these two practices though it is possible that this was the purpose of the perforation. The holes in the ear and nose often contained pieces of wood or small ornaments but were not extended in the fashion of the Nandi and Masai.

Great attention was paid to the coiffure. The enormous chignons of the Suk and Karamojong were not worn, but the former practice was to mix mud with the hair to form a sort of cap, a style still in vogue in Karamoja. This mud pack was painted in different colours.

For ceremonial occasions the body was painted with reddish clay applied after greasing with shea butter nut oil. For dances the whole body was painted, leaving circles round the eyes. For war one arm, one side, and one leg were painted.

2. *Former female fashions*

Ornamentation of the female body was just as elaborate. Women perforated the nose, ears, and lips, and also the tongue. A brass ring was inserted in the hole in the tongue and never taken out whether eating or sleeping.[1] Women tattooed their foreheads, chests, loins, and stomachs round the navel. There appears to have been no symbolism in the design of the tattoo such as is found in the hoe motif on the breasts of Nilotic women. The hair was always heavily greased and often arranged in ringlets. It was unusual for women to cut their hair except at ceremonies connected with childbirth.

Bracelets and beads were worn by women in more profusion than by men. A small type of bead was worn round the forehead and even under the eyes. According to Roscoe young women used to thread rows of small iron rings through holes pierced in the skin of the chest.[2] Beads were worn round the arm and wrist, neck and chest, and the loins. 'Girls and women of all ages in Teso love to accumulate bead necklaces and strings of shells until their necks are really heavily loaded. . . . Round their waists they are fond of wearing belts made of iron cylinders, such as are used by some of the men; more wealthy ladies will make a belt of the cents issued by

[1] Kruyer (undated).   [2] Roscoe, 1915.

PLATE I

Woman and girls, showing clothing fashions
(*See p.* 105)

Woman at a grind-stone, showing typical clothing style and ornaments
(*See p.* 105)

Government to take the place of the old cumbrous shells. . . .'[1] Anklets of iron or brass were fashionable. They were often an inch thick, forged in position by the local smith.[2]

Women often oiled their bodies but smeared them with mud only for rain-making ceremonies.

There are no early photographs of women, and early description of female dress is lacking. It is certain that the women were always covered. 'Women had a little dress in front made of plaited rope about 4 by 6 inches, though this was often discarded at home. They also wore a very narrow strip of leather at the back like a tail. . . .'[2] This apron was sometimes made of beads.[3] My informants claim that the Teso women wore a small leather apron in front and a goat-skin pleated skirt behind. This fashion is still in vogue in Karamoja where the apron is adorned with beads. A girl is given a tiny apron from the earliest age which is replaced by a larger one as she grows. It is doubtful whether the apron was often discarded at home. Trowell records that 'Teso women wore front aprons of small tin cylinders, but no specimen is available for description'.[4]

3. *Contemporary dress*

Most of the styles described have passed out of fashion. Removal of the two front teeth is nowadays rare. Perforation of nostril and lip is equally rare, but small ear-rings are still worn by both sexes in holes pierced in the ear. Perforation of the tongue by women is not practised any longer. Heavy locally forged anklets and bracelets are no longer worn but beads have, to a certain extent, retained their popularity. It is not, however, usual to ornament the face with beads on any occasion. The bead loin bands of women appear to have acquired a special significance. They are given to a girl by her mother at a very early age and are usually worn even by women who affect European dress. The fashion of tattooing the body is disappearing and but few of the present-day children follow this custom.

Teso men have nowadays copied European fashions of clothing. Many of the more influential and wealthy, however, also wear a kanzu, which was once a garment of authority and respect at the time of the Baganda occupation and during the early days of British administration.

Their womenfolk, too, follow Baganda fashions with long bustle dresses of bright material which cover the shoulders. A few women use print dresses of European style which fit badly and ill become them. But the vast majority of Teso women, as many as 90 per cent., wear a garment which consists of one piece of cloth about 60 inches long and 40 inches wide. This is first wound round the loins and secured by a tape or belt; on a hot walk to market or to fetch water or while working in the fields, the upper part of the body can thus be left uncovered. The folds can, however,

---

[1] Kitching, 1912.   [2] Kruyer (undated).
[3] Roscoe, 1915.   [4] Trowell and Wachsman, 1953.

easily be raised over the breasts and fastened by tucking and rolling, leaving the shoulders bare. The popular materials for this style of dress are often plain or dull in colour, white 'shukas' of Indian origin being preferred. Mature girls and women usually wear an under-skirt as well.

4. *Children*

Babies are carried on their mother's back seated astride a bar. A leather flap attached to the bar keeps them pressed to their mother's back. The flap and bar are secured by thongs to the mother's shoulders. This sling is called *anapet* and may these days be made of rough cloth instead of leather. Nevertheless, among certain clans the material used is of great importance, and the *anapet* must be made of barkcloth or of the skins of sheep, goat, calf, monkey, or mongoose according to the custom of the particular clan. The *anapet* is one of the traditional presents given by her parents to a wife at the birth of her child.[1]

Children of both sexes, except in the houses of the rich, usually remain unclothed except for a string of beads around the loins until the age of about three.

Father Kruyer records various games played by Teso children at the beginning of this century.[2] These include *ediro* (hitting a wooden ball with a stick); a competition to see who is the last to get dizzy when turning round quickly; a game of bumping heads; swings tied in tree branches; sham fights with leather thongs on sticks; making clay figures of cows and naming them; throwing a stick through a moving wooden hoop. Perhaps the commonest toy in Teso today is the wheel of baked clay with a central hole through which a withy is fixed; the child pushes the contraption in front of him. Kitching records an indigenous game resembling hockey (*enyure*) played with a piece of wood instead of a ball.[3] I have only once seen this game played. The tug-of-war has always been a popular pastime. The old games remain. Mission teaching has added many new games. Girls play netball and boys football from an early age at school. Athletic sports are popular and the Uganda record for the high jump has been held for several years by Iteso and an Etesot gained second place for Uganda in the high jump at the Empire Games in Vancouver in 1954.

5. *Slaves*

Slaves were either obtained in raids or purchased and a supply came regularly through Pallisa from Busoga. The price of a male slave was a bull, of a female slave one heifer and five goats.[2]

Slavery was not a harsh condition. A man made no distinction between his slaves and his children; he helped his male slaves by giving them the bride-price for marrying, and married out his female slaves like his own

---

[1] Engulu, 1937.   [2] Kruyer (undated).   [3] Kitching, 1912.

daughters. No man would ever think of making his own female slave his wife or concubine. No slave was maimed or killed. If a slave was unmanageable he was simply told to go, as a man would do with his own son as an extreme measure.

6. *Feminization*

'Among the Iteso, people of hermaphroditic instincts are very numerous.'[1] There are no statistics and I have myself seen and heard of such people but rarely. The men are impotent and have the instincts of women and become women to all intents and purposes; their voices are feminine and their manner of walking and of speech is feminine. They shave their heads like a woman and wear women's ornaments and clothing. They do women's work and take women's names. I myself know of no cases in which they live with men as a 'wife'. One seen in Serere prison was treated entirely as a woman and kept in the women's cell. It was stated by the warders that the male prisoners would assault him were he imprisoned in the men's cell.

7. *Narcotics*

Early recorders have all noticed the addiction of the Iteso, men and women, to hemp smoking. It was customary to grow hemp for the purpose in every compound. This is now illegal, but there are many people prosecuted for the offence every year. The pipe consists of a bowl for the hemp below a perforated tray for hot embers. The smoke passes through a gourd containing water (see illustration on p. 163).

The Iteso have long been fond of tobacco. At the present time Teso is the largest cigarette-consuming district in the whole of East Africa. In former times each homestead grew its own tobacco and it is not uncommon to see tobacco growing in the family garden, especially in Amuria, today. 'Neat tobacco pipes are made of a kind of fine red clay that resembles terra-cotta when baked; geometrical patterns are cut round the top edge by way of decoration.'[2] The stem is usually of wood set into the bowl at an acute angle. Pipes are comparatively rare because cigarette smoking is the vogue. Both sexes smoke, though formerly only old women used to indulge.

[1] Driberg, 1923.   [2] Kitching, 1912.

CHAPTER II

THE HOME

1. *The former homestead* (ere)

FORMERLY homesteads were surrounded with a stockade (*abwas*) or euphorbia hedge (*apopong*) with a small defendable doorway (*erute*).

The villages of the Akum are also entirely different from those of the Lango, being always built on the same ordered plan. This consists of two large circles enclosed by strong euphorbia hedges and leading into one another by an arched gateway in the euphorbia. To enter an Akum village, the visitor first passes by a broad opening into the smaller of the two enclosures. In this there are no buildings, but several shade trees affording pleasant resting places. This is the dancing enclosure and in it the cattle are gathered in the evening for milking and preparatory to their being passed through the second gateway one by one into the circular kraal, which is built in the middle of the rearmost enclosure.

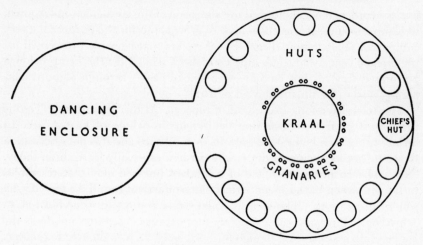

DANCING ENCLOSURE

HUTS

KRAAL

CHIEF'S HUT

GRANARIES

PLAN OF AKUM VILLAGE

Round the kraal the granaries are neatly arranged, generally two or three to a house, and the houses are built on the inner side of the euphorbia hedge, the doors facing towards the centre. The chief's hut is on the side opposite from the entrance gate. The houses are much larger than the Lango houses, are built on a different technique with doorways three feet high, and are surmounted on top with an antelope's head. There are no raised bachelors' houses[1] nor unmarried

---

[1] In spite of this assertion, raised houses presumably did exist, for isolated examples are still to be seen in Amuria and Kumi. They are small huts, raised on stilts and entered by means of a step through a very small doorway. The purpose of these houses is obscure and one of the few seen was occupied by an old woman.

women's quarters. In addition to sheep and goats, cattle are also sometimes kept in the living houses.[1]

Driberg claims that the Teso villages were identical with those of the Kumam described above. According to Father Kruyer, writing about the same time, houses were built round the cattle kraal, doorways facing the latter. The number of houses depended on the number of wives and importance of the pater-familias. The whole was surrounded by a euphorbia hedge to keep out animals and thieves.[2]

Teso villages are usually small and compact, except in the case of a big chief, who is the owner of many wives. As each wife must have a house to herself, the compound of a wealthy man makes a huge circle, perhaps two hundred yards in diameter, the centre of which is occupied with the numerous granaries, each standing on stones raised on edge to keep out the rats. As a rule, a large anthill is made the centre of a village, and round the hill is made the kraal; this is to ensure drainage in bad weather, as no attempt is ever made to clean out a kraal, and if there is no hill in the centre to throw off the rain water, the whole area soon becomes a sea of mud into which the unfortunate cattle sink knee-deep. A fence of thorns surrounds the kraal at first, and outside that is planted a hedge of prickly euphorbia, which will be grown up by the time the thorns have rotted. The same plan is followed with respect to the village itself; every Teso village is ringed with a hedge of this euphorbia, which is not only prickly but exudes, when wounded, a white milky juice which is so caustic as to take the skin off a cow's back or destroy the sight of any eye splashed with it. This hedge is planted round the village in a rounded heart shape, with the gateway at the indentation at the top. The two lines of euphorbia are brought round and continued inwards for a few yards, and end in a low archway made of heavy logs, which is just high enough and wide enough to allow of the passage of one cow at a time.[3]

There is no indication that the interior of the homestead was divided into small fenced compounds as is the custom in Karamoja today. It is probable that what I have described as the extended family, i.e. the descendants of one great-grandfather, occupied a homestead in former times. Nowadays the homestead is considerably smaller and is occupied by a family only, that is, by a man, his wives, and children, and other dependent relatives.

2. *The contemporary homestead*

The homestead is no longer enclosed in this way, though wise householders often plant cassia, nsambya, or cape lilac trees close together round the circumference of the compound to ensure a supply of building poles. Stockaded and euphorbia fenced enclosures are rarely found and only then in Usuku. The houses, outhouses, and granaries are grouped around the largest house which is that of the head of the homestead. The wives or married relatives have their own houses. The cattle kraal which formed the centre point of the old-time homestead is nowadays sited anything up to

---

[1] Driberg, 1923.   [2] Kruyer (undated).   [3] Kitching, 1912.

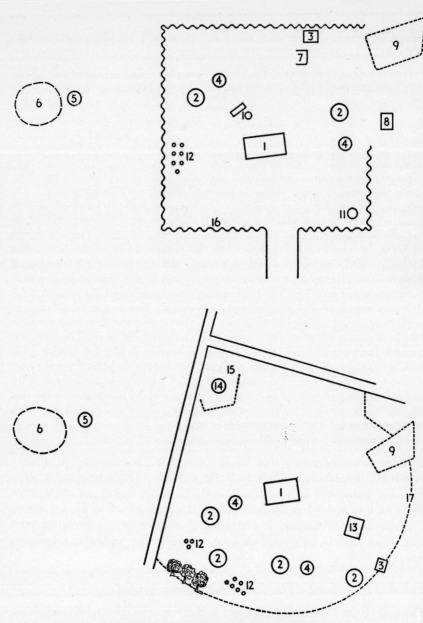

TYPICAL LAYOUT OF TWO MODERN HOMESTEADS

1. Householder's house.
2. Wives' houses.
3. Latrine.
4. Kitchen.
5. Kraal watchman's house.
6. Cattle kraal.
7. Ablution.
8. Calf pen.
9. Vegetable garden.
10. Grave.
11. Chicken house.
12. Granaries.
13. Householder's former house.
14. House of aged and sick relative.
15. Garden of aged and sick relative.
16. Cassia fence.
17. Edge of swept area.

150 yards away. Separate huts are often built for goats and even occasionally for poultry. Food is cooked in a separate kitchen and many homesteads boast a latrine and a screened washing-place. Granaries of the whole homestead are grouped together somewhere near the houses.

3. *Former methods of house building*

When Europeans first came to Teso all houses were bee-hive in shape, thatched with thin layers of grass in flounces to within a few inches of the ground. The frame was constructed of withies set in the ground and bent and secured at the apex of the hut. The mud-plastered doorway was so low that it was necessary to go on all fours or to stoop double to go through it. The peak of the thatch was usually ornamented in some way, often by fastening the horns of a buck on it. Bishop Kitching records how the interior of the house was much cumbered with poles used for propping weak places.[1]

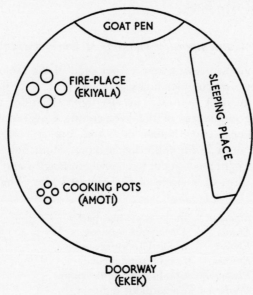

PLAN OF OLD-TIME TESO HOUSE

Inside the hut the lower part of the wall was plastered with mud and cow dung up to a foot or two above ground level. The floor was plastered with cow dung. A mud platform, raised about 3 inches above the floor, served as a bed when covered with skins. Near it, at the farthest point from the door, was a small platform with a mud lip round it in which the goats were tethered to stakes in the ground. A small aperture allowed the urine to run outside the house. On the opposite side to the bed was the hearth (*ekiyala*) formed of conical cakes of mud about 9 inches high. The cooking

[1] Kitching, 1912.

utensils rested on these cones while the fire was kindled underneath. In plastered depressions in the floor stood the earthenware jars of water and beer. It was customary to construct a mud niche above the door in which the remains of the evening meal of cooked millet could safely be left until morning. Household belongings and the weapons of the menfolk were stowed in the rafters of the hut or hung from the notches on the poles which shored the roof.

This type of house no longer exists, but the District Agricultural Officer in a village survey of Toroma in 1937 records that 'Teso houses are of two types, one the round bee-hive type with a long step-thatched roof coming down to within a few inches of the ground. This is an old type and fast going out of fashion. The more popular type is a round house with a four-foot wall, a two-foot verandah and a step-thatched roof. . . .' The low door-ways had begun to disappear by 1915 and it is probable that the round hut with walls, which is still common throughout the district, began to appear about the same time. The photograph in the 1913 Uganda Handbook shows 'bee-hive' type huts.[1]

4. *Contemporary methods of house building*

I estimate that at the present time 72 per cent. of the Iteso occupy round huts, 15 per cent. rectangular houses, 10 per cent. semi-permanent, and 3 per cent. permanent houses. The last figure includes the permanent houses built for employees of the Protectorate Government and of the Teso African Local Government in Soroti and at rural headquarters. Round huts are built in the following manner. Stout building poles each with a Y-shaped joint are first cut to convenient lengths and inserted in the ground in the form of a circle of the required size. The best building poles are:

Ekungur	Butyrospermum parkii
Ekoboi	Terminalia torulosa
Ekimeng	Combretum ghasalense
Ekworo	Combretum gueinzii
Ekulonyi	Combretum binderanum
Epeduru	Tamarindus indicus
Etiti	Lannea schimperi or L. merstingii
Elicerai	Crossopteryx febrifuga
Ebobori	Ficus guaphalocarpa

Eryeco (Bridelia scleroneuroides), *ebwolo* (Annona chrysophylla), and *ebata* (Albizzia zygia) are also used but are not so popular. The roof of withies is constructed separately on the ground and then lifted onto the upright poles to rest between the Y-joints. The uprights are strengthened with horizontal withies, the more usual of which are *ekulonyi*, *ebwolo*, *esalang* (Ziziphus abyssinica), *emuturu* (Heeria reticulata), and *ekisim* (Acacia seyal). The

[1] Uganda Protectorate, 1913.

PLATE II

Teso homestead at Gweri
(*See p.* 110)

'Beehive' hut, a former type of Teso house
(*See p.* 111)

latter is not much favoured as it does not last long. The withies of roof and wall are tied in position by tree fibres, the most common of which is *eparis* (Grewia mollis). *Ebonori* (Ficus species), *ebiong* (Ficus glumosa), *ekwanga* (Lachnophylis oppositifolia), *epapai* (Piliostigma thonningii), and *etiti* are also used. When the frame is thus complete the thatching takes place. Step thatching is practised only where the grass is suitable; elsewhere the thatching is plain. Hyparrhenia filipendula is the commonest thatching grass. When the thatching is complete the walls are filled with black mud which cracks when it dries. The walls are then plastered with a fine mixture of mud and cow-dung inside and out. There is a modern tendency to decorate the exteriors with coloured drawings or designs. This practice is particularly noticeable in Kaberamaido and Amuria.

Preparation of the frame and thatching are the recognized tasks of the menfolk except in Usuku where the women thatch. Plastering of floors and walls and collection of grass is the women's share. It is common practice to invite neighbours to help in all stages of house building and to provide a beer party for them at the end of their labours.

Inside the hut the sleeping platform has now given way to the moveable wooden bed. The goats may by law no longer be tethered in a house occupied by humans. The houses are lighter because the doors are as high as the walls; but windows are still a rarity. If windows are required, a space is cut in the wall after the frame is in position. The doors themselves may be made of woven withies or rough boarding. There is usually a separate place for cooking outside the house. There is never a partition in round huts but the bed is often screened from the rest of the room by a large cloth hung from a rope. Apart from a small table and a box for clothes there is seldom any furniture.

The wealthier Iteso have copied European fashions in house-building by adopting a rectangular-shaped house with separate rooms. There is little difference in the method of construction between the round hut and the rectangular house except that the roof of the rectangular house which requires stout timbers must be built into position instead of being constructed separately. Usually two stout uprights support the beam which forms the ridge of the roof. It is, however, possible to construct such houses having only one upright on which the four main corner rafters rest. A wall-plate beam is rested in the Y-joints of the uprights and this beam takes the weight of the rafters of the hip-roof. The partitions between rooms, made of wattle and daub, are only about 6 feet high. Windows are much more common in this sort of house than in the round hut.

Within the last twenty years corrugated iron has begun to replace thatch on many of these rectangular houses and, for ease of construction, gable-roofs are favoured rather than hip-roofs. But no other changes in method are involved and only unshaped indigenous wood is used. Fully permanent houses are still a rarity but are becoming increasingly common as living standards improve and local artisans become available.

5. *Granaries*

Granaries have remained unchanged in form and construction since the time of first contact with Europeans. The normal type (*edula*) is constructed on the site and cannot be moved. It is built solely of grass (Loudetia simplex) and mud and cow dung, built up and shaped like a huge water pot on a base of timber, which rests on posts or stones as protection against termites. The hole at the top is sometimes fitted with a lid constructed of grass and mud and protected with a thatch cover. More often a thatched roof constructed of withies rests over the top of the granary. This roof may be supported on separate posts set in the ground or may rest on the granary itself. This type of granary averages 5 feet in diameter and 5 feet in height. There exist, however, outsize granaries as much as 12 feet high and correspondingly wide. It is said that in former times these outsize granaries were common and a sign of high standing.

A portable wicker granary also exists (*ekerei*). It is similar in size and shape to the *edula* and may be plastered with mud and cow dung. Occasionally the wicker basket consists of sides only without a bottom. In such cases the wicker frame is set in a mud base raised off the ground. Granaries are occasionally built like huts with mud held by a wicker frame; they are built up from mud floors raised off the ground.

There is a special type of granary (*epem*) which is usually found only in Usuku and Tisai Island. This consists of a very large wicker basin, about 18 inches high, woven from the sticks of Harrisonia abyssinica and raised on poles. A steep conical thatched roof, supported on separate posts, provides cover for the grain from the elements. These stores are largely used for sorghum whereas millet is stored in the *edula*. It is not uncommon to use this store as a kitchen shelter and to cook beneath it. The smoke from the fire permeates the sorghum and thus prevents damage by weevils.

Sorghum may also be stored in the form of a stack raised off the ground and covered from the elements by a thatch roof supported on poles set in the ground. There is little difference between this stack and the *epem* just described. The same word is used for both.

6. *Furniture*

The sleeping platform of beaten earth, raised a few inches above the hut floor, used to be covered with dry skins. A piece of wood served as a pillow and people slept without covering. Though this type of bed is by no means extinct, bed frames are now made by local carpenters of local woods; the frames are fitted with leather thongs or sisal rope. It is comparatively rare to see a homestead without a bed, and bedding is universally used where beds exist.

The fireplace inside the house or kitchen is known as *ekiyala*. It consists of rounded mud-cones about 9 inches high or of stones of similar size. A

PLATE III

Simsim granary on the veranda of a house
(See p. 141)

Filling a granary with millet
(See p. 114)

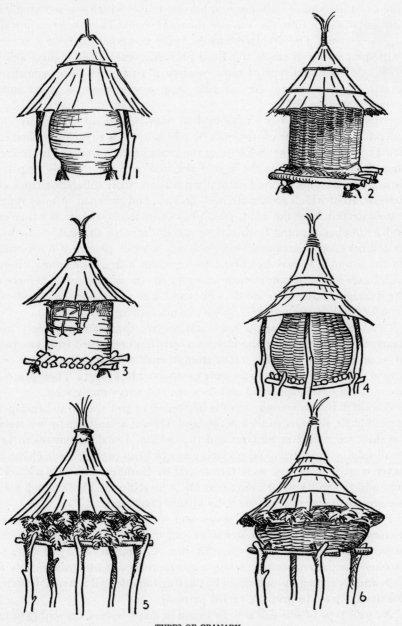

TYPES OF GRANARY

1. *Edula*: grass and mud granary with roof on poles.
2. *Ekerei*: wicker granary.
3. *Edula loirwata*: wattle and daub granary.
4. *Ekerei*: wicker basket with roof on poles.
5. *Epem*: grain stand.
6. *Epem*: flat basket.

wife must use stones until her first harvest home, which is celebrated with beer, after which time she may use the mud cones. There exists a portable type of *ekiyala*. The fireplace outside in the compound is known as *etem*.

In the carving of stools the Iteso probably reach their highest artistic creation. The usual type of stool consists of a top with three, sometimes four, legs. It is carved with an adze from a solid piece of wood and is usually carefully finished. The stool is never decorated with beads or carving but the wood is often polished with simsim oil. Sizes vary considerably, but this type of stool may be said to average 12 inches in diameter and 12 inches in height. Sometimes the branches of a tree, if conveniently shaped, may be taken as the legs of the stool and the trunk is shaped to form the seat. This method naturally produces many different shapes and designs, all of which are usually well finished and polished. A rarer type is a stool carved from the solid, which has short thick-set legs at either end and a crossbar running from end to end underneath the seat. Sometimes an ordinary log is smoothed and used as a stool by placing it horizontally on the ground. It may be carved to represent a figure or animal. Stools with bases resemble cotton-reels and vary in size and design. They are on the average larger than stools with legs. The most popular woods are *ekungur* (shea-butter nut) and *eputon* (Pseudocedrela kotschyi).

Head-rests to support the neck and to save the head ornaments from damage resemble those in use in Karamoja; they are carved from one piece of wood and have two legs, often strengthened with a thong. These rests are carried on one arm and can serve as stools or head-rests. Their practical use in Teso has disappeared and they are nowadays rarely seen.

Although the indigenous stool is beginning to give way to the European type of chair, it is rare to see a homestead without at least one or two stools, for they are useful in milking and in cooking. Local carpenters make a small folding chair from old packing cases or bush timber. Cane chairs are never seen. Tables, too, were introduced by Europeans but are not yet in common use and are not used to eat off at meal-times. Those which are in use are small and roughly made by village carpenters.

Papyrus mats are used on floors and beds and for ceilings in larger houses. The dried papyrus stems are put side by side and then tied together with fibre down each side. Alternatively, the fibre may be threaded through the papyrus stems. Another common type of mat used mainly for beds and for sitting upon is made by plaiting together palm strips. Different colours are used to produce varied patterns.

A crude type of sun-dial is to be found in many homes, consisting of two upright sticks about 18 inches high and a cross stick from which hangs a piece of string with a nut, stone, or small fruit on the end. Grooves are marked on the ground under this contraption and as the shadow cast by the nut moves across the grooves it indicates the hour. Although this contraption is laughingly attributed to children's games, its commonness indicates that it has a practical use.

STOOLS

1 and 2. *Eicolong lokisu*: bobbin stools.
3–6 and 8. *Emakuk*: legged stools.
7, 9, and 10. *Eicolong lotuba*: horizontal stools.
11. *Eicolong loketem*: natural type stool.
(The average height of the bobbin or legged stools illustrated is 12 inches. Other stools are in proportion.)

CHAPTER III

FOOD AND DRINK

1. *General*

THE main meal of the day is taken in the evening about sunset. The remains of this meal with perhaps a baked sweet potato or cassava root must often serve for the morning food, for it is unusual, except for the wealthy, to eat at midday.

Cooking and serving food is entirely the concern of women. If there are male guests present the master of the house will eat apart with them, otherwise he may eat with his womenfolk. Tables are not used for food and the members of the family squat round the common platter, a large wooden tray with edges (*atuba*), and help themselves. Food is eaten in the fingers and no implements are used. Ladles are, however, made by cutting in half the hard shell of gourds (*adere*). A small variety of these ladles (*aokit*) is used for drawing water or ladling food.

2. *Cooking pots*

In a well-equipped Teso house there are at least four cooking pots, one for grain foods, one for starch foods, one for meat and vegetables, and one for beer manufacture; in addition there is at least one water-carrying pot and another larger pot for storing water, which does not leave the house.[1]

All these pots may differ in shape and size according to function. The generic word for pot is *amot*, which also has a particular meaning of water pot. Apart from the specially shaped pots for making salt or for twin birth ritual, all pots may be roughly grouped into two categories according to function, those used for the storage or preparation of liquids and those used for solid foods. The former category is, for the most part, characterized by a narrower neck or a narrower aperture than the latter. Within these two categories pots may vary in size and shape according to precise function or according to age. Thus pots used for carrying water are sufficiently small and round to enable them to be balanced on the head when full, whereas pots used for storing water or beer may be very large and tall. Old pots are often distinguishable by the grey clay, which is no longer used, the rough and gritty finish, and the absence of lip; modern pots have a smooth finish, are often coloured red or black, and lips are usual.

In the first category, the pots used for liquids, the following pots are found:

amot   a water-carrying pot with a narrow neck, fairly large aperture, and wide belly.

[1] Kruyer (undated).

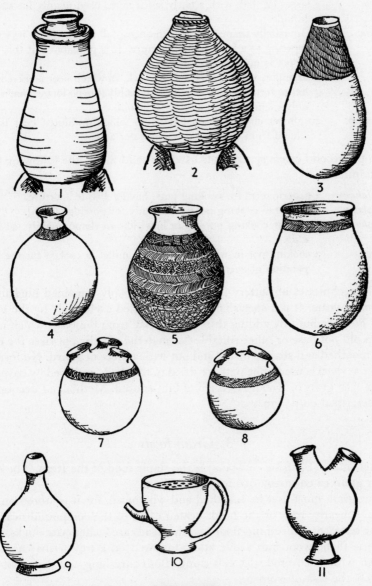

TYPES OF POT

1. *Etuja*: simsim granary (height 3 feet 6 inches).
2. *Etuja loka ekerei*: simsim granary basket (height 2 feet 9 inches).
3. *Ebinu*: pot for liquids (height 2 feet 6 inches).
4. *Eico*: narrow-necked pot for liquids (height 2 feet but usually larger).
5. *Amot*: water-carrying pot (height 1 foot 6 inches).
6. *Akeit*: cooking pot (height 1 foot 6 inches).
7–8. *Adogoria*: twins ceremonial pots (height 13 inches).
9. Water jar: (rare; possibly imitation of a bottle) (height 10 inches).
10. *Atitot*: salt-making pot (height 8 inches).
11. *Adogoria*: twins ceremonial pot on stand (rare) (height 12 inches).

eico   a large pot, tall, with a fairly small neck, used mainly for storing liquids.

ebinu   an unusually shaped pot with no neck, tall in relation to its width, tapering to a fairly small aperture. It is probable that this type of pot is no longer made.

eli   a large pot, with a fairly narrow neck, in which beer is mixed and left to ferment for a few days. Possibly it is no longer made; the only examples seen appear to be old.

abarak   an almost circular-shaped pot into which undiluted beer is decanted from the *eli* and warm water added.

In the second category, the pots used for solid foods, the following pots are found:

aalakany a generic term for cooking pots, having a wide aperture.

atakwa   a large, tall cooking pot used mainly for porridge (*atap*).

atabo   a smaller cooking pot, more bowl-like in shape, mainly used for *atap*.

akeit   a cooking pot in which germinated millet is cooked for the preparation of beer.

The techniques of pottery making have probably remained unchanged for many years. It is a specialist trade, performed exclusively by the menfolk. Pots are built by adding thin coils of clay from the base, which is set on an old pot base or other suitable flat material. As the pot rises the coils are smoothed and shaped inside and out with a piece of gourd. No form of potter's wheel is used. The pots are dried in the shade and fired by covering them with grass or wood. No form of kiln is used. Methods of decoration are described on p. 170.

3. *Grain foods*

Finger millet (Eleusine coracana) is the staple food of the Iteso. The only other grain eaten in any quantity is sorghum.

The grain must first be threshed and winnowed, for it is stored on the stalk. A nearby rock or the hard, beaten earth of the compound near the house serves as a threshing-floor and the heads are beaten with sticks. The grain is then swept into a pile and winnowed on a tray (*eritei*) made of woven withies covered with cow dung. Both threshing and winnowing is entirely the task of women.

The grain must then be ground. The base of the grindstone (*amoru*) consists of any piece of hard, gritty stone of suitable size. Sometimes grinding is done on a nearby rock, but usually a grindstone is kept in the kitchen or on the veranda of the house. It is usual to set the stone in a base of hard mud to raise it off the ground and to give it a suitable lip to catch the flour. The upper stone (*atapen*) is a rounded, flat white stone about 1 inch thick quarried at Ongino and sold in quantities at Kumi market. The grindstone outfit is not really complete unless there is an *ekekep*, **a**

PLATE IV

Stirring porridge
(See p. 121)

Winnowing millet
(See p. 120)

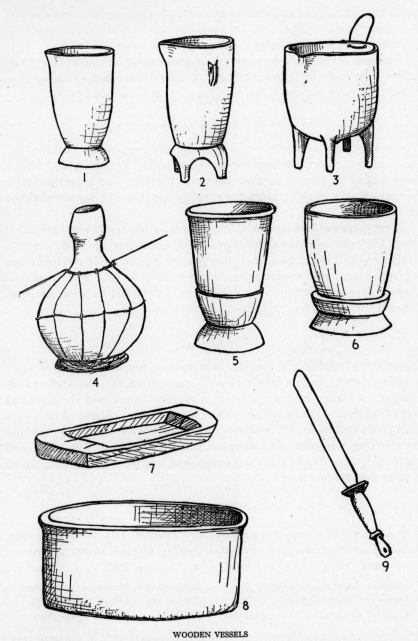

WOODEN VESSELS

1–3. *Elepit*: milk pails (average height 14 inches).
4. *Ekeret*: milk churn (height 10 inches).
5–6. *Ekisu*: mortars (average height 14 inches).
7–8. *Atuba*: dishes (length or diameter 14 inches). (8 is probably a copy of the modern aluminium cooking pot.)
9. *Akingol*: stirring implement (elaborate example) (length 16 inches).

small hard stone held in the hand and used for chipping the *amoru* to give it a gritty surface. The wise housewife always stores some of the flour (*akiria*) in a special pot (*edonero*) in case guests arrive suddenly.

The flour is cooked with water to a thick dough-like consistency (*atap*) and is then rolled by hand into balls of suitable size and so eaten. It is, however, almost invariably flavoured in the ways described below.

4. *Starch foods*

The grain crops are harvested in June or July and seldom last until the next harvest. Sweet potatoes are harvested about November and form a large part of the diet in the first months of the year. Just before the grain harvest, cassava often becomes the main food as it can be harvested at any time.

Sweet potatoes (*acok*) are either eaten fresh, or dried and sliced for making flour. The removal of the skin before cooking is supposed to be detrimental to the crop still in the ground. If they are to be eaten fresh, the tubers are washed, placed in a cooking-pot of water, covered with leaves, such as those of *epapai* (Piliostigma thonningii), and left to boil for about an hour. Cassava (*emuogo*) is treated in a similar manner.

5. *Oil foods*

Groundnuts (*emaido*) and simsim (*ekanyum*) are prepared by pounding in a mortar (*ekisu*) with a pestle (*arukit*) made from the wood of *eputon*, *ekungur*, or *ekisim*. Before pounding it is usual to dampen the nuts and seeds slightly and then dry them over a fire. They are usually eaten mixed with green vegetables. If it is intended to keep the oil separate for cooking or smearing purposes, the pounded material is put in hot water and thoroughly stirred until the water evaporates, and the oil remaining on the pulp is then skimmed off.

6. *Vegetables*

A great variety of wild plants are eaten as vegetables. The leaves are usually pounded and stirred with a rammer-shaped instrument (*eipiret*), made by fastening a stick into a round head of hard wood. Plants so used include:

Ejatoto	Asystasia schimperi	*Egwanyira*	Hibiscus cannabinus
Ekelio	Celosia argentea	*Emalakany*	Hibiscus sabdariffa
Ecaboi	Gynandropsis pentaphylla	*Ekilitoni*	Sonchus bipontini

The leaves of cassava plants and cow peas (*eboo*) are treated in the same way.

7. *Flavouring*

Atap is often flavoured by cooking the flour in milk or ghee instead of in water or by adding the juice of *elemai* (Ximenia americana) or *epeduru*

PLATE V

FOOD PREPARATION
Foreground: threshing millet, winnowing millet, and crushing groundnuts
Background: grinding millet to flour
(See pp. 120 *and* 122)

Grinding millet on the veranda of a house
(See p. 120)

(tamarind) when in season. *Alilot* or *etigo* (Corchorus trilocularis), *ekoropot* (Ancilema beniniense) and *emorosi* (Lissus adenocaulis) are all used as flavouring materials with green vegetables.

The most important flavouring, however, is salt. This valuable commodity can nowadays be bought in the shops but the old method of manufacture from plants is still practised. The plants are first dried and then burned and the resultant ash is used as salt. Wild plants are used but most homesteads possess a small garden of special seasoning plants for this purpose. The following list contains only some of the many plants used:—

Atilo	Hygrophila spinosa
Etutumu	Vemonia amygdalina
Ekwira (or *Akaramoto*)	Achyranthes aspera
Eboga	Amaranthus spinosa
Edwaroi	Vemonia grantii
Eririo	Lippia adoensis
Abokeboke	Asystasia gangetica
Atiraja	Ageratum conyzoides
Apungula	Coreopsis
Okwarasi	Aspilia motschyi
Aurukoroi	Laggera alata
Ayileyile	Trichodesma zeylanicum

A special pot known as *atitot* is used for baking salt. It is in two parts, the top half having a perforated base and the lower portion a spout. It resembles a teapot. It is illustrated on p. 119.

8. *Meat and Fish*

The Iteso used to draw blood from their cattle, as the Karamojong still do, by tying a rope tightly round the beast's neck and piercing the main artery with an arrow shot at close range. 'As much as three or four gallons of blood was often taken from one animal; some of this was used fresh, mixed with groundnuts, but most of it was boiled well and cooked in a mixture of groundnuts with vegetables.'[1] Blood is no longer part of the Iteso's diet.

Meat, however, is a favourite food, but few can afford to eat it regularly. Figures of hides and skins exported from Teso in 1952 (29,942 hides, 37,700 skins) give a rough indication of the number of domestic animals slaughtered for consumption in that year. The figure has risen rapidly during the years following the end of the 1939–45 war. All portions of the animal are eaten. Meat is sometimes roasted in the hot ashes but is often boiled. 'Fat is sometimes eaten raw as soon as the animal is skinned.'[1] The fat is often preserved both for use in cooking and as a delicacy.

Although meat is always popular, clan taboos often prevent women and sometimes men from eating duiker, oribi, reedbuck, kob, and some other animals. Kitching records how two or three boys attributed their sickness

[1] Kruyer (undated).

to hartebeest.[1] In a recent court case the complainant, a woman, is recorded as saying 'they made me eat sheep's meat without my knowledge and so I vomited, that is why I must not leave his home because I am spoiled now'. Hippopotamus and buffalo meat are eagerly sought after and often purchased from poachers. Of the smaller mammals, hyrax and edible rats are popular. The latter 'were eaten with groundnuts; only the entrails were removed; skin and bones were eaten'.[2]

Flying ants (*ikong*) and, to a lesser extent, locusts (*emase*) are considered a great delicacy whether cooked or raw. The former are caught over the ant-hill at dusk by hand or by scorching their wings with grass torches. *Airam emome* (to beat for the ants) is another method of catching them. A log is beaten with two small sticks. The ants mistake the sound for rain and swarm up a tube which has been put over the hole in the hill and which leads into a pot. The usual method of preparation is to fry the ants in oil, dry them in the sun, and then pound and eat them with groundnuts. Locusts are prepared in a similar manner.

The flesh of domestic fowls, game birds, and water birds such as cormorants, herons, or egrets is enjoyed by men but is mainly taboo to women. Eggs are also taboo though old women past child-bearing may be permitted relaxation of this rule.

All species of fish are now eaten. In former times the Iteso obtained only mud fish from swamps in the dry season. But the lake waters are now fished by immigrant fishermen who smoke and sell their catches locally (see p. 132).

9. *Non-alcoholic beverages*

'Milk was taken mostly when sour, or as butter milk, though the men when milking often milked straight into the mouth and drank the milk in this way.'[2]

The churn is a gourd (*ekeret*) suspended from a post, and the necessary movement is given by jerking the gourd with a string. Milk is added to the churn as available. Tall milking pails (*eiciret* or *elepit*) are hollowed from the wood of any hardwood tree. These pails stand on legs or on a moulded base. They closely resemble mortars (*ekisu*) but have a lip for pouring. Milk is also carried in calabashes (*adere* or *aokit*), or a gourd bottle (*etwo*).

Tea is a popular beverage but the most important ingredient is the sugar rather than the tea-leaves. A form of tea is often made from lemon grass (Cymbopogon citratus).

10. *Alcoholic beverages*

Beer (*ajon*) is commonly brewed from finger millet though occasionally sorghum is used. The process has three distinct stages.

The millet is threshed and winnowed on the usual tray (*eritei*) made of

[1] Kitching, 1912.   [2] Kruyer (undated).

PLATE VI

(i)

(ii)

(iii)

(iv)

DRAWING BLOOD FROM CATTLE

(i) Preparing to shoot the arrow into the vein
(ii) Blood is let out into a bowl
(iii) A tourniquet controls the blood flow
(iv) The blood is consumed

(These photographs were taken in Karamoja district by Mr. V. E. Blad. The custom of drawing blood from cattle for human consumption is now almost extinct in Teso)

(See p. 123)

twigs of *ederun* plastered with cow dung. After winnowing the millet is placed in a heap, water is added from a gourd, and the grain is mixed in the same way as cement is mixed by a builder. The heap is left for two or three days and kept damp until germination takes place. It is called *asip* at this stage.

After germination the millet is dried in the sun and ground into an exceptionally fine flour. The ground *asip* is then mixed with water to the consistency of porridge and buried in the ground in a hole lined with leaves and left for ten days or a fortnight. The earth is beaten hard above the hole to prevent damage from rain or chickens. Instead of placing the mixture in a hole in the ground it may be put in a pot or large basket (*amurat*) well plastered and with the mouth sealed with leaves. The pot or basket is then left in the shade. After about two weeks the *asip* is removed from the hole or receptacle and cooked over the fire in an earthenware pot (*akeit*) and then put out in the sun to dry. At this stage it is called *akiria*, dry beer. This process marks the end of the second stage.

To make beer, germinated millet (*asip*) seed is ground and mixed with the *akiria* and cold water is added. When sorghum instead of millet is used the sprouting grain is first mixed with wood ash which is said to have the effect of darkening the colour of the beer. Approximately one part of germinated grain (*asip*) is added to forty parts of *akiria*. During fermentation, which takes place within a day, the mixture is covered with leaves. The beer stands for at least three days before it is ready for consumption. The pot in which the beer ferments is called *eli*. *Eli* pots are often very large; one example was 36 inches high and 28 inches wide. The few seen appear to be of some age and nowadays an ordinary water pot may be used for the purpose. When required the fermented beer is decanted into a smaller pot, almost circular in shape and averaging 22 inches in width, which is known as *abarak*. Warm water is added at the time of drinking.

It is unusual but nowadays not unknown for men and women to drink together. The drinkers squat or loll round the pot and suck the warm beer through a stick (*epi*) with a filter bowl (*esosot*). The stick is made from a plant called *emanit* and is usually wound with coloured raffia and sometimes carried in a hollowed walking-stick.

The consumption of *waragi* (Nubian gin) is unfortunately increasing in Teso. It is distilled mainly by immigrant Africans, particularly Nubians and Baganda, often women. The method does not differ from that employed elsewhere in Uganda.

CHAPTER IV

WAR, HUNTING, AND FISHING

1. *Warfare*

THERE are traditions that the Iteso of Usuku fought the Karamojong and the Iteso of Bukedea the Bagishu, whom they called Kumam. There are more detailed accounts of battles between the Lango and the Kumam.[1] But most of the warfare of former days was on a much more local scale, one *etem* or group of *itemwan* against another. Attackers always had the advantage of surprise and usually saw to it that they had numerical superiority. Villages were surprised, food, women, goats, and fowls forced off, and houses burnt. Those attacked would later combine with neighbouring villages and organize a counter expedition. 'Reasons for warfare were many, ranging from an accusation of stopping rain (the most serious one) to beating somebody else's dog.'[2]

The leader in small-scale raids was the *apolon ka ajore*. The size of his command depended on his reputation; it might range from an *etem* to several *itemwan*, and he held his position by popular consent. The commander for larger expeditions was known as *apolon ka ebuku* 'leader of the shield'. His command included several *apolok ka ajore* and he retained it by success in the field. When in about 1937 Luganda terminology was replaced by Ateso in the administrative machine, the title *apolon ka ebuku* was coined to represent the chief in charge of a *saza* or county, and hence the word *ebuku* has nowadays acquired a secondary meaning of 'county'.

2. *Weapons used in warfare*

Weapons used in warfare consisted of a shield and two spears, one for throwing and one for stabbing. Bows and arrows were never used. Shields are rarely seen nowadays, even on ceremonial occasions. They were invariably made of hide, usually of buffalo but also of giraffe, in shape like those of the Acholi or Lango, rectangular with elongated corners bound with metal wire. The hide was stitched to a stout stick which ran from top to bottom and protruded at one end. On this protrusion was an ostrich feather pompom, which was carried downwards in war and upwards in hunting. The shield was not decorated. In two examples the size averages 32 inches by 9 inches.

The commonest type of spear (*akwara*) has a long shank, butt, and haft. The blade is narrow; the average length of blade, shank, haft, and butt is 7 feet. Though once part of every man's accoutrements, the spear is now

---

[1] Tarantino, 1949 (ii). [2] Kruyer (undated).

becoming rare. It is no longer allowed at dances and is only used when cattle herding in the remoter parts of the district and in hunting.

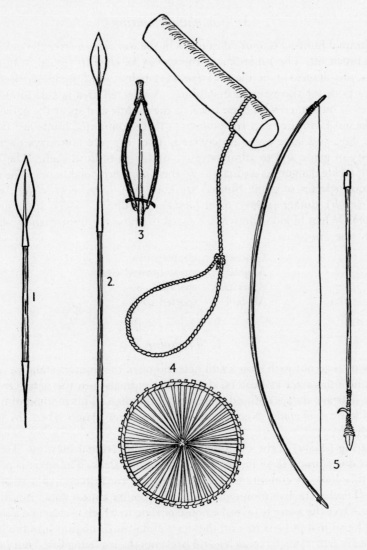

HUNTING WEAPONS OR TRAPS

1. *Akwara*: stabbing spear.
2. *Akwara* or *aliru*: throwing spear (length with shaft 6 feet).
3. *Akuraru*: sheath for spear blade.
4. *Etirir*: spiked wheel trap with noose and log (diameter of trap 12 inches).
5. *Akabwa*-bow and *emal*-arrow (used for piercing a vein in cattle to draw blood).

The short stabbing spear is even rarer. It has a broad, heavy blade, short haft, and heavy butt. A spear with a long haft but a very small blade is to be seen occasionally. It appears to have no particular purpose and no specific name. It is perhaps carried more often by youths than by full-grown men.

3. *Communal hunting*

Communal hunting (*eriga*) takes place in the dry season after the grass has been burnt off. The functions of the *apolon ka eriga* in regard to hunting rights are described in Part VI (p. 253) below. The weapons used are spears both for throwing and stabbing. A selected area is surrounded by parties of huntsmen who close towards the middle and spear the game as it breaks out from the ring. In some areas these communal hunts last two or three days and large areas are covered. They are rare nowadays owing to scarcity of game and to administrative measures to limit them. The Iteso do not tackle dangerous animals as do their northern neighbours. The most common species of game hunted are kob (*etil*), hartebeest (*eloba*), water buck (*epoli*), duiker (*amor*), oribi (*amiam*), reedbuck (*ekali*), and warthog (*eputir*). When blood is drawn it is usual to praise the huntsman by shouting in staccato tones:

Orotokol	dappled cow
Angole	white-browed cow
Ameritaok	speckled cow
Akolkol	spotted cow[1]

4. *Trapping*

A few men go out with spears and nets. Some of the hunters stand near the nets and others act as beaters, driving the animals into the nets. Owners of the nets are always entitled to a share of the meat. This method of hunting is known as *etoda*. Nets are used in the rainy season when the grass is high.

Snaring (*atacit*) is the commonest form of individual hunting. A small hole is dug about 6 to 18 inches deep in the game track. The snare is placed over this hole. It consists of a ring in which are fastened thorns of the *etirir* (Dischrostachys glomerata) with the points almost touching in the centre. Over the snare is placed a noose of rope to which is attached a heavy log. The animal puts its foot on the snare and goes through it into the hole. The snare (*etirir*) sticks to its leg and prevents the leg being lifted out of the noose before it has tightened. The frightened animal then runs away with the log trailing behind it. If it goes fast the log bruises its body and soon tires it. The huntsman follows up and spears it. Most species of game, including giraffe, are snared in this manner. This type of snare is illustrated on p. 127.

String and wire nooses (*esilot*) are used for smaller animals and game birds. These nooses are set from sticks put in the tracks of the animals or

[1] Lukyn-Williams, unpublished notes, 1921.

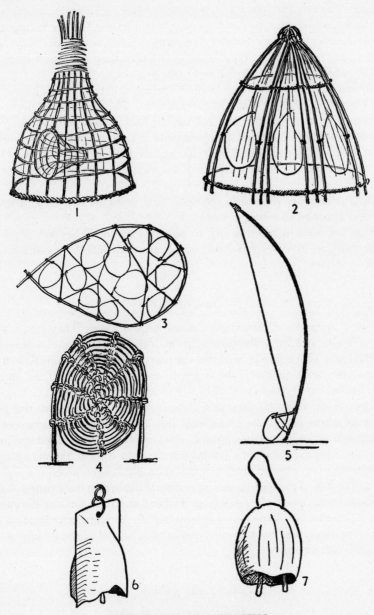

HUNTING TRAPS AND CATTLE BELLS

1. *Aruja*: 'no return' trap for small birds (height 16 inches).
2. *Erukutu*: multiple snare for small birds (height 16 inches).
3. *Atacit*: ground snare for small birds.
4. *Erojo*: trap for edible rats made of fibre.
5. *Eic*: snare for edible rats.
6. *Edongot*: metal cow bell (height 6 inches).
7. *Ekuma*: cattle bell made from borassus palm nut (height 4 inches).

birds. Edible rats and hyrax are caught by balancing stones on a little stick. The animals move the stick and are caught and crushed by the falling stone. Father Kruyer records a rat-trap consisting of a hollowed piece of wood set in the path taken by the rats; once in the trap they could not back out. These traps caught as many as eight rats at a time.[1]

Various types of bird traps (*aruja*) are constructed from withies. One type consists of a basket with a funnel entrance. The bird is lured in through the funnel in search of the bait and cannot find its way out. Another consists of a number of string nooses suspended from a circular frame in the midst of which is the bait. Both types stand about 15 inches high. Doves and weaver birds are the most common victims. Ants are often used as bait.

Hippopotami are hunted in the water and never on dry land. A special harpoon attached to a float is used.

Dogs are used in hunting but to no great extent. They are employed particularly to 'tree' guinea-fowl, which are then killed by hunters with sticks or stones.

5. *Swamp fishing*

The Iteso have never gained proficiency on the water. They rarely know how to swim and leave the construction and the use of canoes largely to the Bakenyi. The Bakenyi, with the immigrant fishermen from Kenya and Tanganyika, are responsible for nearly all the lake fishing in Teso. But the Iteso have always been fond of fish, and swamps are regularly fished during the dry season from January or February to the beginning of the rains. Large numbers gather for communal fish hunts, and the channel of the swamp is dammed at various points. The stream is then 'walked up' to the dam. The men use spears and when near the dam conical baskets (*eisogwa*) which are thrust into the mud. If a fish is caught it is removed through the hole in the side of the basket near the apex. Women also use a canoe-shaped dip basket with which they scoop up the mud and then sort out the catches of small mormyrids, haplochromis, and barbel. An alternative method is to fasten a semicircle of basket-traps across the channel of the swamp and to drive the fish into them.

6. *Lake fishing*

The very few Iteso who fish in the lakes (estimated at 200 in 1950) follow Bakenyi methods. The commonest method is the long-line baited with small fish (haplochromis) caught in unbaited basket-traps. The line consists of three-stranded sisal or papyrus ropes with hooks fastened by snoods at 6-foot intervals. Some lines are over 100 yards long. The catch consists mostly of mamba, male, and semutundu. While operating long-lines, the

[1] Kruyer (undated).

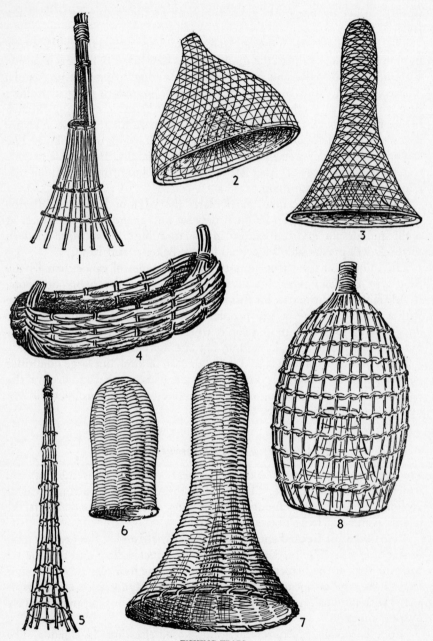

FISHING TRAPS

1. *Eisogwa*: swamp trap operated by hand (length 3 feet 6 inches).
2, 3, and 8. *Aruja*: moored 'no return' traps (various sizes from 2 to 6 feet in diameter at the base).
4. *Eijang*: fishing scoop (length 3 feet).
5. *Erojo*: moored trap (length 3 feet).
6 and 7. *Ekodo*: plunge or scoop baskets (average diameter at base 2 feet 6 inches).

men often live in temporary grass huts built on the floating islands of the lake.

The Bakenyi also use unbaited basket-traps for the larger fish; these are put between stakes sunk in the mud, often as many as fifty baskets in a row. Fishing is then carried out by a system of seining, using floating islands. These are punted into open water; then, with bundles of papyrus trailing beneath them, they are taken back towards the baskets, sweeping the fish before them into the traps. This is a communal task, for at least six men are required. This method is used at night and is a hazardous undertaking. The catch is chiefly Tilapia esculenta and Tilapia variabilis. Individual basket-traps of various types are also left in likely stretches of water without any effort to drive fish into them.

The immigrant fishermen, particularly the Jaluo of Kenya and Baziba of Tanganyika, use cotton or linen nets set and anchored in the water at night and drawn in from canoes in the morning. These more modern methods will presumably be copied by the Bakenyi and Iteso.

The immigrant fishermen import their own types of canoe, usually the Sese type or Koki type. Locally made canoes are invariably dug-outs. Mvule is the favourite tree for this purpose. Canoes vary in size from those with a capacity of one or two people, which are used for fishing, to large ones holding twenty or more people, which are used for ferry work. Dug-out canoes are usually leaky and do not last more than about ten years.

Much of the fish landed is sold fresh for cash or kind, but large quantities are smoked. The smoking is done on wooden grids over a wood fire and the fish is cooked rather than smoked. The smoke-blackened product will last up to a month before it goes bad.

7. *Weapons used in hunting and fishing*

For larger game the Iteso use the same spears which were used in war and which are described above. There is in addition a light throwing spear or javelin, having a blade about 4 inches long. With the wooden haft the length averages 3 feet. There is no butt.

A small double-headed spear (*ekojo*), usually twisted at the neck, is used in stabbing fish. The blades are only about 2 inches long and may be set with the flats of the blades parallel or in line. The haft may be of wood or iron. This type of spear has a magico-religious significance and is associated with rain making and according to some informants has an exclusively magical function.

Hippo harpoons (*edobo*) resemble those used elsewhere in Uganda. The blade with barb is fixed to a long pole. A rope is usually fixed to the blade and the end of the rope is fastened round a large float of ambach.

Bows and arrows do not appear to be used by the Iteso except for birds and drawing blood from cattle.

A gaff (*egolu*) is used for landing mud fish. It consists of a metal hook to which is attached a string. The base of the hook is set in a stick about 2 ft. long. Should the fish pull the hook out of the stick, the owner can still secure the fish with the rope.

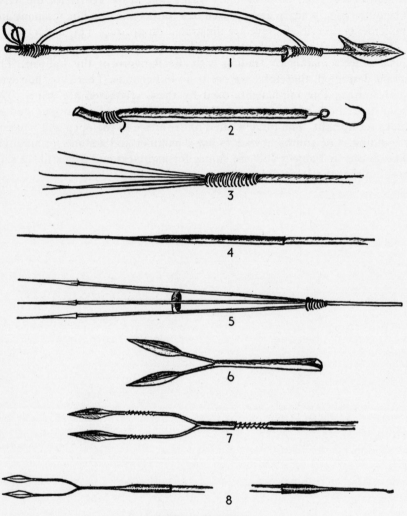

FISHING IMPLEMENTS

1. *Edobo*: harpoon (length 4 feet 6 inches).
2. *Egolu*: gaff (length 2 feet 6 inches).
3. *Imacarin*: pronged stabbing instrument (length with shaft 5 feet 6 inches).
4. *Emacar*: stabbing spear (length with shaft 6 feet).
5. *Imacarin*: multiple stabbing spear (length with shaft 6 feet).
6–8. *Akwaras* or *ekojo*: twin-headed spears (average length with shaft 4 feet).
(6–8, although said to be used in fishing, appear primarily to have a magico-religious significance.)

A hunting knife is a common possession. It is exactly like a spear blade, pointed and with a double cutting edge. It is used for flaying and for cutting up meat. The handle is of wood and the blade is enclosed in a leather sheath. The knife is nowadays carried on a belt or attached to the trousers. Before trousers were worn it was fastened to the arms.

Finger knives are used for harvesting. There also exists a wrist slasher formed of a circular piece of metal with a hole in the centre for the wrist. The outer edge is sharp and encased in a leather sheath. The weapons and implements described above are illustrated on pp. 127, 133, and 137.

The Iteso are not metal workers. They obtained their spears and other metal objects mainly by trading with the Banyoro or the Labwor. The spears described, therefore, are not truly indigenous. There are, however, local smiths. The implements used by these craftsmen are crude. The bellows are built of burnt clay with a goat-skin cover and are pumped by sticks set upright. The forge is sited under a tree in the open and never in a building. The smiths nowadays use a hammer and a stone for an anvil. The smiths in Labwor still use stones for hammers and it is a likely supposition that the Iteso did too.

CHAPTER V

AGRICULTURE

1. *Agricultural practice*

WHEN during the second migration the Iteso spread over most of Teso district they used to practise a system of shifting cultivation. The staple crops were millet and sorghum. Groundnuts, sweet potatoes, and cassava were at that time unknown. These grain crops were grown on the same piece of land until there were signs of deterioration in the yield. The family then moved to new land and the fields returned to bush. Agricultural implements used in this subsistence agriculture were of a primitive kind. The value of metal hoes was appreciated but the manufacture of them was not practised. They were bartered from the Banyoro and Lango and were scarce. Those who could not obtain them had to scratch the soil with wooden hoes or pointed sticks (*akuta*).

This primitive system has given way within fifty years to a universal system of rotational cropping. Standard rotations have been worked out by experience. The commonest rotation is cotton in the first year and finger millet in the second. In the third year the field is usually split up and crops of groundnuts, cassava, sweet potatoes, or beans grown on it. Then follows a three-year resting period.

Crop	Acreage	Market value (shillings)
Finger millet . . .	339,198	
Cotton	271,514	27,625,609
Sweet potatoes . . .	235,114	
Cassava	179,827	
Sorghum	168,065	
Groundnuts	154,565	706,720
Beans	130,202	605,248
Simsim	49,463	27,081
Maize	18,078	
Rice	8,218	
Bulrush millet . . .	6,953	221,311
Bambara groundnuts . .	5,007	

The fertility of the soil is further safeguarded by a universal system of strip cropping on contours with grass bunds between strips. Primitive home-made implements have given way to the plough and other imported manufactured tools. In spite of this spectacular advance in technique it is noteworthy that there is no appreciation of the value of cattle manure on the land.

The Iteso now grow a large variety of field crops. The 1951 acreages and market values give an indication of the relative importance of each crop. The market value is of course only obtainable in the case of economic crops sold for export. Whereas cotton is wholly an economic crop, simsim, groundnuts, and bulrush millet are only partially economic crops. The market value represents the money received only for that part of the crop actually marketed as surplus to domestic needs.

2. *Labour in agriculture*

There is a certain amount of give and take in the division of agricultural labour among members of the household. 'Although in the case of a large patriarchal family unit, all food crops are assigned to definite individuals, the distribution is somewhat ill-defined, whereas with cotton plots there is never any doubt as to their owners. The proceeds from the food crops are common property within the unit, but the return from the cotton plot is the sole possession of the individual.'[1] The family head is responsible with the menfolk for choice of plots and for clearing and breaking the land. The wives have their respective plots in which they sow the crops. If labour is employed on one of these plots, the wife concerned must provide food from her granary in payment. The women are mainly responsible for weeding the crop but are often helped by the men. Should extra labour be necessary the family head must make arrangements. The women harvest the crops and each wife has her own granaries; all wives must, however, contribute to the famine granary required by law (*emono*). Each wife must feed herself, her children, her husband, and relatives as required from her granaries. Older girls help their mothers. Boys are mainly employed to herd cattle and goats. Only the more influential chiefs employ labour on their fields. Nowadays payment may be by monthly wage, but in former times it was by beer at the end of the task, which is known as *eitai*.

3. *Preparation of the ground*

In choosing new land for crops there are various points for which to look. The height and density of trees will indicate how long the land has been resting and the depth of its soil. Light sandy soils are unpopular and thick black soils preferred. Grasses give the most accurate guide to fertility. *Asisinit* (Hyparrhenia filipendula), *ekode* (Chloris gayana), *ebia* (Imperata cylindrica), and *elele* (Setaria sphacelata) are favourable. *Emoto* (Striga) and *edwan* (Rhynchelytrum repens) mean that the land is unsuitable for crops.

Though hand-operated winches have made their appearance in the last few years, the methods employed to clear land are still traditional. The task belongs to the menfolk. Trees are felled with axes and the roots dug out. Larger trees are first ring-barked to kill them, and when they are dry, a fire is kindled against them and the trunks are burnt through. The

[1] Watson, 1937.

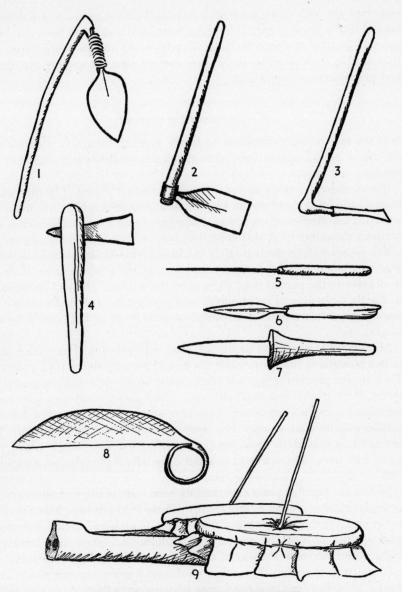

AGRICULTURAL AND HOUSEHOLD IMPLEMENTS

1. *Engit*: heart-blade hoe (handle 3 feet long).
2. *Ekidima*: imported type hoe (handle 3 feet long).
3. *Erokon*: adze (handle 18 inches long).
4. *Aep*: axe (handle 2 feet 6 inches long).
5. *Emutu*: needle (14 inches long).
6. *Ecilikiki*: double-edged knife (total length 12 inches).
7. *Ekileng*: single-edged knife (total length 11 inches).
8. *Ekurupeta*: finger-knife (total length 3 inches).
9. *Acukut*: forge bellows (total length 3 feet).

imported axe with socket has largely displaced the locally made axe which is tanged into a wooden haft. The trees, branches, and scrub thus cut down are seldom used to fence the field. Weeds, roots, and trees are burnt and the ash dug into the ground. No propitiatory rites accompany the choice and preparation of a new plot.

4. *Breaking the ground*

It is the task of the menfolk to break the ground, though it is customary nowadays for women to help with ploughing by driving the team or by handling the plough.

Two indigenous types of metal hoe were formerly used. The first was a heart-shaped flat blade tied to the end of a long stick which was manipulated in a kneeling or sitting posture. Kitching records it as being used in the north of the district.[1] It still exists but is very rare. The commoner type, which is still widely used, consists of a similar flat blade attached by fibre rope to a wooden haft (*amusenu*) bent so that the blade is at an angle of 60 degrees to the part of the haft held by the worker. The end of the tang is usually bent over. The imported hoe with socket still ranks second in popularity to this type of hoe, probably on account of the latter's lighter weight.

Most families nowadays break new land with ploughs. There are nearly 40,000 ploughs in the district and the hire of ploughs is accepted practice. The value of ploughing was not immediately apparent to the Iteso and the spread of the plough was slow; although introduced in 1909 there were only 200 ploughs in the district ten years later and only in the 1930's did the numbers really start to rise. The Safim plough, which can be drawn by two oxen, is nowadays replacing the heavier Ransome plough which requires four oxen. About a third to a half of an acre is ploughed in a normal working day.

Within the last five years experiments have been made with mechanical methods of cultivation in Serere county. These methods have found favour with a small section of the population which is prepared to pay economic rates for the hire of the tractor and equipment. There are, however, practical difficulties in the way of the spread of mechanical cultivation.

Apart from the plough no other ox-drawn implements are used. The ground is broken for the second time by hand with hoes. A type of bush harrow made of thorn bushes is in existence in Amuria and is used for covering the millet crop.

5. *Planting the crop*

The Teso calendar is based on the agriculture of the people. There are three seasons of four months each.

[1] Kitching, 1912.

PLATE VII

Ploughing with a heavy type of plough
(*See p.* 138)

Tethered goats
(*See p.* 143)

The Dry Season:

> *Opoo*, when the sun is hot (December).
> *Orara*, when the trees lose their leaves (January).
> *Omuk*, when the leaves grow again (February).
> *Okwang*, when the children become white in the dust (March).

The Wet Season:

> *Odunge*, when rain covers the sun (April).
> *Opedelei* or *Abwataidwe*, when children wait for food (May).
> *Omaruk*, the month of mushrooms (June).
> *Omodokoingol*, the harvest of millet (July).

The Season of Plenty:

> *Otikoik* or *Oloja*, the month of big stomachs (August).
> *Otibar* or *Ocoto*, the month of richness (September).
> *Osokosokoma*, when the grass blocks the paths (October).
> *Osuban*, the month of celebrations (November).

Kitching's recording varies slightly:[1] *Oolo* is May; *Opedelein*, when the millet ripens, is June; *Oseredekalei* July; *Omaruk* August; and *Opo*, the time of stubble, September.

There are many natural indications of the correct time to plant. When the *erere* (Ficus ingens) sheds its leaves is the time to plant millet; also when the *etekwa* (Albizzia coriaria) is flowering. The men decide when the symptoms are right for planting.

There are certain planting ceremonies such as *aitangar*—blessing of the hoe—or wearing of *emoros* when planting. The hoe is blessed by throwing grain over it on the altar (*abila*) and a beer party follows.

There are numerous superstitions connected with planting. To name a few:

(*a*) A tamarind pod should be placed in the gourd with the millet seed just before planting.

(*b*) Porcupine or hedgehog quills should be mixed with millet or sorghum seed in the gourd when planting.

(*c*) Ashes or goat dung should be scattered on the simsim crop in the early morning after heavy dew to deter insects.

(*d*) *Ebomo*, a creeper, should be tied round the wrists before planting.

(*e*) Certain types of swamp grass should be put in the plots.

(*f*) Where there are twins in the family, they must start sowing the millet, then hand over to someone else.

(*g*) Crops should be sown from the end farthest from the house and lead towards the house. This brings the harvest home.

(*h*) Sodom apples thrown over the field before sowing increase the yield.

[1] Kitching, 1912.

(i) If a neighbour praises a man's plot, the owner will get bad results, particularly if the person giving praise is one of twins. Branches of *ekaka* or *ekaikai* planted round the plot nullify any praise and consequent bad effects.

(j) Bones, beer dregs, and cow dung mixed and burnt on a plot will drive away insects, particularly grasshoppers, by the smell.

(k) A sausage-tree fruit buried in sweet potato mounds will help the potatoes to increase in size.

Planting seasons are as follows:

Finger millet (*akima*)	March–May
Cotton (*epaaba*)	May–August (season controlled by law).
Sweet potatoes (*acok*)	June–August
Cassava (*emuogo*)	June–August
Sorghum (*imumwa*)	March–May
Groundnuts (*emaido*)	April–May
Beans (*imare*)	July–August
Simsim (*ikanyum*)	March–May
Maize (*ekirididi*)	March–May
Rice (*emucele*)	December–January
Bulrush millet (*emawele*)	March–May
Bambara groundnuts (*isuk*)	April–May

Cattle are often used after sowing a crop of millet, sorghum, or beans to walk up and down the plot in order to cover and consolidate the seed. In Amuria a type of bush harrow is occasionally used for this purpose, consisting of thorn bushes chopped at ground level and dragged by oxen.

6. *Weeding and protection of the crop*

Weeding is the task of women though it is not uncommon to see a family group of both sexes working together to weed a plot. A short-handled hoe is used which resembles the digging hoe with the blade set back at 60 degrees to the haft; but the blade is much smaller and narrower and shaped like an adze blade (*erokon*)

Trowell records the use of 'a fresh-water mussel shell for weeding between young millet' and 'a wooden rake or hay-fork about 2·5 metres long for clearing weeds and long grass'.[1] I have not come across these tools but their use is confirmed. *Akuta*, a digging stick, is still used for weeding.

In parts of Karamoja fields are fenced with thorn bush, but no attempt is made in Teso to protect plots from the smaller wild animals or from cattle. Crops consequently suffer from stray cattle and from bush pig and small buck, but the most serious damage is from small birds. Scarecrows are used with even less success than in Britain. Children scare away the birds with a form of catapult (*aporocet*), made from the pliant wood of the *etoboco* tree, which hurls a mud ball.

[1] Trowell and Wachsmann, 1953.

Disease or an evil deity may attack crops. To drive away bad spirits, fires are lit in the evening round the millet plots, and members of the family stay by them and shout.

When gourds are attacked by insects the diseased gourds should be mixed with ashes and placed on a path. People walking on the path will carry away material on their feet and thus keep away disease from the other gourds.

7. *Harvesting*

Harvesting is the duty of women. The heads of the grain are cut either with a small double-edged knife or with a distinctive sickle-shaped knife attached to a ring worn on the finger (*ekurupeta*). The stalks are left in the field for the cattle to eat and are never harvested and stored as cattle feed for the dry season.

Crops are seldom left to dry in the field. They are carried in baskets or trays immediately to the homestead where the drying process takes place. Grain, both millet and sorghum, is stored unthreshed but must be thoroughly dried on the winnowing ground or on the roof of a hut or on a nearby rock. Maize cobs are dried and smoked. Groundnuts are stored in their shells but must be dried first.

Simsim requires special treatment. The stalks with the heads are tied in flounces to a large sloping frame sited to catch the direct rays of the sun at its hottest. The frame, when loaded, looks exactly like one side of a thatched roof. The ground under the frame is plastered with cow dung. When the simsim is thoroughly dry it is beaten with sticks. The dry pods burst and the seeds fall on to the plastered floor. They are then swept up, winnowed and stored in a pot or in the miniature granary (*etuja*).

There are no religious ceremonies connected with harvesting.

Types of granaries are described in detail on p. 114 above.

8. *Vegetable patch*

In addition to his field crops, each householder normally cultivates a vegetable patch close to his house in which he grows a variety of smaller plants needed in the home; the majority of these plants are for seasoning or for vegetables and are listed on pp. 122 and 123 above; tobacco and Indian hemp are often grown for smoking.

9. *Trees and hedges*

Many householders also plant trees for domestic use. The most common are cassia, cape lilac, nysambya—all of which are used in house building. These trees are usually planted round the circumference of the compound but are often grouped to form a small plantation near the house or occasionally spaced among the vegetable patch or home fields. In some villages, particularly in south Teso where trees are scarce, the population has planted the sides of bush paths with cape lilac trees. The trees bordering a man's plot are planted by him and remain his property. Once planted and established, the trees receive no further care. Pruning is not practised.

Fruit-trees are rarely seen far from Serere. The labour involved in pruning and mulching the trees deters most Iteso, for of the citrus fruits only oranges are truly popular. There are many banana gardens to be seen, especially in Serere, Bukedea, and Kaberamaido counties. Most of these belong to the Bantu population of Teso; but the Iteso themselves are fond of the fruit and often attempt to grow it where conditions are favourable.

The fruits of several wild trees are used in the preparation of food, but only the shea-butter nut tree (*ekungur*) produces an economic crop.[1] The nuts are picked and sold to middlemen, who supply the oil mills. No attempt is ever made to grow this valuable tree near the homestead.

Live hedges are seldom seen except round homesteads. In parts of Serere and Soroti counties some farmers have had their farms set out in blocks on the contours. The blocks are demarcated with sisal, which, when fully grown, keeps cattle out or in as required. The sisal is used for rope-making at home.

10. *Honey*

Sales of wild honey in 1951 totalled 243,264s. The honey is usually collected from holes in the trees or rocks by smoking out the bees. Bee-hives are, however, in use. There are two types: the first consists of a hollowed log with the ends closed with tin or wood, leaving a small aperture. The second type is made of woven withies and plastered with mud and cow dung. In shape, size, and appearance the two types are similar, being cylindrical, approximately 3 feet long and 1 foot in diameter. They are lodged in trees in a neighbourhood known to contain bees.

[1] Valued at 677,376s. in 1951.

CHAPTER VI

ANIMAL HUSBANDRY

1. *Economic importance of livestock*

As already stated, cattle are not considered to play any part in agriculture except inasmuch as oxen are used to plough. The value of manure to the land is not appreciated and mixed farming does not exist. Agriculture and animal husbandry are two separate pursuits. Nevertheless, cattle are of considerable economic importance. At one time the ritual and social importance of livestock probably outweighed economic considerations; but there is no doubt that the Iteso now regard cattle first and foremost as an economic asset, not only as a source of bride-price whereby the strength of the clan can be increased, but also as a means of obtaining cash for the necessities and luxuries of life. This change of heart occurred within the last twenty years when the Iteso were persuaded to market their surplus cattle. Once the export markets were established exports rose, particularly during the war years, to such an extent that a ban had to be placed on breeding stock leaving the district. Now exports have fallen again and there is serious danger of over-stocking in some areas. The 1952 livestock census showed 645,807 head of cattle and 251,047 sheep and goats in Teso. Exports of cattle from the district averaged 33,000 a year over the twelve years from 1940 to 1952.

The type of Teso cattle is the humped zebu. Throughout most of the district the Nkedi or Eastern Province zebu strain is found. In Kaberamaido the Kyoga zebu, a bigger-boned animal with short horns and drooping ears, is common, while in the north of Amuria the Karamoja zebu strain appears. Cattle in Serere show traces of the Ankole type and have reduced humps. Old men state that before the arrival of Europeans the Banyoro traded Ankole type beasts for the products of Teso.[1]

At the present time there are thirteen markets in Teso at each of which business takes place once a month. Sales are by agreement and not by auction. Dealers must obtain veterinary permits to move stock purchased to the export quarantines near the railway or steamer stations. The majority of Teso cattle leave the district by steamer fortnightly after a two-weeks' quarantine period.

Hides and skins have always been a valuable export. Before the advent of Europeans, the Iteso traded them for metal hoes from the Banyoro. In recent years, owing mainly to the higher standards of living following improved cotton prices, much more meat is consumed in the district than before. In 1952 29,942 hides and 37,000 skins were purchased in Teso for 516,100s. Some were brought from Karamoja but the majority were produced locally. Much of the value of the trade is, however, lost through

[1] Ross, 1954.

faulty methods. Despite continuous teaching on the subject hides are still sometimes pegged out to dry in the sun. But some of the more enlightened buy green hides from those unwilling or too lazy to dry them correctly, and dry them properly on frames.

2. *Religious and social importance of livestock*

The Iteso have in common with other Nilo-Hamitic tribes an innate love of cattle which is evidenced in part by the numerous words in use to describe the different colours and peculiarities of cattle:

Akol	cow with large white patches.
Angole	cow with a white mark on its face.
Aleli	striped cow.
Aese	striped cow.
Apusi	grey cow.
Akori	white and brown flecked cow.
Ameri	white and black flecked cow.
Amuge	dark brown cow, almost black.
Anyanga	brown cow.
Arengan	red-brown cow.
Akwangan	white cow.
Aongor	khaki-coloured cow.

Every beast is named, often after a human being. The warrior calls the name of his favourite beast in the preliminaries to the fight and in the ecstasy of first blood in the hunt. In all the religious and social ceremonies of Teso life, livestock plays a most important part. In the initiation of *asapan*, when the youth takes on his new manhood name, he must suck the udder of a cow to indicate approval. The entrails of the sacrificial ox or goat will tell the future, and the sacrifice of a goat with special markings will help to cure sickness; its stomach contents must be smeared on the patient. If a woman has failed to observe her clan taboos, sickness will befall her and her children; a bull must be suffocated and the woman must wear the skin of the dewlap and tie pieces of meat round the necks of her children. Cattle are an essential part of bride-price; a bull must be slaughtered at burial ceremonies. In the age-set initiation ceremony the stomach contents of a black bullock were smeared over the initiates.

Superstition and religious conviction ensure that the details of these ceremonies remain unchanged. Cattle and goats are needed for birth and death ceremonies and for marriage, in sickness, and to counteract witchcraft. Without them such ceremonies cannot be performed and the possession of them is essential.

3. *Cattle brands*

In former times each clan (*ateker*) had its own cattle brand. With the spreading of clans all over Teso local variations multiplied and any list

PLATE VIII

Teso zebu cattle
(*See p.* 143)

Cattle kraal entrance
(*See p.* 145)

compiled would contain as many variations and anomalies as a list of clan taboos. For economic reasons the branding of cattle has almost died out, for a branded hide loses much of its value. For this reason information has proved difficult to collect.

In Usuku branding is occasionally still remembered although there are many discrepancies in the accounts given.

It appears that beasts had their ears cut in a distinctive fashion as well as being branded. This nicking of the ears is still practised. Different brands are in some cases believed to have been used for cows and bulls.

The following examples, taken from Usuku, indicate the type of brands used.

Atekok: two half circles on hump, two on haunch. Both ears cut once.
Atekok: circle with diagonal bar on flank. Three nicks in both ears.
Igoria: three half circles on flanks. Left ear cut three times. Tip of right ear cut.
Isureta: no branding. Left ear cut once. Tip of right ear cut off.
Isuguro: large cross across the flank. One further line to the hump. Each ear cut with long split from tip.
Ikarebwok: bull—three parallel lines from base of hump over haunch; cow—two lateral lines across flank over a circle.
Ipalam: no branding. Notch on lower part of right ear. Notch in upper part of left ear.

4. *Care of livestock*

Cattle were, and still are, kept in an open kraal at night. The kraal was once the centre point of the whole village, so sited that it could be well defended against attackers. Nowadays it may be anything up to 150 yards from the owner's house. The kraal is constructed of thorn bush round which euphorbia is often planted. It is usually sited round an ant-hill, which provides drainage and serves as a lick. There is no cover against the elements and no attempt is made to clean the kraal. When the ground becomes too soggy a new site is chosen. Calves are, however, often kept in a separate calf house or occasionally in their owners' homes. Goats, too, are usually kept in a separate hut within the compound. Formerly goats and calves were kept in the house with human beings.

Except in a few scattered herds under the direct supervision of the Veterinary Department, cattle and calves are never fed. They are turned out to graze about 10 a.m., when the labour in the fields is done. It is the task of boys to herd them and take them to water. They are brought back to the kraal about sunset. Calves are allowed to run with their dams and no effort is made to wean them. Milking normally takes place once a day. The benefits of culling stock are beginning to be realized though culling is seldom systematically practised. Castration of bulls, is, however, generally accepted.

The movements of cattle are to a large extent due to herding practice.

Owners tend to put their beasts with others to be herded communally while they break new ground for their crops in March, April, and May. Professional herdsmen, Bahima from Ankole district, often take large herds of many hundreds of cattle in order to build up their own herds through herding fees.

Silage storage methods are taught but not practised. Nor is any effort made to improve grazing, though the value of grass leys is constantly taught. Salt is obtained from natural licks—ant-hills or deposits of grey clay known as *edoot*.

5. *Disease in livestock*

The disastrous rinderpest outbreak of 1890 is still remembered as the first real date in Teso history. Rinderpest (*esotoka*) is still the most feared of all diseases in cattle. It is brought by *Edeke*, the spirit of calamity, from the east and the word *edeke* is indeed synonymous with rinderpest. There is no recognized native cure though the pounded roots of *eusuk* (Fagara chalybea) after boiling, administered internally or externally, or a soup from leopard's meat, are both considered beneficial.[1] Rinderpest has always been the principal killing disease of cattle and as such the main preoccupation of the Veterinary Department. Though it was brought under control in the late 1920's, there have been sporadic outbreaks till the present day. As recently as 1948 4,200 head of cattle perished from rinderpest and the effects of inoculation. The disease is endemic in Karamoja and it was found necessary until 1952 to inoculate periodically all cattle in the areas of Teso bordering on Karamoja to the number of some 220,000 every two years.

East coast fever (*angaarwei*) is responsible for many deaths in calves though not for all those attributed to it. Cattle suffering from east coast fever are drenched with an infusion of the roots of *epejali* (Idigofera endecaphylla) while the juice of *epopong* (euphorbia) is applied to painful swellings. No systematic removal of ticks is practised. Sores made by their removal are smeared with dung. Dips are unknown, and spraying is rarely practised. Such measures are apt to weaken the immunity which cattle must attain to combat this disease.

Trypanosomiasis (*omolimol*) is a condition scarcely recognized by the Iteso and not associated with the presence of tsetse fly. The very word is borrowed from the Lango and the disease is mainly found in the north of Amuria county where it borders on Lango district. There do not appear to be native remedies. The Veterinary Department has of recent years treated cattle in infected areas with antrycide with some measure of success.

Blackquarter (*okwat*) is treated by scarification with a hot knife, but this treatment is admitted to be seldom successful. Blackquarter and, to a lesser extent, anthrax (*atular*) occur all over Teso.

The products of various trees and plants are utilized for dressing wounds.

---

[1] Native remedies in this section are from Watson, 1937.

A slight wound is dressed with the boiled pounded roots of *elilyoi* (Securidaca ongipendulata), while a more severe septic wound is treated with *ebwolo* (Annona chrysophylla) prepared in a similar manner. The pounded leaves, previously boiled, of *eleketete* (Portulaca sp.) are also considered a useful disinfectant.

Worms (*ikitani* and *igoga*), diagnosed by their presence in the dung and the poor condition of the animal, are said to be expelled by administering a cold leaf-infusion of *epeduru loicici* (Cassia negricans).

Sore eyes are treated with a few drops of water mixed with the leaves of tobacco.

6. *Poultry*

Eggs are always, and poultry flesh is sometimes, taboo to women, and men seldom eat eggs. Nevertheless, poultry are kept in every homestead and represent a not inconsiderable source of wealth. No exact figures are available. The returns from fee-nil licences to take poultry and eggs from the district in 1951 show 7,625 birds and 176,950 eggs exported, but these totals are only a fraction of the true figures.

Although there is a high percentage of exogenous types, no attempt is made to breed poultry systematically, and fowls are of a degenerate type and their eggs little larger than a bantam's. Fowls were usually kept in their owner's house at night and often still are. But a type of hen-house perched several feet above ground used to be constructed with a ladder to enable the fowls to enter and leave. This type of hen-house is still common. More elaborate types with nesting boxes and caged runs to protect chickens from hawks are gradually finding favour. Poultry play their part in religious ritual in ceremonial sacrifices, in the ceremony of *asut* during marriage and in the ceremonies to prevent infant mortality. Chickens' liver is an ingredient of harmful medicine.

CHAPTER VII

TRADE

1. *Barter*

ALTHOUGH the Iteso relied entirely on their agriculture and animal husbandry for their food supplies and made their necessary household implements in the home from the skins of their animals or from the trees in the bush or from the clay in the ground, there has existed from ancient times an organized barter system.

In the olden days it was easy for each man to supply his own wants and commerce hardly existed. There were however specialised branches and these articles were usually bought from the artisans who made them. Payment was invariably in baskets of millet or fowls. Specialised branches were:—pottery, smith-work, door making (from plaited twigs), basket work, hoe handles, shoe, or rather sandal, making (leather soles with strips for tying), chair making, mortar making, cutting of *adere* from a marrow, making of gourds, fishtraps, tattooing, drum-making and harp-making. Drums sold for a goat (or a bull for a very large one); 25 baskets of unthreshed millet equalled 1 heifer, 10 baskets of unthreshed millet equalled 1 bull, 2 or 3 baskets of unthreshed millet equalled 1 goat or sheep. Two goats bought an ostrich feather hair-dress. Two heifers and 1 bull bought a live ostrich (Lake Salisbury), 1 cow bought 1 donkey (used formerly for carrying water and firewood especially in the parts near Karamoja). In the present days there is quite an amount of commerce and the currency is the rupee. The introduction of cotton brought quite a lot of money into the country and brought the want of European articles from bicycles to cigarettes. Besides the cotton there is quite a considerable trade in groundnuts, simsim, cattle, goats, sheep and hides.[1]

The Jopaluo bartered iron hoes with the Lango who passed them on to the Kumam in exchange for cattle; three hoes were exchanged for one heifer.[2] Ironwork was particularly in request. There were local smiths but there is no indication that iron was smelted in Teso as it was in Labwor. The Iteso obtained their spears from Labwor and from Banyoro traders in return for hides, skins, goats, and ivory.

Though money is nowadays the usual medium of exchange, barter is by no means a custom of the past. In the food shortage of 1953 it proved impossible to obtain fish except in return for grain. Cattle are regularly obtained by traders in exchange for bicycles. Though an owner is often unwilling to part with a beast for 600s. he is usually prepared to accept a bicycle valued at 300s.

[1] Kruyer (undated).
[2] Driberg, 1923.

2. *Modern marketing methods*

The export value of crops and livestock and the necessity to ensure high quality in outside markets and to prevent the spread of disease has in the last forty years necessitated an ever-increasing element of governmental control. Cattle may only be sold in recognized markets; movements are controlled and movement outside the district necessitates a period in quarantine with necessary inoculations against disease. Hides and skins are graded according to quality and method of preparation and may only be sold at licensed stores. Food export crops must be marketed during certain specified seasons at licensed stores and the quantity allowed to be purchased may in some cases be limited. The most complicated marketing system relates to cotton, which is sold in two qualities, safi and fifi, at licensed stores during a specified season. Owing to the necessity to keep the seed pure, the district is divided into a number of cotton zones; the movement of seed cotton from one zone to another is prohibited. In this manner it is possible to keep separate different types of seed. As much of the experimental work on cotton is performed at Serere experimental station, the zones in Teso are smaller and more numerous than elsewhere to enable a gradual increase of seed production.

The only successful African retail traders in the district are of tribes other than the Teso. It is not that Teso traders lack capital but rather that they lack aptitude. Since 1950 producer co-operative societies have become popular. The movement was started by unregistered groups in Buganda, such as the Federation of Uganda African Farmers and the African Farmers Union, spreading their influence into Teso. Latterly, as a result of the work of the Department of Co-operative Development, a number of true co-operatives have been formed and registered.

PART V

CULTURE

CHAPTER I

MUSIC AND DANCING

1. *Percussion Instruments*

IT is probable that drums came to be used by the Iteso only in comparatively recent times after contact with Nilotic and Bantu tribes. The local dance of the Iteso of Usuku is the *edonga* in which drums are not used; in Karamoja drums are rarely, if ever, seen. Drum making is a specialist and rare trade. In former times the cost of a large drum was one bull, and even today such drums are expensive and ownership of them is a mark of high prestige. Various local woods are used of which the commonest are *etekwa* (Albizzia coriara) and *ekum* (Diospyros mespiliformis).

Drums are made by hollowing logs of suitable dimensions and fixing skins over both ends. Goat skin is generally preferred for the purpose. The two skins are kept taut by leather thongs connecting them. Only the skin on the top or larger end of the drum is beaten. The only exception to this process is the *emidiri* drum which will be described below.

There are four distinct types of drum which vary in size and shape and in the purpose for which they are used.

(i) The *atenus* drum is from 5 to 8 feet long and about 2 or 3 feet in diameter at the top. It is played only by women, who beat a slow, deep note with the flat of one hand while a quicker rhythm is beaten by male drummers with sticks on the *ideteta*, rather in the same way as a big drum is used in a European dance band in company with a side drum. Ownership of an *atenus* is a mark of high standing. It is the most important drum in Teso and is of universal distribution.

(ii) The *ideteta* drums (sing. *idetait*) are much smaller than the *atenus* and vary in size according to the tone required. There are usually four *ideteta* to each *atenus*. The skin is beaten by sticks. *Atenus* and *ideteta* together provide the accompaniment for the most important Teso dance, the *ajosi*. They rest lengthways on the ground when played.

(iii) The *etida* is a large squat drum 3–4 feet long and about 3 feet in diameter, which is played together with a tiny drum (*itelele*) by one drummer. The tiny drum is only about 9 inches long and 3 inches in diameter and contains two pebbles. Both drums are set lengthways on stick-rests, and the drummer sits cross-legged in front of them on the ground. Both drums are sounded with sticks and the high note of the tiny drum is kept up by frequently heating the skin over a fire kept alight for the purpose. The *etida* drum provides the accompaniment for the *etida* dance, which is performed to cure the sick. The dance is banned, but persists in Usuku, Tisai, and Bukedea, and to a much lesser extent in the rest of Teso.

(iv) The *emidiri* drum is played on the occasion of the birth of twins. It is a long, cylinder-shaped drum, held between the drummer's knees and played with the flat of the hand. There are usually two partner drums (*ideteta*), similar to the *ideteta* used with the *atenus*, but strung from the drummer's body and played with the flat of the hand. They average 1 foot in diameter and 3 feet in length. The skin of the *emidiri* is invariably that of the water lizard and is fastened to the body of the drum with wooden studs. The base of the drum is open.

Rattles are made of gourds filled with dried peas or pebbles and are used mainly for the accompaniment of songs for healing the sick or for other magical occasions such as rain making. The narrow neck serves as a handle.

Pellet bells are described as part of dancers' regalia on p. 164 below. The only other type of bell in use is the forged metal bell hung round the neck of cattle.

The sansa (*akongo*) is one of the commoner musical instruments of Teso. It is believed to have been introduced in recent times from the Congo, as its name implies. It does not differ in construction or technique from the sansa found elsewhere in Uganda.

2. *Wind instruments*

The Iteso make an end-blown trumpet from a hollowed tube of euphorbia about 4 feet long, set in a calabash with a hole in the bottom of the same size as the tube. The joints are sealed with the juice of the *ebule* tree (Ficus platyphylla). The notes are produced by blowing with lip vibrations. This instrument is called *asukusuk*, presumably because its note resembles the booming call of the ground hornbill (*esukusuk*), although the same instrument is known as *atoros* in Toroma. It is not in my experience ever played by 'men in sets of three or more'[1] nor is it confined to Usuku,[2] for I have seen it also in Amuria; it is, however, a rare and local instrument. Of an *asukusuk* seen by him Coutts observes:

The *asukusuk* sounds five different notes; the lowest is meant to imitate the growl of a lion. It sounds just beyond the compass of a normal bass voice, probably about low C. The most commonly played notes, however, are about E flat, the octave above that and a third again above that. This last is usually preceded by an appogiatura a second below it. The usual method of playing these notes is thus:

The *asukusuk* is played to mark the rhythm of the *edonga* dance in which no drums are used; more often it is played to do honour to a celebrated visitor or to mark a ceremonial occasion.

[1] Trowell and Wachsman, 1953.   [2] Coutts, 1950.

DRUMS

1. *Atenus*: main drum with accompanying drums (*ideteta*) (main drum 5 feet long; accompanying drums 19, 14, 13, and 12 inches long).
2. *Etida*: healing drum with accompanying drum (*itelele*) and fire and grass (*akalasia*) for tuning (main drum 2 feet 6 inches long; accompanying drum 7 inches long).
3 and 4. *Emidiri*: twins ceremony drums (average 3 feet long).

There is another trumpet in use, which is side-blown; this is the *arupepe*. It is distributed throughout the district but is nevertheless a rare instrument.

It is made of two pieces of the *edodoi*, a tree with sausage-like pods. These pieces are chosen, hollowed out and fitted together, so that the whole is shaped like, and is about the same size as, a Bach D trumpet or a herald's trumpet. The wood is covered in two parts by skins, the long part with duiker, and the 'bell' part with goatskin. They are fashioned with beads. The mouthpiece is an egg-shaped hole about six inches from the end of the pipe. The whole instrument is about three feet six inches long. The player blows vigorously into the mouthpiece, holding the instrument horizontally to his left side. The note is single toned, but is played in a pressing rhythm:

or similarly.[1]

In some examples seen there has been a pronounced bell while in others the instrument tapers evenly from the bell to the end of the pipe. Bead or shell ornamentation is not universal.

The *arupepe* is used, as is the *asukusuk*, to call people to a gathering, especially to a hunt. It is said to have given warning of Karamojong raids. I have seen it used as an accompaniment to a dance both in Karamoja and in Teso, but only rarely.

A third trumpet is fashioned from an animal's horn, either a game animal's or a cow's; it is side-blown and the notes are produced by blowing into a hole drilled in the side of the horn and by stopping or opening another hole drilled in the end. This instrument is probably confined to Usuku and is called *aluut*. It is not used at dances. In Karamoja it is played by herd boys to frighten away hyenas,[2] and in Teso it is blown to call people to gatherings or on ceremonial occasions.

The *esosi* is a cone-flute or whistle, and is distributed throughout the district though nowhere is it common. It is usually made from a goat's horn with the tip pierced by a small hole. It is only a few inches long and is held vertically with the tip downwards and the note is produced by blowing across the top. It is said that the *esosi* is also made of baked clay or of wood. Normally it has no stops other than the basal hole but examples have been recorded in Serere of *esosi* with two or three stops.[3] It is, however, possible that this description refers to the *alamaru*; for according to one informant the *alamaru* is also called *ebilo*, from the name of a reed used in its manufacture, whereas the name for the *esosi* among Nilotic tribes is *bilo*. The *esosi* is played on ceremonial occasions or during dances.

A small flute is made from the hollowed stem of the castor-oil plant,

[1] Coutts, 1950.
[2] Trowell and Wachsman, 1953.
[3] Watson, 1937.

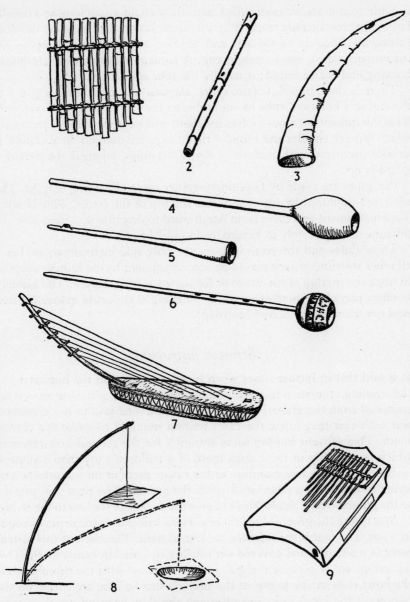

MUSICAL INSTRUMENTS

1. Pan pipes (not indigenous) (length 6 inches).
2. *Alamaru*: flute (length 10 inches).
3. *Aluut*: horn (length 11 inches).
4. *Asukusuk*: bass trumpet (length 4 feet).
5. *Arupepe*: side-blown trumpet (length 3 feet).
6. *Alamaru*: bass flute (length 3 feet 6 inches).
7. *Adeudeu*: arched harp (overall length 2 feet 6 inches).
8. *Aunene*: ground bow (height when standing 2 feet 6 inches).
9. *Akongo*: sansa (not indigenous) (length 10 inches).

suitable reed grass, or even millet stem. It is about a foot long and usually has two, three, or four stops. The sound is produced by holding the flute (*alamaru*) obliquely to the left and blowing across the open top of the instrument which has a straight rim. A similar flute but with a notched blowing end is also found; it usually has four stops.

There is also a bass flute (also called *alamaru*) made by fitting a gourd to the end of a hollowed tube of euphorbia in the same way as the *asukusuk*. This instrument averages $3\frac{1}{2}$ feet in length and has four stops. The gourd, which is much smaller and rounder than the gourd used on the *asukusuk*, is usually decorated with pattern or figure drawings, whereas the *asukusuk* gourd is not.

Pan-pipes are made by fastening together reeds of varying lengths. The notes are produced by blowing across the top of the stems. This is not a Teso instrument and there is no Ateso word to describe it. I have seen the instrument played only in Serere by an old Musoga.

These flutes and the pan-pipes are the only solo instruments in Teso; all other instruments are played as accompaniment to the human voice or to mark the rhythm of the dance or for some specific purpose. The *alamaru* is often played by herdsmen while watching their cattle graze. Neither *esosi* nor *alamaru* are played in groups.

3. *Stringed instruments*

It is said that in former times when songs were sung in the homestead in the evening, the singers were accompanied by the plucking of strings stretched from the granaries in the compound. The skill of the musicians was such that they knew the exact tension required to strike the correct notes. This account implies some antiquity for the ground-bow (*aunene*), which is probably in these days more of a children's toy than a musical instrument. In the few examples seen a square piece of tin was attached by string to the top of a pliant stick set in the ground. The plate was pressed to the ground over a shallow hole to give the necessary tension to the string.

Apart from the ground-bow there are two stringed instruments in vogue in Teso. The first is the *adeudeu*, an arched harp. The bowl of this instrument is made of wood covered with duiker or goatskin neatly sewn. The six strings are of cord, not of gut, and are plucked with the thumbs while the bowl rests in the palms of the player's hands. The arch rests on the bottom of the bowl and comes through the skin covering which is sewn round it. The strings are stretched from the tuning pegs in the arch through the skin covering of the bowl to the base of the bowl. The Teso instrument differs from that of neighbouring districts by the long shape of its bowl and its slim shoulder. There are two types within Teso: the usual type in North Teso has a rounded end to the bowl; this type gives way in the south of the district to the 'Pallisa' type with a squared end.

The second stringed instrument is a tube-fiddle known as *adigidi*. 'The *adigidi* is a patent copy of the Ganda *edingidi* or fiddle. It is, however, interesting to note that its tone is lower and it corresponds to the *edingidi* much as the viola to the violin. This is because a largish calabash is used to form the bowl, instead of a hollowed, smaller piece of wood. Teso modifications include the use of half a groundnut as bridge, and the resin of the *ecomai* tree as bow resin, stuck in a large lump like chewing gum on the bowl of the fiddle.'[1] The *adigidi* is played as accompaniment to the human voice; it is a rare and local instrument in Teso; I have seen it in Usuku and Tisai only.

'The voice sings in concert with the *adeudeu* songs of love and war or topical subjects, usually in 5/4 rhythm. The normal pitch is baritone, but a sort of tenor begins a new phrase and from time to time a bass growl is interposed an octave lower than the main tune of the song, giving a most amusing affect like that in the slave's love-song in "Il Seraglio".'[1] *Adeudeu* players are usually professional musicians who are hired for the entertainment of guests at weddings or other social functions; many of them are women. *Adeudeu* songs are the only songs in Teso which are not sung as accompaniment to dances.

4. Songs

With the exception of the drum bands described on p. 153 the Iteso make no attempt to form orchestras of several similar or different instruments. All the instruments described are played singly. Apart from flutes and sansas they are used, inasmuch as they have a purely musical use, as accompaniment to the human voice in dances. Print is an inadequate medium to describe the melody and rhythm of song or the colourful action of dances. Nevertheless, for the sake of completeness I have made an attempt.[2]

The words of the *adeudeu* songs may range from the tribal ballads of the six generations (see p. 7 above) such as:

> *Epude, epude adau akima, epude.*
> *Epude, epude adau ikanyum, epude.*
>
> (Mice, mice have finished the millet.
> Mice have finished the simsim.)

or

> *Tikir, tikir da, eleli; imanymany acoman, eleli,*
> *Papa ka Onyangaese eleli.*
>
> (Gallop, gallop, he is happy; he folds his apron happily,
> The father of Onyangaese is happy.)

[1] Coutts, 1950.
[2] The results of scientific recordings are not yet available and commercial recordings are few. I am indebted to Dr. K. P. Wachsmann of the Uganda Museum for permission to publish the song melodies which follow.

to modern scurrilous or topical verses such as:

> *Eee! Apiot, Apiot naaa, Apiot*
> *Araun apese amalayat.*

> (Oh dear! This Apiot.
> The girl has become a whore.)

or

> *Yospina, inyoin ibore ikwangunia ijo?*
> *Arai ekolo? Arai ekolo?*

> (Josephine, why have you turned pale?
> Is it jealousy?)

or

> *Iboie ijongo erono ogali, apese na,*
> *Iboie ijongo erono ogali aserebede.*

> (You are seated badly on the bicycle, girl;
> You are seated badly on the bicycle; you will slide off.)

The following songs were recorded in Bukedea:[1]

(i) ARAI KIGIRO ANGOR

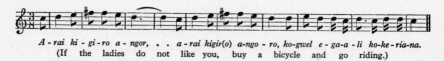

A - rai ki - gi - ro a - ngor, . . a - rai kigir(o) a-ngo - ro, ko-gwel e - ga-a - li ko-ke - ria-na.
(If the ladies do not like you, buy a bicycle and go riding.)

(ii) KWABO IMUSUGUN IMUNONITO

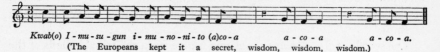

Kwab(o) I - mu - su - gun i - mu - no - ni - to (a)co - a   a - co - a   a - co - a.
(The Europeans kept it a secret, wisdom, wisdom, wisdom.)

Verse:
Ejok Ojilong kikia akan; abong konye Atuturi. Aeeee Obilangolees!
(It is good Ojilong put up his hand; Atutur has been restored.)

(iii) YENADONGI ABWACIT

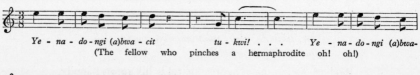

Ye - na - do - ngi (a)bwa - cit   tu - kwi! . . .   Ye - na - do - ngi (a)bwa-
(The fellow who pinches a hermaphrodite oh! oh!)

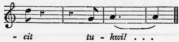

- cit   tu - kwi! . . .

[1] I chose a few from a number of songs collected and recorded in tonic sol-fa by school-teachers of the Native Anglican Church in various parts of Teso. Arrangements were then

O - ko - ku   lo   bo   e - ba - ngaa - nar   a - mi - na   a - dong   ab - wa - cin.
(The   lad   is   a   fool   to   love   to   pinch   hermaphrodites.)

Verse:
Konye moi tupuruc iituni erai ekiliokit. Aeeeeee!
(But in the morning he remembers it is a man. Aeeeeee!)

The following two songs, also from Bukedea, are sung to the accompaniment of a gourd rattle (*akaene*) only:

(i) ALOMA TOGO

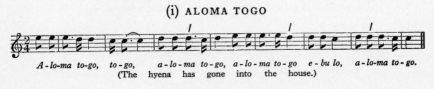

A - lo - ma to - go, to - go,   a - lo - ma to - go, a - lo - ma to - go e - bu lo, a - lo - ma to - go.
(The   hyena   has   gone   into   the   house.)

(ii) ETEMOKIN EIGO

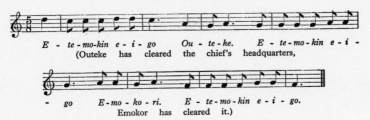

E - te - mo - kin e - i - go   Ou - te - ke.   E - te - mo - kin e - i -
(Outeke   has   cleared   the   chief's   headquarters,

- go   E - mo - ko - ri.   E - te - mo - kin e - i - go.
Emokor   has   cleared   it.)

The following *adeudeu* songs were recorded in Amuria:

(i) IJO LOICEDI KOTO

SOLO.   CHORUS.

I - jo lo - i - ce - di ko - to, (o)co - i - te (i)cak(i) i - mi - ot.
(You who tread stealthily inside the house, beware lest you step on a chicken.)

(ii) SAYO

SOLO.   CHORUS.   4ˣ

Sa - yo, sa - yo, sa - yo ma - li - go,   o . . o . . sa - yo ma - li - go.

made for the songs chosen to be sung to Dr. K. P. Wachsmann, who kindly provided the recordings which appear on this and the following pages. Certain symbols used by Dr. Wachsmann require explanation. Vertical dotted bar lines indicate subdivisions of time signature and some clear rhythmical stress which cannot otherwise be fitted into the pattern of time signature. Plus or minus signs indicate that a note is distinctly sharp or flat and cannot be shown otherwise in the stave system of the score. A sloping straight line shows that there are notes connecting the two notes at each end of the line which cannot be shown otherwise. Vowels in brackets are elided in singing.

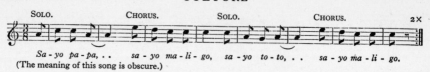

Sa - yo pa - pa, . .   sa - yo ma - li - go,   sa - yo to - to, . .   sa - yo ma - li - go.

(The meaning of this song is obscure.)

(iii) KIMANYA ABERU

Ki - many(a) a - be - ru   da,   mam   i - bor(e) e - jai to - ma.

Ki - gwel a - mu - ka . . da,   mam . . i - bor(e) e - jai to - ma.

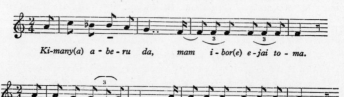

E - bal(a) O - gi - ro,   o . .   O - gi - ro,   ti - a, ti - a.   E - bal(a) O - gi - ro,   o .

. .   O - gi - ro,   ti - a, ti - a.

E - bal(a) O - gi - ro,   o . .   O - gi - ro,   ti - a, ti - a.   E - bal(a) O - gi - ro,   o .

. .   O - gi - ro,   ti - a, ti - a.

(If one marries a woman, one gets nothing out of it.
If one buys shoes, one gets nothing out of it.
So says Ogiro.)

Other verses with slight variations in tune exist:
If one buys clothes, if one builds a permanent house,
If one buys a car or an aeroplane, one gets nothing out of it.

5. *The* ajosi *dance*

This is the commonest Teso dance and is often known by the generic name *eikoso*. Accompaniment is provided by the *atenus* and *ideteta* drums which are sited in the centre of the dance arena under a platform of poles. On the platform stand the master of ceremonies and the judges, for the *ajosi* is usually danced as a competition between different sub-counties or villages and great store is set by the different teams' turn-out.

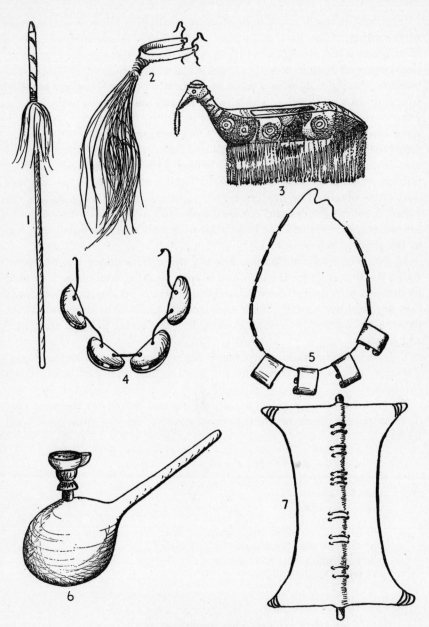

PERSONAL ACCOUTREMENTS

1. *Ebela*: dancing stick (length 4 feet).
2. *Eula*: dancing switch (ring fits round the arm).
3. *Apel*: dancing arm band (arm is inserted through the hole).
4. *Icirin* or *Isiman*: dancing pellet-bells (length of bell 3 inches).
5. *Itibine*: ornament worn by women round the waist (metal rolls 1 inch square). See p. 104.
6. *Etuo loka ejai*: bhang pipe (diameter of tray at the top of the pipe 2 inches). See p. 107.
7. *Ebuku*: shield (length 2 feet 9 inches). See p. 126.

The well-dressed male dancer must ordinarily have four emblems of the dance. The first, a dancing stick (*ebela*), is indispensable. It is usually about half an inch or a little more in diameter and about 5 feet long, decorated near both ends with a tassel of hair. Pellet bells (*icirin*) should be worn on the right leg over a piece of cloth or a puttee. They are made of iron and fastened together with a rope of water buck's (*apoli*) skin. On the left arm is worn the arm-band (*apel*) carved in the form of a bird and decorated with brightly coloured beads. On the right arm is worn a switch (*eula*) made of the hair of a cow's tail and fastened to a ring worn over the arm. Faces and bodies should be daubed with clay. Formerly, colobus monkey skins were part of the regalia but these are nowadays rare and difficult to obtain. The modern regalia is varied and the more bizarre the better. Football jerseys and coloured sashes are common. Wooden masks are sometimes worn and one lucky man possessed a service-type respirator as the modern equivalent.

In the centre of the dance arena are the drums under the platform; round the drums dance the girls and women and the outer circle is formed by the men with their sticks waving up and down till at the end of the dance they are held horizontally above the dancers' heads. The more important dancers are carried on servants' shoulders the better to show their skill and regalia.

Both female and male dancers sing during the exertions of the dance. The men alone sing as they enter the arena to take their part in the dance competition.

The words of the songs are usually topical and consist for the most part of extemporary praise of the dancers themselves or of a prominent local leader.

(i) *Oo! acoa! oo! acoa! Eliling Engulu.*
Oo! acoa! Eur nee Dakabela;
Mam lem isio imora
Amabus Idakabelai.

Oo! wisdom! oo! wisdom! Engulu is quiet.
Oo! wisdom! this place smells of Dakabela;
It is not usual for us to share the
gaol with Dakabela people.

(ii) *Itigoi oo! oo! Itigoi ooo!*
Emoru loo, emoru loo, emoru loo, kolimokinai akiro,
emoru loo, emoru loo, emoru loo, kolimokinai akiro,
Itigoi oo! oo! Itigoi ooo!

The Itigoi oo! oo! the Itigoi ooo!
This hill, this hill, this hill, tell me words,
This hill, this hill, this hill, tell me words,
The Itigoi oo! oo! the Itigoi ooo!

PLATE IX

Ajosi dance scene
(*See p.* 164)

Beer drinking
(*See p.* 125)

At the dances at the Coronation celebrations in Soroti in 1953 the dancers sang mildly scurrilous songs about their chiefs.

(iii) *Ejoku, oo! Ejoku, ooo! Ejoku, oo!*
Ebwaikini akabaka oicolong.
Amunaun Amuria, amunaun Amuria,
Elagano kede Kaberamaido, ooo! elagano kede Kaberamaido,
Ejoku, oo! Ejoku, ooo! Ejoku, oo!
Ebwaikini akabaka oicolong.

Ejoku, oo! Ejoku, ooo! Ejoku, oo!
The Queen has been crowned.
Amuria is spoiled, Amuria is spoiled.
There is striving with Kaberamaido, ooo! striving with Kaberamaido,
Ejoku, oo! Ejoku, ooo! Ejoku, oo!
The Queen has been crowned.

(iv) *Elagano, elagano, oo! oo!*
Nepe kolo ayaunere Edielu, apolor aswam 'show', oo!
Oo! Edielu, oo! Edielu.
Eturitai elagano oo! Edielu, eturitai elagano.
Ayauni lolo elagano oo! oo!
Nepe kolo ayaunere Edielu, apolor aswam 'show', oo!

Competition, competition, oo! oo!
Since Edielu was brought the show work has increased oo!
Oo! Edielu, oo! Edielu.
Competition is good oo! Edielu. Competition is good.
Competition is being held to-day oo! oo!
Since Edielu was brought the show work has increased oo!

(v) *Mam ipedorete Igweritok luka acoa, luapote okide,*
Mam ipedorete Gweri, ooo!
Ebala eong etau dusu nuebalare bee,
Itelekarit Kaberamaido Epido, o! itelekarit Kaberamaido Epido, o!
Ebala eong etau dusu ebe nuebalare bee,
Itelakarit Kaberamaido, Epido, o! itelekarit Kaberamaido Epido.
Mam ipedorete Igweritok luka acoa luapote okide,
Mam ipedorete Gweri, ooo!

You cannot manage the clever Gweri people, who come from the east,
You cannot manage Gweri, ooo!
My heart beats at the saying that
Kaberamaido beats Epido, o! Kaberamaido beats Epido.
My heart beats hard when I hear that
Kaberamaido beats Epido, o! Kaberamaido beats Epido.
You cannot manage the clever Gweri people, who come from the east,
You cannot manage Gweri, ooo!

6. *The* ekuma *and* ikacui *dances*

The *ekuma* is said to be danced by more elderly people, generally at night. According to Father Kruyer the melody and words are sung by one girl, chosen on account of her voice, accompanied occasionally by the *atenus*, but often without accompaniment. It is a family dance performed according to mood and not to mark any specific occasion.[1] I have not seen the dance. The words recorded resemble English nursery rhymes inasmuch as they appear meaningless, perhaps because the original meaning has often been lost.

> *Obiiko—Obiko—Biikoo!*
> *Alu bo nat ikaboro agwelia olope arupian*
> *Alu bo nat ikaboro agwelia olope arupian*
> *Alu bo nat ikaboro agwelia olope arupian*
> *Obiiko—Obiko—Biikoo!*
> Where is my property so that I may sell it for money.

There appears to be a variant of the *ekuma* dance called *ikacui*, which I have never seen and which is not mentioned by Kruyer or other observers. My informants state that it is similar to the *ekuma* and is danced in south Teso, while the *ekuma* is more usual in north Teso.

7. *The* etida *dance*

The *etida* dance is properly performed to cure the sick. It is danced to the accompaniment of the *etida* drums, often at night. The men and women shuffle round the drummer executing steps rather like those of the 'Charleston' and singing. The rhythm of these drums induces a frenzy, especially in women, which causes them to commit excesses. In daylight after only half an hour of the dance I have seen girls strip off the upper part of their clothing and roll in the dust stuffing dust and dirt into their mouths. Far more revolting excesses have been recorded from Usuku and the *etida* dance has accordingly been officially banned for many years; but it is still danced, especially in Usuku and Tisai and parts of Bukedea.

The following *etida* songs were recorded in Bukedea.

(i) OKWE! ADONGO

(O)kw(e)! A-do - ngo, . . A-do-ngo, (A)-do-ngo. (O)kw(e)! A-do -
- ngo, . . ngol e-ta-le . . ko-je-nu ca bo.
(Alas! Adongo, you must know every clan taboo.)

(ii) INGAI AYAUNI IMO?

I - ngai (a)ya-un(i), i - ngai (a)ya-u-ni I - mo lu?
(Who brought these foreigners?)

Verse:

> *Okwe! Koryengutu kere.*
> *Okwe! Kocoutu kere.*
> *Sekeri.*
> (Wake up, everybody! Become wise, everybody! Sekeri.)

[1] Kruyer (undated).

(iii) EROKO APESUR EPOLOETE

I - jo lo! E - rok(o) a - pe - sur e - po - lo - e - te ba, . . . (e)po -

- lo - e - te ba, ... (e)po - lo - e - te ba.

I - jo lo! E - rok(o) a - pe - sur e - po - lo - e - te ba, . . (e)po - lo - e - te ba. . .
(You there! The girls are still growing.)

(iv) ECUDEE

A - ee - ee - e! (O)kw(e)! E - cu-dee, O - gi - re. . .
(Aeeeee! Alas! Sorcery, Ogire.)

Verses:
Aeeeee! Icakete ibuin etogo, itaete ibuin etogo.
Aeeeee! Eipone Ogire, eipone ka toka, ka toka bo.
Aeeeee! Icakete ibuin elupe, eipone ka toka, ka toka bo.
(Hyenas are making mud for the house, they are building a house together.
Ogire's habits, my mother's habits.
Hyenas are making mud, my mother's habits, my mother's.)

8. *Twins' dance*

This is an unusually animated dance. The dancers are grouped round the drummers who carry the drums (*emidiri* and *ideteta*) slung from their person so that they too are mobile. The formality and ritual of the *ajosi* is absent. The dancers rush about and dance individually. The words of the songs are often insulting, such as the following song in Kumam:

> *Onywalo bangin bala alee! ooo! bala alee.*
> *Onywalo bangin bala alee! ooo! bala alee.*
> *Onywalo bangin bala alee! ooo! bala alee.*
> *Onywalo bangin bala Opio! ooo! alee.*
> *Onywalo bangin bala Odongo! ooo! bala alee.*

> She has borne twins like an animal, ooo! like an animal.
> She has borne twins like an animal, ooo! like an animal.
> She has borne twins like an animal, ooo! like an animal.
> She has borne twins like Opio! ooo! an animal.
> She has borne twins like Odongo! ooo! like an animal.[1]

9. *The* edonga *dance*

The *edonga* is danced in Usuku and Tisai island only. It is unusual inasmuch as no drums are used but the male dancers wear bells (*icirin*) round

[1] Schut (undated).

their ankles and calves which sound as they jump and, with the beat of feet
on the hard ground, give an effective rhythm. The dance starts with one or
two of the dancers singing the words. All the men stand in a circle and the
women stand outside the circle. The rhythm of the song is taken up by hand
clapping: three claps—pause—three claps—pause. One or two of the male
dancers then leap into the centre of the circle and are joined by one or two
of the women. The men's dance consists of leaping into the air with legs
kept together and straight, in time to the music. This leaping into the air
is then taken up by all the dancers who form the ring, and they join in the
song. One half of the dancers are in the air as the other half touch the
ground. The dancers hold hands as they jump. No sticks or ornaments
other than bells are carried.

The following songs and tunes were recorded in Katakwi in Usuku.

(i) OGURATOME

A - ki-ding ng - un.   E - lo - i - lo - ok   O - gu-ra-to- me   a - ma - ga -
(All   is   nonsense.   Pretending   to   bite   is   Oguratome   the   horns,

la   a - ma - ga - la   I - rwa-ta - ngu - ra   e - ku - ri a - kwap.
the   horns   of   Irwatangura,   piercing   the   ground.)

(ii) LODOMO

An - i - ca ki - lo - to - no,   an - i - ca ki - lo - to - no,   an - i - ca ki - lo - to - no,
(If   you   are   a   good   traveller,   old   will   you   be,   Lodomo.)

. . .   i - mo -jo - ngi Lo - do - mo.

(iii) OKORILIMA

A - ra-ma - s(i) I - mo,   e - ri-nga ke-a - nyu - na, . .   e - ko - si-ma - se - nik, O-ko-ri- li - ma.
(Before   we   saw,   the   foreigners   took   our   bull,   Okorilima.)

(iv) OMAGAL

Ko - ny - am   i - nya . .   ko - tum,   O - ma - ga - li! . .   E -

- tio-n(o) e-ko-ni - te-ngei,   e - tio-n(o) e-ko-ni - te-ngei,   e - tio-n(o) e-ko-ni - te-ngei.
(Eat grass to fatten yourself, Omagal, for severe is your hunger.)

10. *Age-set dances*

The songs sung at the age-set ceremonies concerned the totem animals of the age-sets or the associated objects. Some of these songs have already been recorded on pp. 80–83 above. Other examples are:

(i) *Esirut oditeku enyami ejakait kiyakiya.*

(The mosquito has a small head but it eats the chief.)

(ii) *Kibwokere ekelai ka etom, aup,*
Kamautu aikit kibwokere ekelai ka etom, aup.

(The elephant's tusk is to be carried, friend;
Let us seek a head pad to carry the elephant's tusk, my friend.)

(iii) *Angolemuge emonyi kocor bala ikoku*

(The little black bird cries on the lake like a child.)

Since the age-set ceremonies are no longer performed the dances are rare. I have seen them on Tisai island only. The dancers imitate the cry of the beast and its actions as they sing the songs. Thus in a song concerning a lion the dancers made roaring noises and pretended to claw each other. The dance was accompanied by the *etida* drum and dancers of both sexes took part. It is possible that the use of drums is modern and that formerly age-set dances were performed, as I have seen them in Karamoja, without drums and by men only.

CHAPTER II

VISUAL ART

UNDER this heading is included only what is created for art's sake, such as the patterns on pottery and gourds, the mural drawings in houses or figures carved in wood or moulded in clay. The highest artistic achievement of the Iteso is probably in the carving of traditional stools (see p. 117 above); in all other forms of art standards are primitive.

The custom of painting representations of men and animals on the walls of houses must of necessity be modern since walled houses only appeared in comparatively recent times. The custom appears to be spreading; it is most common in Kaberamaido and Amuria counties but is now universal. Colours are produced in various ways. For white, lime may be available; otherwise crushed dried cassava or banana is used. Ashes and water give a grey, and black cotton soil and water a black colour. The juice of the *emurie* (Carissa) berry provides a red stain. Other colours are made by crushing stone or soil of the required colour and mixing the powder with water. A wide variety of colours can be produced in this way. Drawings are often stereotyped, perhaps because the number of house painters is small. Lions are heraldic in appearance and, with leopards, surpass all other animal subjects including cattle in popularity. Among human figures the District Commissioner or local chiefs are represented and often named; policemen are also popular subjects. Europeans are usually depicted wearing ties and glasses. Of domestic scenes beer drinking is by far the commonest, and the absence of cattle herding scenes is perhaps remarkable. The drawings, some of which are illustrated on p. 171, display no knowledge of perspective.

There is no indication that wood carving was practised in the past except to manufacture toys for children, although, as has already been mentioned, logs used as stools were sometimes fashioned in the shape of animals. The only examples of such stools seen by me were crude, but two examples in the Uganda museum[1] and the Cambridge museum[2] show some artistic skill. Modern handicraft competitions produce fantastic creations in wood ranging from ploughs to aeroplanes and bicycles, carved in detail and proportion but poorly finished and of no merit. Clay figures are if anything of a higher standard than wooden carvings but less common, and the best of them show European influence. Outstanding among Teso artists in clay modelling is Flora Aulagot, an Atesot of North Nyanza district. Some of her graceful and artistic figures of Teso people engaged in their everyday activities are illustrated opposite.

The commonest method of decorating pottery is to roll a plaited rope

[1] The stool in the Uganda Museum is illustrated opposite.
[2] Dr. K. P. Wachsmann, personal communication.

PLATE X

Group of clay figures by Flora Aulagot
(i) Eating porridge   (ii) Drinking beer   (iii) Drumming for ants
(See p. 170)

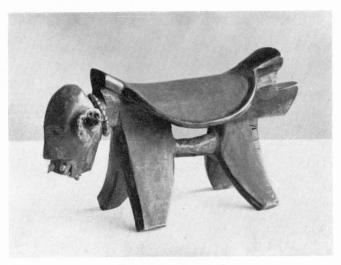

Carved wooden stool
(See p. 170)

EXAMPLES OF MURAL DRAWINGS

1. Owl.
2. Dog.
3. Beer-drinking scene.

4. Lion.
5. Old man walking.
6. Geometric designs.

DESIGNS ON POTTERY AND GOURDS.   1–3. Pottery designs.   4–6. Gourd designs.

over the clay while still wet, thereby producing a herring-bone effect. Small bones or notched pieces of wood are also used in a similar manner to give varying patterns. The patterns on the lower part of the pot are often picked out with a sharp instrument such as a piece of broken pot.

Patterns on gourds are executed by burning with a hot needle or piece of wire. Although figures are often portrayed on gourds, no attempt is ever made to decorate pots in this manner.

CHAPTER III

LANGUAGE

1. *Classification*

ATESO is classified as one of the Nilo-Hamitic languages, a large linguistic group which contains, among others, the languages spoken by the Bari, Toposa, Lotuko in the Sudan; Teso, Karamojong in Uganda; Turkana, Masai, Nandi, Suk, and Kipsigis in Kenya. The group is termed Nilo-Hamitic because all languages in it have a large common vocabulary of Nilotic stems, a large common vocabulary of non-Nilotic stems, and a large common vocabulary of Hamitic-like prefixes and suffixes.[1] The term indicates the mixture of language resulting from the racial mixture between the invading Hamites and the Negro peoples and, though in essence a linguistic term, it is often used of the peoples who speak Nilo-Hamitic languages. Authorities differ, however, as to whether the Nilo-Hamitic languages are essentially Nilotic affected by Hamitic influences or Hamitic affected by Nilotic influences.

The main points of similarity which maintain the grouping and differentiate it from other groupings are:[1]

(i) A nine-vowel system in which the vowels normally represented by *e, i, o, u* have each two values.

(ii) Dynamic accent (stress), accompanied by high or falling tone, apparently plays as big a role as syllable pitch.

(iii) Words are formed mainly by prefixes and suffixes. Roots usually consist of consonant—vowel—consonant, though many non-Nilotic roots are disyllabic.

(iv) There are numerous affixes used to form nouns common to all languages in the grouping.

(v) There are numerous and varied suffixes indicating number in nouns, which may point to a class system of nouns now broken down.

(vi) Grammatical gender in nouns is present.

(vii) There is tonal (but no other) inflexion for case, which may also be shown by position in the sentence.

(viii) Verbs fall into two morphological classes, one of which is characterized by an actual or latent stem-prefix *i-*.

(ix) There are numerous derived forms of verbs, indicated mostly by changes in suffix, which show close similarity throughout the grouping.

[1] Tucker and Bryan, 1948; Dr. A. N. Tucker (personal communication).

(x) Basic tense forms are few in number, although in the Teso group there is a multiplicity of tenses built up on differences of intonation or stress.

(xi) Conjugation for person is effected by prefixes which vary according to the two verb classes.

(xii) Sentence order is usually verb—subject—object.

Within this large Nilo-Hamitic family there are five language groups: Bari, Lotuko, Masai, Nandi, and Teso.[1] The Teso language group contains the Teso, Turkana, and Toposa languages, and the group of dialects spoken by the Karamojong, Jie, Dodoth, and others, known collectively as the Karamojong dialect cluster. Similarities within the language group are very close both in vocabulary[2] and grammatical forms, and all languages are mutually intelligible.

This is the usual classification.[3] It has recently been challenged on the grounds that the differences in grammatical structure between the Nilo-Hamitic and the Nilotic languages are insufficient to warrant separate grouping:[4] both in vocabulary and in morphology there is close resemblance between Nilotic and Nilo-Hamitic languages whereas there is little that points in the direction of the Hamitic-Semitic. The Nilo-Hamitic, and the Nilotic languages, which latter term includes Shilluk, Nuer, Dinka in the Sudan, Acholi, Lango, Alur in Uganda, and Luo in Kenya, should be classified together as the southern branch of the eastern Sudanic family. Moreover, the term 'Nilo-Hamitic' is vague and misleading and should be replaced by a geographical term such as the 'Great Lakes' languages.[4] This view is in turn challenged by Tucker and Bryan who produce their own evidence for retention of the term 'Nilo-Hamitic'.[3]

2. *Dialect*

The four main divisions of the tribe (*ineresinei*) have differences in dialect, which in the case of the Ikokolemu division are so considerable as to make their language unintelligible to the remainder of the Teso people. Ateso as spoken by the Ingoratok division is now officially adopted as standard Ateso.

The main differences are in vocabulary; thus the word *edula* over much of Teso country means the common granary made of grass and mud, but in the south *etuja* is used to describe this type of granary; in north Teso *etuja* means the pot-shaped miniature granary made of clay and used for storing simsim. Other differences which distinguish the speech of other *ineresinei* from that of the Ingoratok are the substitution of *gw* for *bw*

[1] Tucker and Bryan, 1948.　　　　　　[2] Wilson, 1947; Johnston, 1902.

[3] Accepted by Tucker and Bryan in the *Handbook of African Languages*, vol. iii (to be published in 1956).

[4] Greenberg, J. H., 1950, *Southwestern Journal of Anthropology*, vol. vi, no. 2 (Studies in African Linguistic Classification).

among the Iseera (e.g. *aigwok* for *aibwok* 'to carry'), the omission of *k* in initial prefixes among the Iteso of Usuku (e.g. *aipi* for *akipi* 'water'), which is often extended to other parts of a word (e.g. *adukoin* for *adukokin* 'to marry') and a preference for the vowel sound *e* among the Ikokolemu (e.g. *etwen* for *etwan* 'man'). But the language of the Ikokolemu or Kumam is now so influenced by Lango that it is properly classified as a Nilotic language; indeed, the Kumam refer to their own language as *leb Lango* (Lango language), and although they and the Lango, too, retain Ateso words for some relationships, for some numerals, and for many animals and plants, most of the vocabulary and all construction is Nilotic.[1] I can find no acceptance among the Iteso that their language was once known as *Dum* and that of the Kumam as *Lale*.[2] It appears more probable that the divergence in language occurred comparatively recently after the Kumam came into contact with the Nilotic Chopi.

3. *Orthography*

The first person to attempt to reduce Ateso to writing was the pioneer linguist of the C.M.S., the Rev. W. A. Crabtree, in 1901. His short Ateso reader was presumably the only written aid available to the Rev. A. L. Kitching when he began his study of the language, which resulted in 1915 in the publication of *A Handbook of the Ateso Language*, for forty years the only textbook published in English on the language.

By the time Father Kiggen published his *Grammar nak' Ateso* in 1927 for the use of Teso school-children, those divergences in spelling and word-usage between Roman Catholic and Protestant missions, which are a common feature of the Uganda linguistic scene, had already begun to appear. The complexity of the language and the fact that it is spoken only in one or two districts of the Protectorate has always discouraged government officials from learning it. The language of officialdom was, and to a large extent still is, Kiswahili, although more and more English is being used. There was thus little interest or effort on the part of the Government to check these divergences, which concern not only words of religious significance but also common words such as *nes* ('he' or 'him'). Until recently little in the way of literature has been published and that mainly by mission presses, a fact which has tended to spread and perpetuate the differences.

At last in 1947, in an attempt to remove these differences, the Teso Orthography Committee was formed under the chairmanship of a senior officer of the Education Department to find an accepted method of writing Ateso. Differences in dialect were resolved by the decision to take the dialect of the Ingoratok as standard Ateso. A recognized alphabet was agreed upon in keeping with that of the Nilotic and Nilo-Hamitic languages

---

[1] This view is held by Tucker and Bryan and expressed in the *Handbook of African Languages*, vol. iii (to be published in 1956).

[2] Huntingford, 1953; Walshe, 1947.

in Uganda and the Sudan. The committee then decided that, regardless of how they were pronounced in speech, words must be written in full; it followed that the apostrophe, which hitherto had indicated the elision of one vowel before another, would no longer be used. This principle may eventually have to be modified, for there is a tendency in Ateso for the letter *k*, with which the language abounds, to disappear in certain circumstances. Rigid adherence to the rule would in time result in an unrealistic orthography. The committee also agreed upon the spelling of a number of disputed words and formulated rules for the assimilation of foreign words into the language. Differences in spelling, in word usage, and in religious terminology persist, however, and it cannot be claimed that the orthography is firmly established; but at least it exists and will spread as more literature is produced in it.

4. *Proverbs and Riddles*

Ateso appears to have very few proverbs; allusions to a person or to a story, which are a feature of such Lango proverbs as 'Joy killed Atile',[1] are seldom found in Teso proverbs, which, for the most part, display little ingenuity of thought. Many of them are tritely moral:

Ikoku yenimam epupi papake, mam emojongi.
The child who does not listen to his father never grows old.
(Used of a subordinate in relation to his superiors.)

Mam imwangi yenejai okekwa juai.
You do not despise the fellow on the opposite bank.

Lomam elimokino, edokikini ataker naka alupot.
He who is not warned may embark in a canoe made of earth.

Mam ikepi anapet eringa ikoku kidouna.
You do not prepare the baby sling before the child is born.
(Do not count your chickens before they are hatched.)

Others are more colourful:

Icaki emun ekori   You tread on a snake's tail.

This and the three following idioms are used of a person in trouble:

Aibobon otwo   To secrete in a gourd.
Alekun emanyi   To vomit a liver.
Alekun aep   To vomit an axe.

This paucity of proverbs is, however, more than offset by a richness in riddles (*aibukareta*). These are very numerous and popular; there are well-known riddles about life in the villages, about the body, about wild animals, about plants, and about the whole sphere of natural existence. That riddles continue in popularity is shown by the number which concern modern

---

[1] Atile discovered the secret of beer making. The chief drank the beer and passed out. His followers thought he had been poisoned and killed Atile.

inventions; there are many of a 'Christmas cracker' variety, containing a verbal catch or pun. Only a few examples can be given here.

Riddles about life in the village:

Q. *Inyo ibore iboiei koicolongoi iuni?*
A. *Amot*

Q. What is it that sits on three chairs?
A. The pot.
(The cooking pot rests on the three stones of the fire-place.)

Q. *Ingai eoja ikokuke aitelekar totoke?*
A. *Arukit.*

Q. What child is taller than its mother?
A. The pestle.
(The pestle always stands higher than the mortar, its mother.)

Riddles about the parts of the body:

Q. *Inyo ibore yen arai enapit karai mam enapit isingirono noi?*
A. *Akoik.*

Q. What is it that, whether clothed or not, is very bothersome?
A. The stomach.

Q. *Inyo ibore yen karaida kemutono akwap, mam ipedori aolikin?*
A. *Akituk.*

Q. What is it that, even though it is dark, you can never miss?
A. Your mouth.

Riddles about animals, insects, or reptiles:

Q. *Ingai aberu mam elosi atan, mam erarai akito, mam inoki akim, konye do enyami inyamat luekokitos?*
A. *Akingok.*

Q. What female does not go to the well, does not collect firewood, does not light a fire, yet eats cooked food?
A. A bitch.

Q. *Ingai iirana akinyet?*
A. *Ecucut.*

Q. Who is always tasting the butter?
A. The fly.

Riddles about plants and trees:

Q. *Inyo ibore yenimam eurio ido kimwaas nukatotoke aarei?*
A. *Edia.*

Q. What is it that is not born yet has two mothers?
A. Vegetables.

(The mothers are the soil which makes them grow and the mother of the family who cooks them.)

Q. *Etogo eleleba inyamat ido emamei ekek, kikonakinete inyamat elomarete toma ai?*

A. *Apoloet naka emaido.*

Q. A house full of food and no door; how did the food get in?

A. The growing of the groundnut.

Riddles about the elements and natural phenomena:

Q. *Inyo ibore ebenen kwape ajulot kwabo mam itunga ipu epedorete aikamun nes?*

A. *Ekwam.*

Q. What is as light as a feather yet many men cannot hold it?

A. The wind.

Q. *Inyo ibore yenikidedengikini ijo noi ido komam ijo ipedori aanyun nes?*

A. *Etengei.*

Q. What is it that causes you intense pain yet you cannot see it?

A. Hunger.

Riddles about modern inventions:

Q. *Inyo esisianakini Imusugun ainap atai?*

A. *Ekuruk.*

Q. What teaches the Europeans to wear a tie?

A. The pied crow.

Q. *Inyo ibore yenimam enyami, ediding akituk, kopol akoik?*

A. *Ecupa.*

Q. What is it that does not eat, has a small mouth but a big stomach?

A. A bottle.

Riddles containing catches or puns:

Q. *Inyobo iloseneno ijo duc oitada?*

A. *Naarai eitada mam epedori abunere neijai ijo.*

Q. Why do you always go to bed?

A. Because the bed cannot come to you.

Q. *Inyo mam epedori abongun moi karaida moikace?*

A. *Bian.*

A. What cannot return tomorrow or the day after?

A. Yesterday.

5. *Folk tales*

The three tales which follow are taken from a number of such tales recorded by Father Kruyer, the earliest source on this subject.[1] Many of the stories recorded by Father Kruyer show a marked resemblance to the Lango folk tales recorded by Driberg.[2] One of them, which concerns some girls who went to pick cherries, is identical. Many of the tales have animal heroes

[1] Kruyer (undated).   [2] Driberg, 1923.

—the hare, the tortoise, and others, and resemble similar tales told among the Baganda and other Bantu tribes; nevertheless, these animal fables are probably of some antiquity; for they were common in Teso in 1912 only a few years after the first contacts with Baganda.[1]

(i) *The Story of Nyagilo*

Once upon a time a wizard was cooking dog's meat, when his wife's relations came visiting and found that he had just finished. They were invited to sit down and eat, but they realized that the meat was not edible and hid it behind them; only a younger sister of the wife, called Nyagilo, ate the dog's meat. After the meal the wizard said 'give me my meat back'. All did so except Nyagilo who had eaten it. As a punishment she was told to grind some millet for the wizard and the others left. The wizard also went out to cultivate his fields. When Nyagilo saw she was alone she ran away; but as she ran a cock started crowing, 'Nyagilo is running away'. She returned quickly and the wizard, called by the cock's crowing, found her grinding the millet. He went back to his work and Nyagilo was so annoyed with the cock for giving her away that she seized hold of it and cut it to bits, which she threw in all directions. She then prepared to run off again, but the bits of the cock joined up again and she was hardly out of the enclosure when she heard the cock crow, 'Nyagilo is running away'. She hurried back to her work again just in time and the wizard found her grinding millet. She again cut up the cock but the cock stopped her a third time. She was very afraid then and her elder sister, the wizard's wife, when she came home, found her still grinding millet. Nyagilo told her all that had happened and her sister advised her to hide in a granary, because her husband would be sure to eat her. The girl did so. When the wizard came from the field and found that Nyagilo had left the grindstone, he took up a little drum and beat it in front of the house singing 'My wife's sister is in the granary'. He did not take her out, however, and Nyagilo stayed in the granary for two days. On the third day the wizard went visiting. The elder sister then released Nyagilo, gave her a parcel of simsim, and said to her 'Run away quickly; if you hit your foot against a stump throw some simsim there; if you hear a bird, throw some simsim'. The girl walked and walked and at last came to a big lake. There was no boat and she did not know what to do. At last she implored the lake saying 'Please let me pass, let me through, they want to eat me'. She had hardly finished when she saw the water in the lake dry up and leave a path for her, and she went safely across to the other side. In the meantime, the wizard had noticed her escape and gathered his friends together and followed her tracks with spears and shield. They came to the lake and took the path through it, but when they were in the middle the waters joined and they all perished. Thus Nyagilo's life was saved.

[1] Kitching, 1912.

(ii) *The Man-eating Sheep*

It happened once upon a time that a child took his father's sheep out to graze. The sun was very hot and he sat down in the shade of an ant-hill. Whilst sitting there he heard an old ram say to the other sheep, 'Now times have changed, formerly we used to eat men, now they make us eat grass'. When the boy heard this he was afraid and ran home to his father and told him 'The sheep want to eat me'. The father said 'You lazy boy, do you leave the sheep in the care of the wild animals and come to tell me such silly tales? Go back quickly.' The boy went back, but again he heard sheep talking about eating men, and again he ran to his father. His father sent him back again a second time, but when the boy came for the third time the old man thought, 'Let me go alone and see whether the boy tells stories'. He hid himself nearby and he also heard the old ram tell the other sheep about eating men. He said nothing, but at night he tied the sheep in a separate house and burnt that house. When the rains set in, an enormous amount of marrows started growing on the plot where the burnt house had been. People came from afar to take away the gourds obtained from the marrows but they could not exhaust the supply. Some were put in store houses and others were simply thrown away.

It happened one day that everybody was out at a beer party. The gourds then got together, including those in the store houses and those which had been thrown away, and came and executed a dance, knocking against one another. When the people came back from the beer party they found the gourds still at their dance and were very afraid. They took all the bewitched gourds, smashed them, and burnt them and hurriedly left the spot which had been the scene of such witchcraft. But the pieces joined together again and came to life and followed the owners wherever they went. These they smashed again and burnt and dug a deep pit for the ashes and beat the earth down very firmly; this was the end of the matter.

(iii) *The Magic Bird*

Once upon a time a man sent his wife to clear a plot for cultivation. In the afternoon he went to see how she had done, but he saw only high grass. He was very annoyed with her and beat her, though she assured him that she had cleared quite a large plot. Next morning the man thought to himself 'Let me go with her; then she will have to work'. They worked hard all the morning, but in the afternoon the man found that where they had cleared the grass had grown up again. 'I have beaten my wife without reason', he thought; 'I will call all my friends and together we shall clear a very large plot.' This was done but in the afternoon everything was as before. He called his friends again and told them, 'Where we have cleared the grass is just as high as before'. Then he decided to clear a small plot and to hide himself nearby and see what would happen. He did so and saw a little bird called *edidit*[1] come and plant the grass again. When it came near

[1] A weaver-finch (Pytilia).

the place where he was hiding he caught it. 'Don't kill me', it cried, 'I have plenty of food, and I will give you everything which would otherwise have grown on the plots you cleared. Go and make large granaries.' The man took the bird home and locked it up securely and started making the granaries. When they were ready the bird produced all kinds of food. The stores filled up and the man became very rich because people came from afar to buy his food.

It happened one day that a neighbour's child came to play and asked the man's children to have a look at the magic bird. They opened the storehouse in which it was locked and it escaped. The man's son tried to follow it and catch it, but while following it he stuck in a swamp and was nearly drowned, whilst the bird disappeared altogether.

Fortunately he heard a woman who had come to fetch water. He cried out to her 'I am here in the water; please go and tell my relations to kill a large black bull and fetch me out; the mud fishes have nearly eaten my ribs away'. The bull was killed and the child was saved but the man had to work again as before, and the little bird was never seen again.

The earliest recorded information on Teso folk tales appears in Bishop Kitching's book.[1]

The Teso people also have fables, and ascribe most intelligence to Iculi, the weasel, who in one tale produces water by stamping after all others have failed. Another story is interesting in showing how the want of implements is supplied by the use of natural objects. The yarn begins with a cannibal episode, in which a woman kills and cooks her mother-in-law and gives the meat to her relatives to eat. Fearful of the consequences of her act, which is detected by a blind man, she flees away and at the first village she comes to has an axe thrown at her. Picking it up she continues her travels, which then provide a series of incidents, in which she always exchanges what she carries for some object given in gratitude. Her axe goes to a man whom she finds chopping honey-comb out of a dead tree with an ox rib. The honey goes to the children eating sand, who give her an egg, which is passed on to an ostrich rolling along a stone. An ostrich plume, a palm pole, and an ox figure successively in the next transactions, out of which she brings a razor; this is given to a man who is trying to shave his children with a potsherd, because his razor is all used up; the spear-head received in exchange is welcomed by men who are trying to cut up their meat with strips of reed grass. And so on and so forth.

[1] Kitching, 1912.

CHAPTER IV

RELIGION AND MAGIC

1. *Religious beliefs*

MAN turns to God mainly in time of trouble. Though the Iteso used to believe vaguely in a god on high (*Apap* or *Akuj*), whose power was beneficial, it was the god of calamity (*Edeke*) who was remembered, dreaded, and propitiated. If sickness fell on a family, if rinderpest killed the cattle or drought withered the crops, *Edeke* was angry and must be propitiated. 'One of the chief Teso observances is *aremori edeke*—to offer sacrifice to *Edeke*. If, for instance, the crops are doing badly, a mess of porridge may be cooked at the side of a field and then broken up and scattered about the paths leading to the plot of land, or ashes may be used to sprinkle the paths in the same way. . . .'[1]

Gods are served at altars (*abila*) constructed in the homesteads. They may be of stones or sticks of a varying design. Before the crops are put in the granary a thanksgiving is put on the altar. Before sowing, the seed may be blessed. The plough may be blessed by putting it in front of the altar and throwing seed on it. At Kateta a 'devil hut' (see below) was found with an altar inside it; on the altar was the witch-doctor's regalia.

The effect of Christianity on pagan beliefs is difficult to assess. Perhaps 70 per cent. of the menfolk have been baptized into the Christian faith, although the number of women who profess Christianity is considerably less.[2] Children are therefore still brought up by mothers steeped in superstitious fears of the supernatural. Belief in the evil powers of witchcraft (*ecudet*) is still universally as strong among the well-educated as among the ignorant peasants. Nor is this surprising when it is remembered that witches were burnt in Europe after 1,700 years of Christianity. Faith in the curative powers of witch-doctors is decreasing with the increase of understanding of the true causes of disease and the availability of proper medical treatment. Those who truly believe the witch-doctor's power to foretell the future are perhaps not more numerous than those in Britain who believe in the ability of gypsies and fortune-tellers. Rain making is still an important ceremony both to Christians and pagans. This association of religion with nature is, after all, not uncommon in Christian countries, particularly among agricultural communities where harvest festivals are among the most important religious occasions of the year.

There is no ancestor worship although food and beer are often placed

---

[1] Kitching, 1912.
[2] This figure is a rough estimate only. A survey of taxpayers in Kasilang in 1953 showed that out of 215 only 117 (54·4 per cent.) were Christians.

near the graves of dead relatives. These offerings and the celebrations at
the memorial ceremonies (*asuban*) are designed to keep on good terms with
the spirit of the deceased, which in some manner might cause harm. Not
that there is any idea of immortality, for unimportant men, women, and
children are incapable of causing harm—their spirit ceases to exist on
death; but the spirit of important men may last for many months or years
and must be propitiated at several memorial ceremonies.

2. *Superstitions*

Superstitious beliefs are too numerous to attempt to record. Some of those
connected with agriculture have already been described above on p. 139.
Some of the better known superstitions are:

To see a snake disappearing quickly	Journey will not be prosperous.
To hit the right foot against a stump	Good omen.
To hit the left foot against a stump	Bad omen.
Black bird (*acikwa*) crosses the path	The journey should be postponed a day.
Small rat (*eleli*) on the path	Beer at journey's end.
Insect (*aijang*) on the path	Beer at journey's end.
Grasshopper jumps on a person	Present of goat or cow likely.
Barking of a jackal at night	Death in the family.
Hyenas sporting in a food plot	Bewitchment.
An owl (*etukur*) on the house	Bewitchment.

Special superstitions centre round lightning. A person injured by a flash
had to wear bells round the ankles for weeks afterwards. When thunder
threatens he must parade the village with a papyrus wand.[1] A victim of
lightning is buried apart at the swamp edge and his household utensils put
on the grave. A sacrifice of hoes is put at the door of his hut.

3. *Witch-doctors*

A witch-doctor (*emuron*) is a person who uses magical powers for good ends,
such as foretelling the future, curing sickness, providing charms and love-
potions, or bringing rain. One of his main functions is to counteract the
activities of a wizard (*ekacudan* or *ecudan*) who uses magical powers for evil
purposes.

Those who suffer from continual sickness in youth are deemed to be
possessed by some superior power; they are noted by practising witch-
doctors and in due course initiated into the profession.[2]

The majority of modern witch-doctors appear to be women. Their
paraphernalia is varied but usually consists of a bark skin robe ornamented
with cowrie shells, long necklaces and bracelets of cowrie shells or hard nuts,
gourds containing dried peas, and fronds of grass or leaves around their

[1] Kitching, 1912.   [2] Kruyer (undated).

brows. Male witch-doctors often wear a white cotton robe and grass or leaf garlands. Faces are often daubed with clay taken from a special magical spot. All carry a number of magic objects concerning which they are naturally reticent. One basket when examined revealed certain types of bark, pieces of string, shells, and paper packages. According to Bishop Kitching, witch-doctors used to dress as women and wore women's ornaments. In a photograph a witch-doctor is shown wearing heavy chains of beads and shells and a cloth tucked over the breasts and under the armpits like a woman.[1]

On initiation witch-doctors are said to enter a special clan, Imokolya. The members of this clan were once gifted with the art of making barren women fertile.

4. *Curing sickness*

Witch doctors are, as a rule, only appealed to in cases of sickness. The witch doctor gets a small part of the sick man's house screened off, where he can consult his particular spirit (*ajokit*). Each has his own assistant spirit which he names by his clan names; there are male and female spirits. The witch doctor mutters over the sick man, consults with the spirit, whom he makes to speak in a high-pitched voice and eventually 'extracts' a snake, a large insect, hairy caterpillar or other monstrosity from the stomach of the sick man, by which the cause of the disease is removed. A goat or sheep is killed; the witch doctor takes the hind legs and skin; part of the food is consumed by the spirit in the little set-off room and the rest by the witch doctor himself. The removal of the cause of the disease is done in darkness and no one is allowed to get near. A witch doctor's reputation grows or decreases in proportion with the success he has with his patients.[2]

This spirit (*ajokit*) is the medium between mankind and the deities, and can be contacted only through witch-doctors. According to some it is said to live in blindworms or snakes and to it is ascribed anything abnormal or mysterious affecting the life of man. Of a childless woman or a madman it is said that she or he has an *ajokit*.

The ritual of the cure varies slightly. The colour of the goat is often important, black being a popular colour. The goat may be slaughtered by piercing its throat with a sharp knife. The stomach contents are used by the witch-doctor to smear his patient on the face, chest, and legs; part of the skin is often worn by the patient.

Since sickness is believed to be caused by an evil spirit the most important element of cure is the removal of the spirit. Witch-doctors nowadays often rely on what Bishop Kitching describes as a 'devil hut' (*abila*, pl. *abilai*), a small hut only about 4 feet high and usually made of grass, to tempt the spirit away from the sick person. This form of cure appears to be employed mainly in the case of mental disorders and mainly for women. When a woman suffers from any form of mental derangement, her relatives

[1] Kitching, 1912.   [2] Kruyer (undated).

summon a witch-doctor and under his or her directions build a 'devil hut'.
The witch-doctor then goes to work. The sick woman is brought into the
compound and curing songs are sung to the accompaniment of rattling
gourds. A specially marked goat is slaughtered and the patient is daubed
with the stomach contents and must wear an amulet made from the skin.
She then eats some of the food and puts some in the 'devil hut'; beer is
drunk. The 'devil hut' stays where it is built but is not repaired. The site
is, however, usually marked with a fig pole which easily sprouts. The door
of a 'devil hut' may be blocked to keep out dogs and jackals but there is no
idea of imprisoning the spirits. Indeed, most 'devil huts' have two doors
to allow the spirit, transferred from the patient to the hut, to take its
departure.

The *etida* drum is properly used in the curing of disease, though the
dance is officially banned and the drum is not often used outside Usuku,
Tisai, and Bukedea.

The magical approach to healing appears still to be universal, especially
in dealing with sick women. Witch-doctors also rely on vegetable cures,
prepared from leaves, roots, and bark, particularly in the curing of out-
wardly visible ailments such as ulcers, syphilitic sores, leprosy, and small-
pox. Each witch-doctor has his own stock of remedies, which probably vary
in different parts of the district according to the availability of plants. The
application of the various medicines is usually accompanied by magic
ritual. The examples which follow are taken from Usuku unless otherwise
stated;[1] it has not proved possible to identify all the plants concerned:

Cough: Root or leaf of *ekworo* (Combretum queinzii).

Cold: Mixture of leaves of *ekore* (Gardenia jovis-tonantis) and *ekere* (Harrisonia
abyssinica) with *ebata* (Albizzia zygia) and *imomwakajele*, pounded and
watered and applied as nose-drops.

Smallpox: Leaf of *okuwara* (Acacia pennata) mixed with root of *engerengeruai*
(Cassia singueana) and *eruopokoto* applied as a liniment.

Leprosy: (*a*) Root of *omoti* as a potion. (*b*) Root extract of *etudole* (Hymenodictyon
floribundum) (Serere county).

Mumps: Leaf of *edodoi* (Kigelia aethiopica) applied as a liniment.

To accelerate childbirth: A potion made by mixing the root of *acaboi* (Gynan-
dropsis pentaphylla) with the root of *ecilaboi* (a vegetable).

To accelerate expulsion of the placenta: A potion made with the root of *epongai*
(Dombeya rotundifolia) mixed with the root of *aleet*.

To increase a woman's milk: A potion made with *eleketete* and natural salt.

Nebula of eye: Root of *ekere* (Harrisonia abyssinica) and root of *adulia* are mixed
with water and used as eye-drops.

Hydrocele: The root of *esikarukaru* (Vitex doniana) is taken as a drink.

Toothache: A gargle made from *ekoboi* (Terminalia torulosa).

To kill pain during tooth extraction: Leaf of *egwangira* (Hibiscus cannabinus)
rubbed on the cheek.

[1] Brother K. Ludger, Mill Hill Mission, personal communication. Serere examples
are taken from Wilson, 1953.

Earache: A mixture made from the leaf of *ejoroi* (Teclea nobilis) and *ekere* (Harrisonia abyssinica) and applied as drops. Drops can also be made from the root of *ejotait* or the stem of *etulelut* (Solanum aculistatismum).

Wounds: Contraction of a wound caused by stepping in excrement can be treated by rubbing the leaf of *emoros* (Cissus adenocaulis) into the wound. Other plants used as dressings or rubbed into the wound are: root of *ekaka* (Lonchocarpus laxiflorus), root of *ekoboi* (Terminalia torulosa), root of *engite* (Stereospermum thunthianum), and *elele* (Setaria sphacelata), a grass.

Syphilitic wounds: The leaf of *emou* is used as an embrocation.

Gonorrhoea: (*a*) Leaf extract of *ekisim* (Acacia seyal) mixed with an extract from Piliostigma sp. (Serere county). (*b*) Latex of *epopong* (Euphorbia candelabrum) taken orally (Serere county). (*c*) Root extract of *eputon* (Pseudocedrela kotschyi).

Ulcers: The root of *ekoboi* is put on the ulcer.

Burns: The excrement of hares (*acin apoo*) is smeared on the affected part.

Lumbago: *Enokorokote*, which is a poison, is rubbed on to the body and produces warmth.

Rheumatism or sciatica: A liniment is prepared from the root of *ebusubus* (Steganotaenia araliacea) or the root of *eukot*.

Indigestion: A potion made from the root of *asurulac*.

Thread-worm: A potion made from *epeduru lodidi* (Tamarindus indica).

Guinea-worm: A mixture made from the grass, *omusenu*, is used either as a potion or as a liniment.

Jiggers: The root of *ekulwas* is made into a liniment.

Purgatives: Leaf extract of *emus* (Mystroxylon aethiopicum). Purgatives can also be made from *amo*, *elokile* root, and a variety of *epopong* (Euphorbia candelabrum) and are taken as potions.

Emetics: *Elokile* root is taken as a potion but in a heavier dosage than is used for purgatives.

Anti-diarrhoea: (*a*) A mixture is drunk made from *ebiong* root (Ficus glumosa), *ekulony* root (Combretum binderanum), and *ekungur* (Butyrospermum parkii). (*b*) The root of *aurengo*, a Teso vegetable, is also beneficial. (*c*) Chewing the bark of *eryeco* (Bridelia sceleroneuroides) (Serere county).

Hair stimulator: An embrocation made from *etakalari* leaf.

5. *Charms and potions*

Witch-doctors are often consulted in order to obtain love potions, for which there are numerous recipes. A small long-tailed bird (*ekiriojing*)[2] may be caught and killed; its meat is dried and ground and mixed with butter and the ointment so made is smeared on the girl's chest. Or the root of a shrub (*erutotan*) may be pounded and mixed secretly in a man's food or beer to ensure his love. The anus of a crocodile, cooked and powdered and put in a girl's food, will win her love.

Witch-doctors also conduct a trade in lucky charms, particularly 'amulets, worn by young and old for good health, though they are not considered to be very effective . . .'.[1] Young children in particular are given such trinkets to wear round their neck or waist.

---

[1] Kruyer (undated).   [2] Probably the Paradise Flycatcher (Tchitrea viridis).

That there is still belief in mumbo-jumbo magic, even among well-educated adults, is shown from the records of the 'money-making' cases in 1953. Sundry tricksters persuaded their victims to hand over enormous amounts of money and cattle in return for initiation into the secret of a magic money-making book. The interesting point about these cases is the ritual which impressed initiates; examples are:

(a) to abstain from sexual intercourse for seven days;
(b) roasting the liver of a sacrificial goat or sprinkling 'medicine' on it and eating it;
(c) cutting of the body with a razor blade;
(d) insistence on some odd figure in the initiation fee such as Shs. 752/77, Shs. 1,252/77, Shs. 852/77;
(e) smearing of the body;
(f) not to shake hands when greeting for forty days;
(g) not to allow a woman to touch the magic book.

One witness described the prayer: 'I brought a leaf from the mango tree and he shaped it and put it in the book. We then put our hands on the book and prayed "Mother, Father, let this leaf become a note according to your wish and not as we wish, a note of Shs. 20/-, Shs. 10/- or Shs. 5/-". After we had prayed he waved over my hand and behind my head twice and opened the book; I saw a Shs. 20/- note.'

6. *Divination*

'Witch doctors are also consulted as seers and prophesy whether journeys will be successful or sick relatives will recuperate. For this, pieces of hide are used, cut into small bits, which are thrown about and the way they fall and dispose themselves tell the witch doctors what the future holds in store.'[1] The only example I have seen of divination by sandals was at Amuria. An equally common method of divination is by examination of the stomach contents of sacrificial goats or oxen or by examining whether a goat defaecates or urinates first. If the former, then the disease of the witch-doctor's patient will be mild, but if the latter, the patient may not recover, for urine signifies tears.

7. *Black magic*

The main duty of a witch-doctor (*emuron*) is to counteract the evil activities of the wizard (*ecudan*). These activities of the *ecudan* are wholly evil and wholly abhorrent. The wizard plies his evil trade and sets his spells in many different ways. The commonest way is to gain possession of the excreta or scabs of the victim to induce disease in him. There are, however, recognized medicines used in spells. These are made from certain reptiles

[1] Kruyer (undated).

associated with witchcraft, particularly snakes, frogs, and lizards. The medicines are concocted by taking certain portions of the reptiles, drying them, and pounding them together. Chickens' livers are also used. Dogs, hyenas, and jackals are all associated with the occult. A wizard is believed to have the power of sending hyenas to do his bidding. (The story of Nyagilo quoted above illustrates this belief in the magic properties of dogs and cocks.) The act of striking a closed door at night or of dancing round a house at night is believed to cast a spell on the occupier of the house.

The commission of sexual abnormalities such as incest or bestiality is associated with the powers of wizards and those who commit them are deemed wizards. Unintentional incest may, however, be pardoned if a purifying ceremony is performed as described on p. 209.

Wizards are universally feared and detested. In former times, a wizard caught in the act was speared and his family sought no redress. 'If seized he may be instantly killed or tortured in ways too horrible to write about. He may be impaled upon a sharp stake and die miserably of exposure and starvation.'[1] Nowadays, they are punished by normal process of law. Courts invariably award the maximum sentence and wizards are so hated and feared that to call a man a wizard or to suggest that he practises wizardry is in itself a most serious crime.

8. *Rain making*

The ceremony described at Kyere[1] is typical of all rain-making ceremonies in the district.

It is unusual to pray for rain during the height of the dry season; it is only in times of unseasonable drought that recourse is had to this method. For instance, if the rains have broken and seed is sown when a dry spell sets in, then prayers will be offered for rain.

Notice is given by the witch-doctor (*emuron*)—*Kopote moi kere, kanuka alosit amoot edou* (All of you come tomorrow to look for rain). The ceremony often takes place at the grave of a well-known rain-maker, but may take place at a prominent feature such as a granite outcrop. At the Kyere ceremony, both rock and grave were visited.

The assembled people[3] parade round the grave or rock singing *kobala edou kotep kicek kiyakiya, jelele, jelele, jelele* (Let the rain fall throughout the night, jelele, jelele, jelele). *Jelele* is meant to indicate the sound of rain.

The *emuron* puts earth in a calabash and all go to the swamp, singing the while. In the water the *emuron* fills a pail (*elepit*) with water and holds it up and shouts: *Wee! wee! wee! edou, jelele! jelele!* (Wee! Wee! Wee! Rain, flowing, flowing!) The people answer: *Edou eyapuni, sirikibu ededeng, kimonyi isio ijo.* (Rain is near; do not be violent, we cry for you.) The crowd

---

[1] Kitching, 1912.   [2] Wright, 1946.
[3] The following brief account of a typical rain-making ceremony is based partly on local inquiries and partly on Ludger, 1954.

go into the water and take papyrus stalks and decorate their bodies with swamp grasses or lilies. They then gather round a nearby tree or rock and the *emuron* climbs the tree or rock and scatters the water to a chant:

Emuron's chant:	*The people's response:*
Edou lokide (rain from the east)	*Edou* (rain)
Edou lonyakoi (rain from the north)	*Edou* (rain)
Edou lotoo (rain from the west)	*Edou* (rain)
Kobu (come)	*Kobu* (come)

The *emuron* then addresses a spirit in the tree or the rock. There follows a feast. Goats are killed and roasted. Before the feast starts, the *emuron* announces *Edou ibwaitai akipi* (clouds hold water). If rain does not immediately follow, it is because evil men are withholding it. They must be pointed out and made to plunge themselves in the water and then scatter water from the tree. The *emuron* eats some of the goat meat, which must be cut for him.

An account of Ogura, a former rain-maker of Kaberamaido, shows that the ceremony was similar among the Kumam. Ogura, who was born blind, began to practise on Soroti Rock but later moved to Obur Rock in Olomet. On a day chosen by Ogura, the people would gather and dance down to the swamp, wearing grass decorations. They returned with three fishes and while they danced round the rock, Ogura entered a cave with the fishes. He reappeared and scattered water, making the usual incantations.

Whatever the variation in detail of the ceremony, the invariable ingredients are the ceremonial sprinkling of water, the rain-maker's prayer with the people's response, the adornment of the body with water plants, and the sacrifice of the goat. The wagtail and lily trotter are often associated in songs with the arrival of rain.

Songs and responses are similar throughout most of the district. The following songs were recorded by F. Lukyn-Williams in Usuku in 1920 and are thus the earliest recorded:

(1) *Irukonokini kokide edou.* (Clouds are rumbling in the east.)
   Oye! aremere papa ka Aungor awasia. (Sing, they spear the father of
      Aungor outside.)
   Irimonokini kokide edou. (Clouds are circling in the east.)

(2) *Edou iruko, kowo!* (The clouds are rumbling, sing!)
   Edou iruko, kowo! (The clouds are rumbling, sing!)
   Ogiro edou. (The clouds are roaring.)

(3) *Erioniki edou kokide.* (The cloud blackens the east.)
   Erioniki edou kokide. (The cloud blackens the east.)
   Koyau akipi kwap. (Let it bring down water.)
   Ilimi edou, kowo! (It rains, sing.)

(4) *Kowo! agiro agiro akiru.* (Sing! It roars, it roars, the rain.)
   Kowo! agiro agiro akiru. (Sing! It roars, it roars, the rain.)

(5) *Edou ca irukonokini.* (The cloud there is rumbling.)
    Edou ca, wo! wo! (The cloud there, wo! wo!)
    Edou ca, wo! wo! (The cloud there, wo! wo!)
    Kowo! Kowo! ebala akiru jelele. (Sing, sing, the rain makes a noise like torrents.)
    Kodoo, wo! wo! (Fall in torrents.)
    Kowo! kowo! ebala akiru jelele. (Sing! sing! the rain makes a noise like torrents.)
    Kodoo, wo! wo! (Fall in torrents.)

(6) *Solo:*

Edou jelele. (Rain torrentially).	*Jelele.* (Torrentially.)
Edou kangina ta kangina. (Rain there.)	*Kilim.* (Shower.)
Edou kangina ta kangina. (Rain there.)	*Kitokon* (Make ripe.)
Edou kangina ta kangina. (Rain there.)	*Kilim.* (Shower.)
Kitokon imomwa. (Make sorghum ripe.)	*Kitokon.* (Make ripe.)
Kangina ta oKoromojo. (There in Karomojo.)	*Kitokon.* (Make ripe.)
Kangina ta oKoyale. (There in Koyale.)	*Kitokon.* (Make ripe.)
Kangina ta okomor ka Itepes. (There in the mountain of the Tepeth.)	*Kitokon.* (Make ripe.)
(Repeated, or with *kilim* (shower) for *kitokon*.)	
Edou iruko. (The rain clouds rumble.)	*Wo!*
Edou jelele. (Rain torrentially.)	*Jelele.*

(7) *Edou ka Ogulo, oiyoye!* (The rain of Ogulo, oiyoye!)
    Edou ka Ogulo, oiyoye! (The rain of Ogulo, oiyoye!)

(8) *Koribok ajelele abwatu, Emuge.* (Blacken rain make wet, Emuge.)
    Koribok ajelele abwatu, Emuge. (Blacken rain make wet, Emuge.)

(9) *Women only:*
    Aie! aono aono ekitoi ka Ogulo, edou, aie! aie! aie! (Aie! dried, the tree of Ogulo has dried, rain, aie! aie! aie!)

(10) *Ekipie ca, irukonokini. Ekipie ca, wo! wo!* (Lightning, the thunder, lightning, wo! wo!)

PART VI

LAW

Note: The methods employed in making this recording of Teso law have been described in the Introduction. Briefly, the recording is based on an examination of a large number of court cases and has been checked by various assessors, all of whom have had considerable judicial experience. The recording attempts to tabulate the whole body of law at present administered by the native courts in Teso district. In consequence it contains a mixture of customary law, some of it ancient and some of it modern, council resolutions, gazetted by-laws, applied Uganda statutory laws, and formal administrative directions issued by the District Commissioner in his capacity of supervising magistrate of the native courts. In the hope that this recording may be of some practical use, a detailed index showing the subject-matter of each section in each chapter is provided.

Certain abbreviations are used in the quotations. D.C. stands for District Commissioner's Court (District Court), which consists of the District Commissioner or an Assistant District Commissioner and has appellate or revisionary jurisdiction only. D.N.C. stands for District Native Court of Teso, the highest native court in the district, which has appellate and, very occasionally, original jurisdiction. The constitution and powers of this and other native courts in Teso are described in Chapter VIII. I.H.L. stands for imprisonment with hard labour. The number following the name of the court (e.g. Asamuk Sub-County 235/53) indicates the number of the case in the court register for the particular year shown.

INDEX OF SECTIONS

CHAPTER I. MARRIAGE

43. No time limit on claims for children.
44. Pregnancy at marriage.

CHAPTER II. DIVORCE

1. Divorce necessitates repayment of bride-price.
2. Divorce before clan leaders.
3. Witnesses to such divorces.
4. Divorce before the courts.
5. Clan leaders' decision recognized in courts.
6. Contested cases must always come before the courts.

Grounds for divorce

7. Grounds for divorce of wife.
8. A wife cannot divorce her husband.
9. Refusal to perform wifely duties.
10. Adultery.
11. Disease.
12. Desertion.
13. Witchcraft.
14. Excessive cruelty.

Procedure on divorce

15. Bride-price may be paid back before clan leaders in uncontested cases.
16. In other cases it must be paid before the native courts.
17. Witnesses to repayment.
18. Only the legal maximum bride-price is repayable.
19. No time bar on claim for bride-price.
20. Divorce becomes absolute when pronounced by clan leaders or courts.
21. The children always belong to the husband.
22. Children at breast must be left with their mothers until weaned.
23. Wife may plead that husband is unfit to have custody.
24. A woman may sue for custody.
25. A mother can always see her child.
26. Seasonal crops belong to the divorced woman.
27. Divorced women may claim private property.

CHAPTER III. ADULTERY AND FORNICATION

1. *Adultery with married women*
    1. Cases of adultery to be filed in sub-county courts.
    2. Cases of adultery to be filed by the wronged husband.
    3. Direct evidence is necessary to prove adultery.
    4. A confession by the wife is never direct evidence.
    5. Witnesses should declare their presence at the time.
    6. An immediate report must be made to the local chief.
    7. Tendency to make adultery into a business.
    8. Duty of a man to ascertain that the woman with whom he lives or whom he marries has no living husband.
    9. The word of the woman is insufficient evidence in such cases.
    10. Wronged husband acquiescing in the adultery is sufficient defence.
    11. Instigation by husband is sufficient defence.

4. *Claims and debts on estates*

27. Claims and debts are called for at the meeting for division of the estate.
28. There is no time limit for collection of assets or payment of debts once registered.
29. Claims and debts admitted at the clan meeting are inheritable.
30. Debts of bride-price or blood-money are always inheritable.
31. Debts take priority over other claims.
32. Creditors are paid as they arrive and not in proportion to the assets of the estate.

5. *Wills*

33. Wills are not generally used in Teso.
34. Verbal wills.
35. Grounds for disinheritance.
36. Debts must be paid before legacies are met.
37. Written wills.

6. *Guardianship*

38. Appointment of guardians when the heir is a minor or is absent.
39. The mother of the minor is appointed a co-guardian.
40. A woman can never be sole guardian.
41. Guardians appointed by clan leaders.
42. A guardian is responsible for the property of his wards.
43. A guardian cannot claim compensation for services rendered.

CHAPTER V. CONTRACT

1. *Contracts for specific performances*

Cattle herding

1. Cattle herding is the commonest form of contract in Teso.
2. Contracts may be written or verbal.
3. Contracts must be witnessed.
4. A herdsman has the right to dispose of the milk.
5. Offspring of the cattle belong to the owner.
6. Responsibility of the herdsman for loss or damage to the herd.
7. Responsibilty of the herdsman for damage done to property and for building kraals or calf houses.
8. Courts assess remuneration when not fixed.

House building

9. Contracts may be verbal or written.
10. Contracts must be witnessed.
11. Time limits are not fixed and penalty clauses unknown.
12. Procedure when contractor fails to complete work.
13. Contracts for building temporary houses.

Medical treatment

14. Fees are fixed in advance.
15. Fees are not paid until a cure is obtained.
16. If the patient does not recover the doctor has no claim.
17. If the patient grows worse no compensation can be claimed but fees paid are recoverable.
18. A patient has the right to change his doctor.

CHAPTER VI. REAL PROPERTY

1. *Introduction*

    1. Extract from D.N.C. judgement.
    2. Preliminary note.
    3. Basis of land rights.

2. *Definitions*

    4. Land Authority.
    5. Land Authority area.
    6. Ownership.
    7. Newcomer.
    8. User.
    9. User rights.
    10. Unallocated and surplus land.

3. *Rights in land*

    Ownership by inheritance or gift

    11. How ownership may be acquired.
    12. The heir inherits all land.
    13. The heir is responsible for subdivision of the estate.
    14. No limit is imposed on fragmentation.
    15. A father may subdivide his land during his lifetime.
    16. No woman can own land.
    17. A widow may cultivate her former plots.
    18. Ownership does not entitle to sale, rent, or mortgage.
    19. An owner may lend part of his land.
    20. Land belonging to a deceased man without heirs is divided among neighbours.

    Ownership by breaking new ground

    21. Breaking of new ground is subject to rules.
    22. A newcomer must find a sponsor.
    23. Only a sponsor may speak on the newcomer's behalf.
    24. Allocation of land to a newcomer.
    25. Allocation to be made in the presence of witnesses.
    26. No ceremony attends allocation.
    27. A newcomer may be evicted for certain offences.

    Demarcation, disputes, and claims

    28. No form of demarcation is obligatory.
    29. Where disputes come before courts, courts may order boundary marks to be erected.
    30. It is an offence to destroy boundary marks.
    31. All disputes and claims must be referred in the first instance to the village clan leaders.
    32. Courts may not hear cases which have not first been dealt with by parish councils.
    33. A case may only be filed in the courts if the dispute is between two individuals. Individuals cannot sue the Land Authority.
    34. Ownership may be claimed by the presence of ancestral graves.
    35. Ownership may be claimed by the presence of private trees.

73. Presence of a house is a valid ground for claiming title to land.
74. Mortgage is unknown.

CHAPTER VII. CRIMINAL, APPLIED, AND LOCAL LAWS

1. *Criminal*

   Offences against the person

   1. Native courts may not hear homicide cases but can hear blood-money disputes arising from homicide cases.
   2. Blood-money fixed at five head of cattle.
   3. When and to whom blood-money is due.
   4. Intention to kill is immaterial.
   5. Liability of relations to meet blood-money debts.
   6. Blood-money debts are inheritable without time limit.
   7. Punishment for common assault.
   8. Assessment of compensation for assault.
   9. Procedure in assault cases.
   10. Native courts may not hear defilement cases.

   Offences against property

   11. Punishment for cattle theft.
   12. Powers of county courts extended to deal with cattle theft.
   13. Receiving stolen cattle.
   14. Sub-county courts may not hear arson cases.

   Witchcraft

   15. Definitions.
   16. Mystical or occult practices.
   17. Poisons.
   18. Unnatural vice.
   19. Accusations of witchcraft.

2. *Applied laws*

   20. Protectorate Government laws applied by warrant.
   21. Protectorate Government laws commonly administered.

3. *Local laws*

   22. Laws made under the Native Law Ordinance.
   23. By-laws made under the African Local Governments Ordinance.
   24. Preservation of law and order.
   25. Agriculture and soil conservation.
   26. Veterinary.
   27. Public Health.
   28. Beer by-law, 1951.
   29. Cassava by-law, 1952.
   30. Education Tax by-law, 1952.
   31. Ferries by-law, 1952.

CHAPTER VIII. COURTS

1. *Clan courts*

   1. Origin of clan courts.
   2. Territorial jurisdiction.

CHAPTER I

MARRIAGE

1. *Bride-price*

1. MARRIAGE is legalized by the payment of bride-price and is dissolved by the repayment of bride-price (see also Chapter II, Divorce).

2. Bride-price (*iboro luemanyit*) is a payment by the bridegroom (*eteran*) to his presumptive father-in-law (*amuran*) on the occasion of the marriage.

3. The form of the bride-price, whether cash or kind, and the amount of the bride-price are solely matters of agreement between the two families subject to section 4 below.

> *Notes*: (*a*) One recognized method of refusal to allow a marriage is to fix a prohibitive bride-price.
>
> (*b*) Normal bride-price used to range up to twenty-five to thirty cattle, though after a rinderpest outbreak it has been known to have fallen as low as thirty goats and one cow. There was formerly no differentiation between bride-price paid for an unmarried and for a married woman. Payment by instalments meant that even a poor man could afford to marry.

4. The present maximum permitted bride-price is:
(*a*) For an unmarried girl (*apese*), five head of cattle or 500s.
(*b*) For a previously married woman (*akobo*), three head of cattle or 300s.

> *Note*: It is immaterial whether or not the woman is a virgin or whether or not she has borne children; if she has not previously been married, the higher bride-price is legal and if she has been married, the lower.

5. (*a*) Any person convicted of offering or paying bride-price in excess of the amount allowed in section 4 is liable to a fine of 50s.

(*b*) Any person convicted of offering to receive or of receiving bride-price in excess of the amount allowed in section 4 is liable to a fine of 150s.

(*c*) If either of the persons in (*a*) or (*b*) above is a chief he is liable to a fine of 200s.

> *Quotation: Asamuk Sub-County Court 225/51: Court* v. *Adwomu Ekora and G. Olir.*
>
> Adwomu, father of the bride, admitted receiving fifteen head of cattle as bride-price, but attempted to shift the blame to G. Olir, who paid the bride-price and married the girl. G. Olir admitted paying excess bride-price but claimed that he was not a substantive chief at the time and was merely acting as a chief. Nevertheless the Court fined

Adwomu the usual 150s. and fined G. Olir 200s. instead of the usual 50s. 'because he was a chief'.

(*d*) Any person who hides excess bride-price cattle in his kraal is liable to a fine of 25s.

Note: (*a*) Evasion of section 4 is wholesale. Prosecutions do not, however, occur unless a divorce comes before the courts. The fact that all witnesses to the transaction are not punished is a flaw which makes evasion even commoner.

(*b*) See note on section 15 below.

6. When a divorce is granted by the courts only the legal maximum bride-price under section 4 may be reclaimed by the husband and no further suit may lie for any excess paid.

7. But in the case of marriages contracted prior to 1925 or during the period 1 January 1937 to 31 October 1938, when there was no legal maximum bride-price, section 6 does not apply.

Note: Since the recipient of excess bride-price is allowed to keep the excess and cannot be compelled to return it nor is it confiscated by the Court as is done in several other districts, the fine of 150s. under section 5 is no deterrent whatsoever. In practice, however, a private arrangement is made to return the excess cattle along with the legal bride-price.

8. Apart from the bride-price certain presents are customarily given by the bridegroom:

(*a*) To the presumptive mother-in-law: a cloth to cover the breasts (*egoye loerapia ikisina*); for a son-in-law may not look on his mother-in-law.

Note: Formerly this present consisted of a goat-skin skirt as worn by the Karamojong today (*arobai*) or, according to one assessor, a she-goat. Another assessor denies that any gift at all was made to the mother-in-law.

(*b*) To the women who escort the bride (*ateran*) to her husband's house: cloth.

Note: Formerly this present (*enyamit*) consisted of necklaces or bracelets.

(*c*) To the presumptive father-in-law: a *kanzu* or other articles of clothing and a cash present varying from about 20s. to 100s. though no maximum is fixed (*ikisina* 'payment for the breasts').

Note: Formerly this present consisted of a spear, shield, or hoe, or, according to one assessor, a he-goat.

None of these presents is ordinarily repayable in case of divorce except the *ikisina*.

9. The only person legally entitled to receive bride-price is the father or nearest adult male relative of the girl.

Note: But this rule can be varied if no male relatives can be found and especially if the mother of the girl has left her district of origin.

Quotation: Kuju Sub-County Court 38/51: G. Esau v. Ogweli d/o Maraka:

G. Esau sued Ogweli d/o Maraka for recovery of bride-price, which he had paid to her in 1942. Ogweli, a Lango, came to Teso with her husband and bore a daughter. Before the daughter came of age, the husband died and Ogweli did not know her husband's relatives. So she received bride-price for the daughter.

10. It is the duty of the suitor to ascertain that the bride-price is paid by him to the person legally entitled to receive it (see section 9) and if it is paid to the wrong person, no claim to the woman lies, though return of the bride-price wrongly paid may be claimed as a civil debt.

Quotation: Otuboi Sub-County Court 83/50: Omoding v. E. Emesu:

Omoding sued E. Emesu for keeping Omoding's wife, Aleto, in his house and for refusing to allow her to return to Omoding. It was proved that Omoding had paid bride-price for Aleto to Iraitai, Aleto's uncle, whereas her true guardian was E. Emesu, her half-brother. The Court ruled that Aleto should stay with her guardian E. Emesu, as she was not Omoding's lawful wife, but Omoding could ask for the bride-price back from Iraitai.

11. The bride-price must be paid to the legal recipient in person and not through a third party.

Quotation: Otuboi Sub-County Court 203/51: Edou v. Omoon:

Edou claimed that Omoon gave Aoto, Edou's wife, in marriage to Emenyu. Omoon admitted this, but stated she was not Edou's wife, for Edou had paid dowry to Opurotong on behalf of Omoon. Edou lost the case.

12. The payment must be made before at least two witnesses. The official witnesses may receive a monetary fee or a fee of one goat.

Quotation: D.C.'s Revision 4/50 from D.N.C. 114/49: O. Eryatu v. S. Elweu:

It is stated in evidence that Oguti Etotu, official witness, received a goat.

13. If the father receives bride-price for his daughter on remarriage before a divorce is agreed upon before witnesses or ordered by a court, he is guilty of an offence and liable on conviction to a fine of 100s. to 500s. according to the amount of the second bride-price so obtained.

Note: This is a law to prevent greedy fathers from enticing their daughters from their first husbands to marry where higher bride-prices are offered. If, however, the divorce has been regularized, the father can receive bride-price, because it is from this second bride-price that the first will be repaid. The courts usually award only 100s. fine for this offence.

14. The woman in such cases remains the legal wife of her first husband until the marriage is formally dissolved and the man to whom she was illegally given has no claim on any children he may have begotten by her.

15. The legal recipient of bride-price customarily distributes the bride-price among:

(a) his paternal aunt;
(b) his maternal uncle;
(c) his elder daughter (if she exists);
(d) his elder brother (including half brother);
(e) his father;

in that order.

> *Note*: The amount that each recipient gets depends on the bride-price paid (see note in section 3 above). The father of the girl normally keeps at least one good bull himself. The division is made as fairly as possible bearing in mind any previous allocations for previous marriages. This custom serves to stimulate the interest of members of other families in the marriage. By presenting cattle to (a), (b), and (c) it is possible that three different families may be united in a common desire for a successful marriage. The custom is seldom not observed though the modern tendency is to leave the father of the girl discretion regarding to whom he awards the shares and it is not uncommon for a chief or clan leader to be given a portion even though not related. It is this custom above all which tends to cause disregard of the maximum bride-price law. A proper distribution cannot be made with only five head of cattle.

16. Where any of the relatives in section 15 do not exist, the father may keep the share himself; but when the relative has died, the share must be paid to his heir.

17. Claims for these shares are heard only in clan courts.

> *Note*: Virtually the only redress for a disappointed relative is retaliation when his turn to distribute bride-price arrives. But at least one disappointed relative retaliated by bewitching his brother by sundry charms. (Bukedea County Court 98/50 quoted on p. 260.)

18. If a divorce is subsequently granted by the courts, the legal recipient of the bride-price or his heir is bound to return the whole bride-price and cannot legally claim any help from the relatives who have received a share under section 15. He is, however, then entitled to receive the whole of the bride-price paid for the woman on remarriage.

> *Note*: Normally bride-price is not refunded till the woman is remarried.

19. Rights and obligations regarding bride-price are inheritable and an heir is liable for the return of bride-price in case of divorce.

Quotation: Otuboi Sub-County Court 137/50: Kaberamaido County Court 90/50: S. Ebietu v. Otuboi Sub-County Court:

In the Otuboi Court Sulemani Ebietu was fined 150s. under section 5 (*b*) above, because his deceased brother, Mohamed, had received excessive bride-price of five head of cattle, two goats, and 80s. from Kelementi Elyau. Kelementi Elyau was fined 50s.

On appeal the conviction and sentence on S. Ebietu were set aside because he had not been present at the illegal transaction and because he lived in a different parish and was therefore unlikely to know about it. But the fine on K. Elyau stood and S. Ebietu was still liable to return the bride-price paid to his deceased brother.

20. Progeny of bride-price cattle are not returnable but cows with calf at heel are reckoned as one beast.

21. No bride-price is returnable in case of death or incurable illness.

Quotation: Mukongoro Sub-County Court 111/51: W. Olupot v. Odulusi Obang:

W. Olupot sued Odulusi for return of bride-price. Olupot's wife had visited her father, Odulusi, to perform an *asuban* ceremony. She fell ill at her father's house and died. The Court ruled that no payment was due. Olupot knew of his wife's illness and death.

22. If a woman is living with a man at the time of her death without being married to him, bride-price must be paid immediately.

23. The marriage is legalized when bride-price has been paid in full.

Note: This is strictly speaking true but there is a tendency now as in the past to pay in instalments and to regard the passing of *ikisina* (section 8 (*c*)) as the legalization of the marriage. See also the following sections.

Quotation: High Court Civ. Rev. 88/52: D.C.'s 26/52: D.N.C. 30/52: Amuria County Court 23/52: I. Edigu v. E. Okello:

Edigu married Okello's daugher and paid *ikisina*. Agreement had been reached to pay fifteen cattle as bride-price, but Okello demanded more and, during the negotiations, took back his daughter by force from Edigu's home. It was held that the girl was Edigu's lawful wife after payment of *ikisina* and that Okello had no right to take her away by force.

The point was illustrated in the D.N.C. evidence:

'What now shows that Teresa is your wife, if Okello has not taken the cows?'

Answer: 'The 300/- which Okello took.'

24. Notwithstanding section 23 the marriage may be recognized as legal and children of it belong to their father when a portion only of the bride-price has been paid over.

> *Note*: In such cases the legal position is different from that obtaining under section 23. The cattle paid are treated as still belonging to the suitor and the girl as still belonging to her father until the contract is completed. This fact explains the following sections.

25. In such cases the father of the girl may at any time recall his daughter and refuse to allow her to return to her husband until further instalments or the whole bride-price is paid. The husband can then claim back his cattle.

26. In such cases the father can at any time return the husband's cattle and the husband must then return the girl to her father.

27. If the girl returns to her father before the payment of bride-price is completed, children will belong to her husband even if the bride-price already paid is refunded.

> *Quotation:* (a) *Ochero Sub-County Court 127/51: Okiror v. S. Onang:*
>
> Okiror married Imele, S. Onang's sister, in 1939 paying one cow and 6s. to her father. He claimed three children and the part bride-price back. The Court awarded two children and the bride-price.

> *Quotation:* (b) *Ochero Sub-County Court 111/51: S. Elasu v. Odieny Onyega:*
>
> S. Elasu married Odieny's daughter, Adato, in 1944 but bride-price, if offered, was not paid or not paid in full. In 1949 Adato was given to another husband. She was pregnant at the time. S. Elasu sued for the child. The Court considered that Odieny should have sued S. Elasu during the four years for failure to pay bride-price; it took note of the fact that S. Elasu brought his wife's pregnancy to the notice of the chief at the time. The Court awarded the child to Elasu.

28. If the girl dies before the full bride-price has been paid, the husband is liable to pay the remaining part (see section 22).

29. If a man dies and leaves a wife, she may, if she wishes, live with the deceased's close relatives, i.e. members of his extended family (*ekek*) (see Chapter IV, Inheritance).

30. If, however, she wishes to return to her parents or marry outside her late husband's family, bride-price must be returned to the heir of the deceased.

2. *Marriage restrictions*

31. A marriage may be prohibited by:

(*a*) endogamy (sections 32 and 33);
(*b*) consanguinity (section 34);
(*c*) affinity (section 35).

(Tables of consanguinity and affinity appear on p. 54.)

32. No man may marry a woman of the same extended family (*ekek*) or one having the same clan observances or taboos (*etal*) as himself. It is, however, possible for a man to marry a woman having the same clan (*ateker*) name as himself, although in practice such marriages are rare because a man and a woman having the same clan (*ateker*) name and living in the same locality are likely to have the same taboos or to be related.

33. No man may marry a woman having the same clan taboos (*etal*) as his mother had before her marriage.

> *Note*: According to one assessor a man may nowadays marry a woman having the same taboos as his mother had before her marriage provided she does not come within the relationship mentioned in the note in section 35 below.

34. No man may marry:

(*a*) his mother or grandmother;
(*b*) his daughter or grand-daughter;
(*c*) his sister or step-sister;
(*d*) his niece or great-niece;
(*e*) his aunt or great-aunt;
(*f*) his first or second cousin.[1]

But he can marry:

(*a*) his step-mother after his father's death;
(*b*) his sister-in-law after his brother's death;
(*c*) his wife's sister.

> *Note*: This is the view of some assessors. But a wife's sister is usually regarded as a blood relative, as a sister or daughter according to her age, and it would be considered improper to marry her. One assessor writes: '*Enyamit* (a present for escorting a bride to her husband's home) is obtained from one's wife's sister and one could never marry such a girl. If one did, one would be called *ekacudan* (wizard). Perhaps the younger generation of Iteso are marrying in this way, but it was never done in the past.' Roscoe (1915) states that a man is forbidden to marry more than one daughter of the same man.

[1] Such I believe to be the rule although Roscoe (1915) asserted that marriages between second cousins can be permitted provided that they are grandchildren of a brother and a sister respectively, and that the father of the one was the son of that brother, and that the mother of the other was the daughter of that sister. That is to say, a man's son's children may marry his sister's daughter's children.

35. No man may marry:

(a) his wife's mother or grandmother;

(b) his wife's daughter or grand-daughter;

(c) his son's wife or wife of daughter's son.

Note: The barriers of consanguinity and affinity are determined in cases of doubt by reference to the clan head (*apolon ka ateker*). The prohibited degrees are often carried to the fourth degree or even further than those shown in sections 34 and 35 above.

36. Any man who marries a woman or who has sexual intercourse with a woman in contravention of sections 32–35 above is deemed guilty of witchcraft.

Note: This is the general view of assessors, supported by the use of the word *ikacudak* (wizards) in the purification ceremony described below. One assessor stated that in former times both man and woman would have been put to death by spearing. Nowadays there is no sanction which the courts can apply and such offences would not be brought before a court. Indeed, it is almost inconceivable that a marriage could take place in contravention of these binding customs, for the publicity surrounding all bride-price matters would ensure that public opinion was marshalled against it. Nevertheless, reference to these customs is not uncommon in court records and it is a common defence to a charge of adultery to prove that the woman concerned is within the forbidden circle of relationship to the adulterer.

Incest outside marriage does, however, occasionally occur. In such cases the offence is regarded as one against clan taboo and a purification ceremony must be performed. It is stated by one assessor that this purification suffices even if the incest was knowingly committed.

The ceremony is as follows: the incestuous couple are placed in a small grass hut specially erected for the purpose near the man's house. *Ema* grass is used. The hut is then fired by the clan leader in the presence of other clan leaders. When the couple feel the heat of the flames they run out to the cry of *Ikacudak* (wizards) from the onlookers. The couple must not look behind them.

The man's father then kills a bull and the woman's a goat. Beer is provided by both families. Blood and dung of the slaughtered animals are mixed in a small vessel and the man and woman are made to sit near the entrance of the man's house. First the woman and then the man are smeared with the mixture. A feast follows.

37. There is no restriction on the number of wives a man may marry.

38. A man customarily consults his first wife before marrying a second wife.

39. A second wife is customarily given a separate house after her first harvest, when she has put food from her garden into the store.

40. A man would customarily consult his wife before bringing a concubine to live in his house.

3. Custody of children

41. (a) Custody of children on divorce is dealt with in Chapter II, Divorce, sections 21–25.

(b) Custody of illegitimate children is dealt with in Chapter III, Adultery and Fornication, sections 27–32.

42. Children of the marriage invariably belong to the husband even if he could not have been their real father.

Quotation: (a) *Katine Sub-County Court 323/49: Y. Emeu v. R. Atege:*

Y. Emeu sued for custody of a child, Eswau, born to Atoo, Emeu's daughter, who was married to R. Atege. Atoo had left Atege and returned to her father. Five months later she became pregnant by a man named Emechu and bore her son, Eswau, nine months later. The Court awarded the child to R. Atege.

Quotation: (b) *D.C.'s Revision 8/49. D.N.C. 64/49: Eilu s/o Adaku v. Abyong s/o Ewangu:*

Awiliwil was the wife of Ewangu; about thirty years ago Ewangu died and Awiliwil passed to his brother, Igira, but she eloped with a man of another clan named Adaku and bore him two children. Later she returned to Igira with her two children. Adaku's son, Eilu, sued for custody of these two children. The Court ruled that as Awiliwil was in law married to Igira they belonged to him and his family.

43. There appears to be no time limit for claims for children.

Quotation: Soroti County Court 116/49: Edyangu v. Opinya (appeal):

Opinya sued Edyangu in the sub-county court for custody of a child born in 1931.

44. But if a wife was pregnant at marriage the child will belong to the father of the wife.

Quotation: Otuboi Sub-County Court 50/51: Kaberamaido County Court 33/51: G. Eduru v. Eitu s/o Owiny:

Eduru sued Eitu for return of bride-price on divorce and for custody of his wife's child. Eitu admitted liability to pay bride-price but proved that the child was conceived before Eduru had paid bride-price; the woman was, in fact, pregnant at marriage and the child therefore illegitimate. Both courts awarded custody of the child to Eitu.

CHAPTER II

DIVORCE

Preliminary note

DIVORCE was formerly very rare. Then, as now, the distribution of bride-price made several different families interested in the success and continuance of the marriage and consequently a considerable weight of opinion was, and still is, marshalled against the woman by members of her family and every effort is made by them to ensure continuity of the marriage. The only real ground was complete incompatibility.

Thus it was not unusual for a wife to leave her husband to live with another man and to bear him children. Her husband would claim these children as his and eventually the wife would return to him to live with her grown-up children and no objection would be raised.

> *Quotation: D.C.'s Revision 8/49 from D.N.C. 64/49: Eilu s/o Adaku* v. *Abyong s/o Ewangu (quoted above):*
>
> Awiliwil left her husband Igira and lived with a man of another clan named Adaku for several years. Two children were born and eventually Awiliwil returned to Igira. Years later Adaku's son claimed those children and their property. The Court held that they belonged to Igira.

It was not unusual if a man's wife left him in this way for the father of the woman to provide another daughter at a much reduced bride-price.

1. Divorce (*airenge*) invariably necessitates the repayment of bride-price. Suits are always filed as actions, to recover bride-price.

> *Note*: The corollary—that repayment of bride-price invariably indicates a divorce—would naturally, and is universally, considered to be, true; but divorces in marriages under the Marriage Ordinance, which takes no account of bride-price, can only be granted in a first class subordinate court. Matrimonial tangles are therefore not uncommon.

> *Quotation: D.N.C. 90/48: B. Ideet* v. *Apieujo and Oguti:*
>
> B. Ideet, a Roman Catholic, married Sabina Imaidoto under the Marriage Ordinance. The marriage was solemnized in church. Bride-price was, of course, paid. In 1944 he arranged a divorce under native customary law with Sabina's guardian, Apieujo, a pagan. The divorce was undisputed and the bride-price was paid back before clan leaders (see sections 2 and 15 below). In 1948 B. Ideet filed two cases (Achwa Sub-County 107/48 and 111/48) against Apieujo for giving Sabina in marriage to Oguti before a divorce had been granted (Chapter I, section 13) and against Oguti, a pagan, for adultery. It was proved that

Apieujo had repaid bride-price to B. Ideet, that B. Ideet had announced before witnesses that he wished to divorce Sabina, and that B. Ideet had used the returned bride-price to marry another wife. The Court ruled that, since B. Ideet claimed he was still married to Sabina, he must repay the bride-price back to Apieujo. Sabina should return to B. Ideet. Apieujo and Oguti, having acted in good faith, were deemed guiltless. B. Ideet unsuccessfully endeavoured to obtain the customary damages by appeal.

Note: This is, of course, an incorrect ruling. B. Ideet having voluntarily dissolved his marriage under native customary law has no claim under native customary law for adultery or wrongful giving in marriage and the Court should not have heard the case at all. His marriage to Sabina remains valid under Protectorate law alone and his only redress is in the District Court under the Divorce Ordinance.

2. In uncontested cases by mutual consent of the persons concerned, divorce may be regularized by clan leaders without recourse to constituted native courts.

3. Such agreement must be witnessed by not less than two witnesses. There is no witness fee.

4. If either party is dissatisfied with the decision of the clan leaders he may reopen the case before a constituted native court in which case the decision of the clan leaders will carry considerable weight.

5. If either party fails to fulfil a condition of the clan leaders' decision, action may be taken against the delinquent in the native courts, in which case the decision of the clan leaders will be recognized.

Quotation: D.C.'s Revision 17/51 from D.N.C. 56/51: Atim d/o Opolot v. B. Osekeny:

Atim filed a case because her husband, Osekeny, drove her away and claimed return of bride-price for no valid reason. The case had been referred to the clan court which had decided that Atim had done no wrong and should be allowed to return to Osekeny. The D.N.C. and D.C.'s court took cognizance of this previous ruling and ordered that if Atim was forced to live with her parents or on her own, no return of bride-price to Osekeny could be allowed.

6. In contested cases divorce can only be granted by constituted native courts (invariably the sub-county court).

Grounds for divorce

7. Recognized grounds for divorce of a wife may be summarized as follows:

(*a*) Refusal of wife to perform wifely duties (see section 9 below).

(b) Refusal of wife to cohabit.
(c) Continued adultery of wife (see section 10 below).
(d) Epilepsy in wife (see section 11 below).
(e) Syphilis in wife (see section 11 below).
(f) Desertion by wife (see section 12 below).
(g) Practice of witchcraft by wife (see section 13 below).
(h) Repeated arson by wife.
(i) Assault of husband's elderly relatives.

But the only real ground for divorce is complete incompatibility; nevertheless, this incompatibility must involve an element of fault in the woman before it is accepted.

Quotation: D.C.'s Revision 32/51: D.N.C. 180/51: K. Abosi v. M. Asibo:

K. Abosi attempted to divorce his wife because she would not accept the Seventh Day Adventist religion. She was a Roman Catholic. All courts refused to allow a divorce on these grounds and in addition made an order that, if he refused to allow her to live with him, he must bear the cost of building a house for her elsewhere.

8. A wife cannot divorce her husband but can return to her parents' home. Her parents can then bring her husband before the clan courts for certain recognized offences:

These are:

(a) Excessive cruelty by husband (see section 14 below).
(b) Refusal of husband to cohabit.
(c) Desertion by husband (see section 12 below).
(d) Failure of husband to maintain (see section 12 below).
(e) Assault of wife's elderly relatives.

Note: A wife can sue her husband for not divorcing her.

Quotation: Orungo Sub-County 35/52: Debula Agalo v. N. Eilu:

D. Agalo sued her husband, N. Eilu, for not divorcing her thereby delaying her remarriage. She had lived with her parents for upwards of three years. But N. Eilu proved that he had visited her and tried to take her back, but she and her father had refused. The case was dismissed.

9. *Refusal to perform wifely duties:* These duties include:

(a) Fetching water for any purpose.
(b) Cooking food.
(c) Fetching grass for house building.
(d) Smearing daub in house building.
(e) Thatching (Usuku only).
(f) Keeping house and compound clean.
(g) Part of cultivation (weeding and harvesting).

10. *Adultery*: Adultery by the husband is never a ground for divorce. Normally adultery by the wife is never a ground for divorce but the modern view tends to accept repeated adultery by the wife.

11. *Disease*: (*a*) Epilepsy: No example seen.

Quotation: But in *Katine Sub-County 335/49: G. Okanyabalanga* v. *Elyau*:

Elyau agreed to marry Okanyabalanga's daughter but after taking her to his home he discovered she suffered from epilepsy so he returned her to her father. G. Okanyabalanga's claim for damages on this account was dismissed by the Court.

(*b*) No form of venereal disease except syphilis is recognized as a ground for divorce, and it is probable that even this ground is now no longer recognized. (No cases seen.)

(*c*) If the husband can prove who infected his wife with syphilis he can claim compensation whether or not he sues for divorce. (No cases seen.)

Quotation: But in *Kateta Sub-County 152/51: S. Ochungo* v. *M. Euryana*:

Ochungo sent his wife, Atim, to see Euryana's father. It was alleged that Euryana waylaid her on her return and infected her with gonorrhoea. Medical evidence showed that Atim and Euryana both suffered from this disease but other evidence was scanty and the claim was dismissed.

12. *Desertion*: (*a*) The husband must know the whereabouts of his wife before suing for divorce and she must be present at the hearing. But if he can prove that she went from him to her relations and thereafter disappeared, he can sue without her presence.

(*b*) If the wife runs to her father or guardian, her husband must follow within about seven days.

(*c*) In such cases it is the duty of the wife's father or guardian to inform the husband within about seven days of his wife's whereabouts.

(*d*) Desertion by the husband must be for a long period (one year or more) during which time no provision is made for any maintenance.

(*e*) If the husband leaves his wife in the care of a relative this does not constitute desertion however long the period of absence.

(*f*) But if the husband leaves his wife, even though he has made provision for her maintenance, she may if she wishes return to her parents and, if not claimed by her husband within a year, she may be married to someone else. The husband then has no claim on his wife, though he may sue for return of bride-price.

(*g*) If during the period the wife is sheltering at her parents' home her father or guardian refuses to allow the husband to take back his wife, he is liable on conviction to a fine of 10s. and to pay 15s. compensation to the husband.

Note: Section 12 (g) can be stretched to cover cases in which the father though not refusing to allow the wife to return does not force her to do so.

Quotation: Bugondo Sub-County 135/51: Haji Salim Segere v. Jaberi Abdulla:

Mwajuma, Haji's wife, returned to her father, Jaberi, and stayed a week. She then left with Haji's servant and was next found in Buganda with her uncle, Jaberi's brother. She refused to return. Jaberi was fined 10s. and ordered to pay 15s. costs.

13. *Witchcraft*: This term may be taken to include:

(a) The practice of certain rites normally believed to be associated with witchcraft, e.g. extraction of chickens' livers, preparation of poison from herbs, cutting off snakes' heads.

(b) Commission of acts against taboo (e.g. incest, sexual intercourse within the forbidden relationships, unnatural vice), because a person committing them is *ekacudan*, a wizard.

(c) Accusation of witchcraft.

(See Chapter VII, Criminal, sections 15–19.)

14. *Excessive cruelty*: No rules are yet evolved and courts vary considerably in their views as to what constitutes excessive cruelty.

Under Teso Council laws a man may chastise his wife by 'beating her with a small stick in no other part of the body than the buttocks for disobedience of his orders'.

Excessive cruelty may be said to mean:

(a) Severe wounds inflicted intentionally with a spear, knife, axe, &c. (But it is stated in Ngora Sub-County Case 46/49 that A. Okiring wounded his wife Madudu with an axe, causing her to spend one month in hospital; she was awarded 15s. compensation only.)

(b) Permanent maimings.

(c) Tying wife to a post.

(d) Fractures.

Note: Normally a wife brings a suit for compensation only. Such claims are common but return to parents and subsequent divorce on such grounds are rare.

Procedure on divorce

15. In uncontested cases in which a divorce is granted by clan courts bride-price may be paid back before clan leaders. See D.N.C. 90/48 quoted under section 1 above.

16. In other cases it must be paid before the native court.

17. At least two witnesses to the transaction are required.

18. Only the maximum bride-price permitted under Chapter I, Marriage, section 4, is repayable.

Note: See note under Chapter I, Marriage, section 7.

19. A divorced husband does not forfeit his bride-price merely by reason of delay in claiming it.

Quotation: (a) But in *D.C.'s Revision 2/50 (from D.N.C. 69/49): A. Okiring v. M. Ongediya:*

In 1942 A. Okiring obtained a divorce from his wife Madudu. Madudu was then given in marriage to Eyamu, who paid bride-price, and the cattle were duly offered to Okiring; but he refused them. Madudu's father then returned his daughter to Okiring and the cattle to Eyamu. Madudu remained a short time with Okiring and then ran away and died two years later. Okiring claimed bride-price on the grounds that a divorce had already been obtained. His claim was rejected.

Quotation: (b) *D.C.'s Revision 20/52: D.N.C. 7/52: D. Enyagu v. Echoku Eliao:*

Enyagu sued for return of bride-price from Echoku. In dismissing the claim the D.N.C. recorded 'The cattle which Enyangu admits receiving were paid in 1939. This shows that the debt has already been settled otherwise he would not have waited for so many years to file a case.'

20. Divorce becomes absolute when pronounced by clan courts or native courts.

Quotation: D.C. 44/52: D.N.C. 90/52: Eudu Odela v. S. Ikoluot:

Eudu Odela sued S. Ikoluot for adultery. But the sub-county and county courts found that Eudu had already obtained a pronouncement of divorce before the clan court and dismissed the claim. The D.N.C. allowed the claim but the D.C. upheld the decision of the lower courts.

Note: It is often some years before the woman is remarried and the original bride-price returned.

21. All children whatever the grounds of divorce belong to the husband.

Quotation: Wera Sub-County 56/52: Okello Elangut v. Ekwangu Ilami:

The mother of the child in dispute ran away to her father's home and stayed there for two years. Before she was divorced she became pregnant by another man and bore a child. The Court ruled that the child belonged to Okello as he was the legal husband at the time.

Note: The claim must be made by the person entitled in person. In Wera Sub-County 43/52, Y. Elyacu sued for the same child in the quotation above on behalf of his brother, Okello; the Court ruled that Okello must sue in person.

But see Chapter I, Marriage, section 44. When a wife is pregnant at marriage her father can claim the child.

22. Children at breast will be left with their mother until weaned or until large enough to draw water.

23. A wife may plead that her husband is not fit to have custody of the child.

24. A woman may sue for custody of a child taken by the husband in defiance of sections 22 and 23.

25. A mother can always claim the right to see her child.

26. Seasonal crops in a divorced woman's own plantation and her granary may be claimed by her.

27. A divorced woman may claim all private property including all gifts from her husband.

CHAPTER III

ADULTERY AND FORNICATION

1. *Adultery with married women*

1. CASES of adultery may be filed only in the sub-county court within whose jurisdiction the adultery is alleged to have taken place.

> *Notes*: (*a*) By administrative direction cases involving a chief or the wife of a chief must be tried in a court having jurisdiction above the court over which the chief presides.
>
> (*b*) Formerly, when there was less security in the land, it was unlikely that a man and woman would be caught in adultery. Sections 3, 4, and 5 are therefore comparatively recent ideas. If a husband suspected his wife of adultery, he could usually extract a confession, for there existed a strong superstition about lying in such matters.
>
> (*c*) If adultery was admitted by the lover, settlement was reached between the two families. Compensation ranged from three goats to three head of cattle, or even five head of cattle. Refusal by the lover to admit adultery led to a clan feud often resulting in death.
>
> (*d*) Some assessors state that adultery was occasionally punishable by death, the aggrieved husband having the right to spear the lover. In Karamoja district compensation for adultery is fixed at the same rate as compensation for homicide, that is sixty head of cattle.

2. Cases of adultery must be filed by the wronged husband, but by permission of the court a relative or friend may, for good reason, stand proxy.

> *Quotation: Kumi Sub-County Case 29/52: Apolot w/o Y. Ekoroi* v. *Emukade s/o Okwele:*
>
> Apolot, wife of Y. Ekoroi, successfully sued Emukade for adultery with Teresa, another of Y. Ekoroi's wives. Emukade pleaded guilty and was fined 100*s*. and ordered to pay 50*s*. compensation. Ekoroi was stopped by illness from filing the case.

3. To prove adultery the direct evidence of more than one witness is necessary. The direct evidence of the plaintiff alone, even if supported by circumstantial evidence, is usually insufficient proof. Circumstantial evidence alone, however strong, is never sufficient proof.

> *Quotation: Obalanga Sub-County Case 10/50: P. Ochen* v. *A. Otim:*
>
> P. Ochen and one of his wives found that another wife, Agido, was absent from her house at night. With a witness he went to A. Otim's house. The witness saw Otim running away. The wife ran away unobserved but admitted in Court that she had committed adultery with A. Otim. P. Ochen had made an immediate report to several other

witnesses. The Court acquitted A. Otim as there was no direct evidence that Agido and A. Otim had been found together in the house. There was no appeal.

4. A confession by the woman involved is never direct evidence but may be admitted as circumstantial evidence.

Quotation: Wera Sub-County Case 114/53: Isuat Odongole v. Abosi Elungat:

Isuat accused Abosi of adultery with Atii. Atii admitted adultery and Abosi's behaviour when Isuat came to his house was suspicious. He was, however, acquitted.

5. The witnesses should declare their presence to the guilty party at the time. Their evidence may not be admitted if they merely watched the occurrence from a hiding place.

6. An immediate report must be made to the local chief.

Quotation: (a) Otuboi Sub-County Case 220/51: V. Elietu v. Echwou:

V. Elietu saw Echwou running away partially clad from the house of V. Elietu's wife, K. Asayo. K. Asayo admitted adultery. A witness also saw Echwou running away. V. Elietu tried to stop Echwou but was thrown to the ground. Echwou denied adultery and claimed that V. Elietu had attacked him. The Court acquitted Echwou 'because V. Elietu did not make an immediate report of adultery to the village chief'. No appeal.

Quotation: (b) D.C. Petition 23/53: D.N.C. 144/52: Abdalla bin Kanyike v. T. Eyenga:

In the Sub-County Court judgement is recorded: 'The case is decided against the plaintiff. The Court has seen that the accused man and woman were not truly caught in adultery because they were not seized and then taken forthwith to the *etem* chief as is the custom.'

Note: It is normal practice to raise an alarm, catch the adulterer, bind him and take him immediately before the village chief.

7. The rules in sections 3–6 above have been necessitated by the tendency to make adultery into a business. Wives are ready to perjure themselves and many instances occur of deliberate frame-ups.

Quotation: (a) Tira Sub-County Case 37/51: B. Olila v. Z. Okacha:

It was eventually proved that B. Olila pushed his wife into Okacha's home at night to secure adultery compensation.

Quotation: (b) *Asuret Sub-County Case 155/51: E. Opio* v. *S. Okode:*

Okode's bicycle broke down and he sheltered at Opio's house. Opio seized the opportunity to fabricate an adultery charge and took Okode before the chief. The wife of Opio gave evidence in support of Opio. By applying rules 3 and 4 and by reason of the explanation of Okode the Court acquitted Okode.

If the attempt to make adultery into a business is discovered the offender may be punished.

Quotation: *Asamuk Sub-County Case 221/53: Court* v. *B. Okopiton:*

B. Okopiton pleaded guilty to an attempt to incriminate an acquaintance and was fined 50s.

8. It is the duty of a man to ascertain that the woman with whom he lives or whom he marries has no living husband and it is no defence to a charge of adultery to claim ignorance of the woman's status, unless it can be proved that all reasonable steps have been taken to find out the woman's true status.

Quotation: (a) *Otuboi Sub-County Case 94/51: K. Engalu* v. *Epechu.*

K. Engalu sued Epechu for adultery with Achilo. Epechu claimed that Achilo was his own wife and her father, Emayu, supported him. Nevertheless the Court convicted him on the evidence of a previous case 212/49 in which it was ruled that she was Engalu's wife. Epechu must have known about this case and should have verified the true position.

Quotation: (b) *Ngora Sub-County Case 276/48: Omunyin s/o Odu* v. *Otalai s/o Akemo:*

Otalai, sued for adultery, claimed he had married the woman Amidiong in 1940, paying seven cattle to one Okurut. There were two children of the union. But Otalai could not produce Okurut, whereas Magogo, the real father of the girl, testified that she was married to Omunyin. The Court convicted Otalai of adultery and also ordered him to return the two children to Omunyin.

9. The word of the woman herself does not constitute a reasonable step.

Quotation: D.C. 38/52: D.N.C. 47/52: T. Enyangu v. *Abdalah:*

The statement of the defendant, Abdalah, reads: 'I met this woman, Nora, at Soroti and asked her whether she had a husband. She told me she had no husband, so I took her to my home.' Abdalah was convicted of adultery.

Note: Normally a man would have to prove that he had approached the woman's family and that they had given him no indication of her married status.

If, however, he lived with a woman of another tribe, such an approach would be impossible and the Court might admit his contention that the mere fact that the woman was living, a stranger without relatives, was sufficient proof that she had no husband.

10. It is sufficient defence to a charge of adultery to prove that the husband knew of the adultery but failed to take action within one year from gaining such knowledge.

In such an instance the husband may not sue for compensation or the return of his wife, but may sue for divorce only, i.e. return of bride-price.

Quotation: (a) Otuboi Sub-County Case 16/50: Idumura v. M. Oleja:

Idumura sued M. Oleja for adultery, but it was proved that Idumura's wife, Apiso, when she left him in 1939 had gone to her parents and stayed with them for over three years after which time she had been given in marriage to M. Oleja. Idumura knew where she was but made no effort to retrieve her. It was ruled that no claim lay for adultery but that Idumura could sue for return of bride-price.

Quotation: (b) Wera Sub-County Case 150/53: E. Egweru v. Adwomu Echoru:

Egweru knew that Adwomu had been living with his wife, Akano, since 1948 but brought no case till 1953. The claim was dismissed 'because Adwomu lived with Akano with the knowledge of Egweru'.

11. It is sufficient defence to a charge of adultery to prove that the husband instigated his wife to commit adultery in order to obtain the customary compensation.

12. It is sufficient defence to a charge of adultery to prove that the husband has left his wife for a long period without making adequate provision for her maintenance; but if adequate provision has been made a charge may be brought at any time by a relative or friend of the husband.

Note: A long period is usually taken to be a year or more.

Quotation: Otuboi Sub-County Case 141/51: K. Emiedu v. Elunga:

K. Emiedu was married to R. Awicho under the Marriage Ordinance. He claimed compensation for adultery from Elunga. It was proved that R. Awicho left her husband in 1937 when he deserted her, and returned to her relatives. No prior effort was made by K. Emiedu to retrieve her or to sue Elunga, though she was living openly with him. Elunga was acquitted.

13. Even if pregnancy results from adultery in the above circumstances, no charge of adultery will lie against the adulterer if the husband made no adequate provision for the wife.

Quotation: Wera Sub-County Case 274/51: Y. Ejumu v. D. Okiror:

Y. Ejumu sued D. Okiror for adultery with P. Amito. It was proved that Y. Ejumu was Amito's first husband but that he deserted his wife for some years. She had accordingly been given in marriage to Okiror and the two children she bore to Okiror were declared by the court to belong to him legally. The adultery charge was dismissed.

14. Drunkenness has been accepted as a partial defence to a charge of adultery but this principle is not generally recognized.

Quotation: (a) Kabulubulu Sub-County Case 172/51: S. Oula v. Olugu:

Olugu was found with Ailo, Oula's wife, at an hour not stated in Ailo's house. Two witnesses found him in the house but clothed. Ailo denied adultery. The Court accepted a plea of drunkenness and dismissed the case.

Quotation: (b) Kabulubulu Sub-County Case 194/51: M. Edimu v. Erinayo Atur:

Ajoe, the wife, admitted adultery and Atur was caught in the house by the husband and four witnesses. Atur's defence was drunkenness and a 'frame-up' by witnesses. The Court acquitted because witnesses were proved to have lied on certain points and because Atur was proved to have been at a beer party just before the incident.

15. (*a*) Any man who hides or abducts or commits adultery with another man's wife must on conviction pay a fine of 100*s*. or serve three months' I.H.L. in default. He must also pay 50*s*. compensation to the wronged husband.

(*b*) The wife who has consented to the hiding, abduction, or adultery must on conviction pay a fine of 20*s*. or serve one month's imprisonment.

> *Note*: The imposition of a fine for this offence is a recent innovation. Adultery was normally compensated by payment of cattle varying as shown in the note under section 1 above. The imposition of a fine led in turn to evasion which section 18 attempts to cover.

16. For a second offence with the same woman the man must pay a fine of 150*s*. or four months' I.H.L., and for a third offence 250*s*. or six months' I.H.L. Compensation on each occasion remains at 50*s*. and the punishment of the wife in all cases remains at 20*s*. fine or one month's I.H.L.

17. (*a*) Any man who enters another man's house with the intention of committing adultery with the wife of the owner; or

(*b*) Any man who escorts or carries on a bicycle or in a vehicle the wife of another man; or

(*c*) Any man who writes love letters to another man's wife, is guilty of an offence and liable on conviction to a fine not exceeding 20s. or to I.H.L. not exceeding one month.

> *Note*: The courts are tending to misapply this law and often convict under 17 (*a*) without any effort to prove intention. Similarly, little or no discretion is shown in charges under 17 (*b*). A lesser punishment than the maximum, although expressly allowed, has rarely been noted. There appears to be no real basis in custom for this law. Courts have gone so far as to convict for merely standing with another man's wife.

Quotation: Asamuk Sub-County Case 139/52: L. Otikon v. Alibet Elilim:

> L. Otikon sued A. Elilim for adultery with his wife, Ana. Ana was at a shop with some other women and A. Elilim. A. Elilim denied adultery and stated that he was drunk at the time. He was convicted of 'standing with Otikon's wife' and fined 10s. and ordered to pay 15s. compensation.

18. Any person who settles an adultery case out of court is guilty of an offence and both parties to the settlement must on conviction be fined 25s.

> *Note*: (*a*) This section is extended to cover witnesses and accessories also.

Quotation: Tira Sub-County Case 54/51: Court v. Y. Etepu and others:

> In this case the two parties, Y. Etepu and A. Eyobu, were fined 25s. for settling an adultery case out of court and three other accused persons were fined 10s. each for being accessories.

> *Note*: (*b*) When the party to the case or an accessory happens to be a chief the penalty is often enhanced though the Council law makes no express provision for such increased penalty.

Quotation: (a) Mukongoro Sub-County Case 18/52: Court v. N. Otingiro and Odeke:

> N. Otingiro, a parish chief, caught Odeke committing adultery with Otingiro's wife. He forced Odeke to pay compensation of 200s. and a he-goat by beating him. Otingiro pleaded guilty. The Court ordered him to return the 200s. and he-goat to Odeke and fined him 100s. Odeke was acquitted. No appeal.

Quotation: (b) Mukongoro Sub-County Case 14/52: Court v. G. Ogunia and others:

> P. Kateu, a village chief, knew that G. Ogunia settled an adultery case out of court. He was fined 50s. 'because he was a village chief and allowed the others to pay for adultery out of court'. G. Ogunia was fined the usual 25s.

> *Note*: (*c*) When the accessory is a clan leader the sentence is also enhanced:

Quotation: Achwa Sub-County Case 78/52: Court v. Aboele Kunguru, Amisi Enginyu, Adesederio Oluka:

The first two defendants pleaded guilty and were fined 25*s*. each. Adesederio Oluka, who did not plead guilty, was convicted and fined 50*s*. 'because he is a clan head'.

19. If a man takes the wife of another man to another district and there commits adultery with her, he will on conviction be sentenced as in section 15 and in addition to any such sentence will receive three months' I.H.L.

Note: This section refers exactly to the administrative boundaries of Teso; thus a man can take a woman nine miles from Kachumbala to Mbale and be convicted under this section; but when Katine Sub-County Court (216/49) convicted under this section for taking a woman from Serere to Soroti county, the County Court of Soroti revised the case and quashed the conviction and sentence.

20. Any person who allows another man's wife to hide in his or her house, or who knowingly allows a married woman to commit adultery in his or her house, is guilty of an offence and shall, on conviction, be fined 15*s*. and must pay the husband of the married woman 10*s*. compensation.

Note: This section is extended to include any parties who connive at adultery.

Quotation: Kaberamaido Sub-County Case 149/51: Court v. *Elayu, Ochen and Edebu:*

Elayu and Ochen were convicted on their plea of allowing adultery to take place in their house. Edebu was also convicted on his own plea of warning Egobu, the adulterer, that the wronged husband was coming. Egobu thus made his escape. All were fined 15*s*. and ordered to pay 10*s*. compensation to the wronged husband.

2. *Fornication with unmarried women*

21. A man who has sexual intercourse with an unmarried girl from which pregnancy does not result is liable on conviction to a fine of 25*s*. and to pay 25*s*. to the father or legal guardian of the girl.

Note: No case has come to my notice in which the charge has been proved against the denial of the man. Although many men deny the charge at first they finally confess. There appears to be a strong superstition about lying in such cases.

22. If the man who offends under section 21 above is of a tribe other than the Teso tribe and the unmarried girl is an Atesot he is liable on conviction to a fine of 50*s*. and to pay 50*s*. to the father or legal guardian of the girl.

Note: There are no examples of this discriminatory Council law ever having been enforced.

23. The age of the girl in such cases is entirely immaterial.

Quotation: D.N.C. 61/50: K. Engoru v. *Etengu Erusu:*

This case was transferred by an administrative officer from the sub-county court to the D.N.C. because in his opinion the facts of the case warranted a heavier punishment than the sub-county or county court could award. Etengu had had carnal knowledge of a girl of eight years against her will and had infected her with venereal disease. Nevertheless, the D.N.C. awarded compensation of only 100s. and sentenced Etengu to only three months' I.H.L.

24. The consent or otherwise of the girl in such cases is entirely immaterial.

Note: Cases are sometimes revised by administrative officers on this point and some courts have begun to take this point into consideration of their own accord. But only a few.

Quotation: Kateta Sub-County Case 50/51: Mwanika w/o Osilon v. Adesederio Asiga and Etonu Ajokan:

Both defendants had sexual intercourse with Mwanika, a married woman, against her will. They were both fined 100s. and imprisoned for six months and ordered to pay 100s. compensation.

25. A man who has sexual intercourse with an unmarried girl from which pregnancy results must on conviction pay a fine of 20s. and 50s. compensation to the father or legal guardian of the girl.

Note: Only one case has been seen which had to be proved against the denial of the man. The girl is called upon to name the man who made her pregnant. Even if she is a wanton she will name only one man because she will wish to be married to him, and he will not deny the charge because he may wish to establish ownership of the child (see section 27).

Quotation: Katine Sub-County Case 157/53: E. Emitu v. Okello s/o Inuwa:

Okello denied fornication but it was proved that two girls and a married woman were caught in a rain storm. One girl spent the night in Okello's own house whereas the others slept together in a separate house. He was convicted on this evidence.

26. If the man who offends under section 25 above is of a tribe other than the Teso tribe and the unmarried girl is an Atesot he must on conviction pay a fine of 50s. and pay 50s. to the father or legal guardian of the girl.

Note: This section, like section 22, is a dead letter.

27. When the illegitimate child is born it becomes the property of its father if the fine and compensation have been paid. Otherwise it remains the property of the girl's family, though at any time later the real father can pay the fine and compensation and claim the child regardless of how long the child has remained with its mother's family.

Note: This is the modern view. Formerly the child always remained in the mother's clan even if the mother subsequently married the child's father. Many courts still uphold the former system.

Quotation: Otuboi Sub-County Case 50/51: Kaberamaido County Case 33/51: G. Eduru v. Eitu (quoted above):

Eduru sued Eitu for return of bride-price on divorce and for custody of his wife's child. Eitu admitted liability to pay bride-price but proved that the child was conceived before Eduru had paid bride-price; the woman was, in fact, pregnant at marriage and the child therefore illegitimate. Both courts awarded custody of the child to Eitu.

28. If the illegitimate child is reclaimed after a long time it is necessary to pay the father of the girl a sum for maintenance, usually 50s.

Quotation: Otuboi Sub-County Case 32/50: N. Epiru v. E. Esadu:

N. Epiru claimed and was awarded his illegitimate daughter, Atim, who had been in the custody of E. Esadu for eleven years or more; but he had to pay 50s. for past maintenance of the child.

Note: There is considerable doubt as to whether the 50s. awarded in such cases really represents assistance towards maintenance of the child or whether it is merely a late payment of the compensation payable under section 25 in order to secure legal ownership of the child. As stated in the note in section 27, the law is in evident process of change in this very important matter.

29. Even if the father of the illegitimate child has died, his heir can claim the child.

Quotation: Kabulubulu Sub-County Case 30/50: L. Wegulu v. Kiboko Swaga:

L. Wegulu claimed 260s. and three goats bride-price alleged to have been paid by Wegulu's brother, Yozefu Babale, to Kiboko for his daughter, Mwagale. He also claimed two female children. Y. Babale had died in 1937. One of the children was old enough to be classed a prostitute.

The Court held that Y. Babale was never married to Mwagale and that no bride-price should be repaid but that the two children must nevertheless be returned to Wegulu.

30. Even if the fine and compensation have been paid the father may not take away his child until it has been weaned. (This is usually when it is about two years old.)

Quotation: Kateta Sub-County Case 16/52: M. Champera v. P. Kaapa:

The Court awarded the illegitimate child for which M. Champera sued to him 'when it is weaned' (*konye do acamakin nes ailaka ikekoku arai kepolori . . .*).

31. Should the man who has offended under sections 21 or 25 agree to marry the girl, no penalty ensues. (See quotation under section 27 above.)

32. Should the illegitimate child be born dead, no claim will lie for return of fine or compensation paid under sections 25 or 26.

33. Should the girl die in childbirth, the man who made her pregnant is liable to pay blood-money of five head of cattle immediately.

34. This claim for blood-money may be enforced against the relatives of the man who made the girl pregnant if he himself is too poor to pay, or if he dies or absconds before payment.

CHAPTER IV

INHERITANCE

1. *General*

1. INHERITANCE is patrilineal.

2. Women can never inherit though they can act as co-guardians and receive and give property in that office.

> *Quotation:* (*a*) *D.N.C. 138/51: D.C. Appeal 30/51: A. Adusa* v. *B. Osekeny:*
>
> A. Adusa was sued by B. Osekeny for return of bride-price on divorce. The record shows that A. Adusa was the heir of deceased Opiri, whose daughter, Ilakut, was married to B. Osekeny's brother. Bride-price had been paid to Ilekata, mother of A. Adusa, as guardian. Adusa was at the time a minor.

> *Quotation:* (*b*) *D.N.C. 142/51: D.C. Appeal 29/51: Ojilong Isirete* v. *T. Ongwalu:*
>
> This was a land dispute. The original owner, Ongenge, a relative of Ojilong's, died and left his wife, Amuron, on the land. She in turn gave a portion to Ongwalu. This gift was recognized as valid.

3. Women can also sue for debts to an estate.

> *Quotation: Kaberamaido County Court 210/50: Alemo w/o Ocheny* v. *Esaru:*
>
> Alemo sued successfully for a debt of nine head of cattle owed to her deceased husband. Ocheny had sons living.

4. Property of deceased persons is divided by the head of the deceased's extended family, helped by the heir as defined in sections 7–14 below and clan leaders of the locality.

5. The heir inherits all property, though by custom some cattle are allowed to other relatives; the heir is responsible for all debts on the estate.

6. The heir must normally be a member of the deceased's extended family (*ekek*).

> *Quotation: Kamuda Sub-County Court 155/53: Onyige* v. *I. Oniyo:*
>
> Onyige sued his cousin Oniyo for nineteen head of cattle alleged to have been awarded to him in the division of the estate at Elogu's

death. The evidence was conflicting, some witnesses including one clan leader alleging that Onyige was awarded the cattle and others including a clan leader alleging that Oniyo was awarded the cattle. The Court dismissed the claim because it was clearly proved that 'Onyige was not of that clan; he was born in another clan' and had followed his mother when she married Oniyo's father.

2. *Sequence of heirs*

7. The sequence of heirs normally follows the rules in sections 8–14 below but the extended family head and clan leaders have discretion to depart from this sequence if the heir is unsuitable by reason of insanity or known profligate habits. See section 35 below.

8. A man's heir is his eldest son; it is immaterial if the eldest son is the child of the first, second, or any other wife.

9. If a man dies without sons or if the sons predecease him, whether or not they leave issue, his heir is his eldest brother or half-brother.

10. If a man dies leaving no sons or brothers or half-brothers, his heir is his father.

11. If a man dies leaving neither sons, brothers, half-brothers, nor father, his father's brother's eldest son is his heir.

12. The subsequent sequence of heirs is:

(*a*) eldest son of eldest son;
(*b*) eldest son of eldest brother;
(*c*) eldest son of father's sister;
(*d*) eldest son of sister.

Note: It is of course extremely unlikely that an heir could not be found from the relatives listed in sections 8–11. It is very rare for any of the relations listed in this section to inherit.

13. The heir of an unmarried girl is her father; if her father is dead, her eldest brother or half-brother; if she has no father or brothers, her father's brother or his sons.

14. The heir of a childless married woman is her husband or if he is dead his heir as defined in sections 8–12 above. But the son of a married woman can inherit her property.

3. *Division of property*

15. The division of property takes place at the last day of mourning (*asuban*).

16. At the beginning of mourning (*aipuduno*) there is a gathering of all relatives of the deceased and of his neighbours at which debts on the estate are declared. This gathering is presided over by the head of the deceased's extended family and is held at the deceased's home.

17. The heir inherits all wives. Notwithstanding this, older wives are usually inherited by their deceased husband's brothers and only the younger wives are inherited by the eldest son. A widow can, if she wishes, remain in the family of her deceased husband without being inherited by an heir.

18. A widow has, however, absolute discretion to return to her parents, in which case bride-price is repayable to the heir of her deceased husband.

19. The status of an inherited wife does not differ from that of any other wife, nor is her status affected by the fact that she has or has not produced children.

> *Note*: But there are many superstitions regarding wives of deceased husbands. One who has had several husbands all of whom have died is naturally shunned. A woman with hair on her chin is greatly feared. It is believed that if she shaves her chin her new husband will die.

20. If the deceased's wives stay within the extended family (*ekek*) their children stay with them.

21. If the deceased's wives return to their parents, their children belong to the heir and may be taken by him when old enough.

22. For inheritance of children see Chapter I, sections 41–44.

Claims are not frequent and are confined mainly to claims for female children.

> *Quotation: D.C. 1/52: D.N.C. 172/51: Y. Semambo v. Kadhala:*
>
> Semambo sued Kadhala for custody of a girl, the daughter of Ibulaim, deceased. He could not prove that he was Ibulaim's heir, whereas Ramadhani, Kadhala's brother, was undoubtedly Ibulaim's foster father and, in the absence of sons or brothers, his heir. Semambo's claim was rejected by the D.C. and all three lower courts. The D.N.C. judgement states '. . . if Semambo had been a brother of the deceased he would have started suing for his brother's effects immediately after the burial ceremony . . .'.

23. Stock is the sole property of the heir, who is responsible for payment of the sons' or younger brothers' first bride-price from it. It is, however, usual to make allocations to younger brothers at the time of the division of estate (see section 5 above).

24. Crops in the field or store are taken by the wives, who cultivated the fields or who filled the stores, when they go to their new husbands. But if the wife returns to her parents, the food or crops will remain with the heir.

25. Other property, including money which is not the personal property of one of the wives of the deceased, belongs to the heir.

26. Land and houses are the sole property of the heir. But a widow (*apuserut*) has the right to stay in her house and to use the land which she used in her husband's lifetime if she is not taken by the heir and does not return to her parents.

4. *Claims and debts on estates*

27. Claims and debts are called for at the meeting for division of an estate (*aipuduno*) (sections 15 and 16 above) and are acknowledged or denied at the same meeting.

28. There is normally no time limit for collection of assets due or for payment of debts provided that claims are registered at the clan meeting. But if not registered the debts can be barred.

Quotation: (a) D.N.C. Appeal 118/51: D.C.'s Appeal 19/51: Y. Elelu v. *Singoma s/o Nsiyaleta:*

Y. Elelu claimed that his deceased father left four cattle with Nsiyaleta in 1937. He claimed these four head with their progeny. The D.N.C. rejected the whole claim because Elelu did not register it against the estate of the deceased, Nsiyaleta, when he died in 1945. Elelu was living in the same sub-county as Singoma and must have known of the division of the estate. The D.C. upheld this ruling.

Quotation: (b) Kumi County Court 17/50: Ongino Sub-County Court 55/50: C. Ibwala v. *C. Odaka:*

C. Ibwala sued for a debt of three cattle from the estate of C. Odaka's deceased father, Opolot. The following appears in evidence:
'Question by Court: When Opolot died were you present?
C. Ibwala: Yes.
Question by Court: When the funeral celebrations were being held did you mention the matter to the clan relatives?
C. Ibwala: No.
Question by Court: When people die leaving debts or cattle which have been entrusted to them, is it not usual to report such debts to the clan relatives? . . .'
The Court rejected Ibwala's claim because, when Opolot died, Ibwala made no mention of the three head of cattle.

29. Claims and debts admitted at the clan meeting are inherited and can be sued for; other debts and claims are not normally admitted (see quotation in section 28 above).

30. But debts of bride-price or blood-money are always inherited whether or not claims are made at the meeting.

Nevertheless, it would be normal, if a divorce had already taken place, to register the claim for return of bride-price at the clan meeting.

31. Debts against the estate take priority over other claims.

32. If the debt is admitted, creditors against the estate are paid as they arrive and it is not normal to wait until all claims are presented before paying one.

5. *Wills*

33. The custom of making wills is not general in Teso.

34. Verbal wills must be made before the heir and clan leaders as witnesses and would probably only be admitted if the terms conformed to customary procedure.

35. There are recognized grounds for disinheritance:

(*a*) If the heir offers violence to the testator or refuses all social contacts with the testator or commits adultery with the testator's wives.

(*b*) If the heir is guilty of witchcraft.

(*c*) If the heir is a known wastrel or by habitually committing adultery wastes property.

(*d*) If the heir is illegitimate (i.e. although the son of the deceased he was borne by a woman not married to the deceased and therefore belongs to the extended family (*ekek*) of his mother and not to the *ekek* of his father).

36. Whatever the contents of the will, debts against an estate must always be paid before wishes or legacies are met (as in section 31 above).

37. Written wills, though they exist, have not yet been widely tested and upheld in the courts. No clear rules exist regarding the witnessing or the form of written wills. It is given as the opinion of assessors that written wills would not be accepted if they departed in material matters from customary procedure.

Quotation: D.C. Appeal 14/51: D.N.C. Appeal 34/51: Ekeru s/o Egulu v. *E. Esingu:*

Ekeru's father on his deathbed made a will which included reference to a debt of thirty head of cattle owing from Esingu. The will was recorded by one, P. Emwochu. There were no other witnesses. It was stated by Ekeru that Esingu admitted the debt at the clan meeting but there was no evidence on this point. The evidence of the will was rejected by the Court.

Note: This example is quoted merely to show that oral evidence would probably be accepted in preference to a written testament. I have not seen any case in which disposition by written will has been disputed.

6. *Guardianship*

38. Guardians are appointed if the heir to an estate is a minor or if the heir is absent.

39. In the case of minor heirs, the mother of the minor heir may be appointed co-guardian with a paternal relative of the heir. The co-guardian is usually a brother or cousin of the deceased.

40. A woman can never be sole guardian.

41. Guardians are appointed by the deceased's extended family head in consultation with the clan leaders of the locality and can be deprived of office by the same authority if they neglect their duties.

Quotation: Bukedea County Court 22/53: D.N.C. 92/53: Asenyi s/o Owojatau v. A. Parok:

Extract from D.N.C. judgement: '. . . Had the property been handed to A. Parok as guardian, the clan leaders should now be here to testify to the fact as is the Teso custom . . .'.

42. A guardian can be held responsible for the property of his wards, who can ask for an account of their property when they come of age.

Quotation: Bukedea County Court 22/53: Asenyi s/o Owojatau v. A. Parok:

Asenyi sued A. Parok for 25 cattle, 20 goats, 200s., 5 granaries of groundnuts, 2 granaries of millet, 2 wives, 4 girls, 1 plough, 2 yokes, 2 chains, 3 chairs, 4 wooden boards, 12 plates, 6 cooking pots, and 2 drums which A. Parok had received as guardian on behalf of Asenyi. A. Parok, however, satisfied the Court that he had not received all the property and what property he had received he had accounted for satisfactorily.

43. A guardian cannot claim compensation for services rendered as a guardian.

CHAPTER V

CONTRACT

1. *Contract for specific performances*

Cattle herding

1. THIS is the commonest form of contract in Teso.

2. Contracts may be written or verbal and need not necessarily specify the remuneration to the herdsman or the period of the contract.

3. All contracts for herding of cattle must be witnessed by at least two witnesses. No witness fee is chargeable.

> *Note*: This rule is not always followed, particularly when the contract is written. Courts are inclined to accept written contracts without any direct proof of validity.

> *Quotation: D.C. 14/54: D.N.C. 36/54: P. Mulagangabo v. Ewangu:*
>
> Mulagangabo herded thirty-seven head of cattle for nine years for Ewangu's brother, who died. He was awarded one bull in the clan court for this service but claimed a further three head. The Sub-County Court of Kyere rejected this claim. On appeal in the County Court Mulagangabo produced a written contract unwitnessed. He could produce no proof of validity. The County Court of Serere rejected the document because it was spelt Luganda fashion with *l* interchanged with *r*. The D.N.C. accepted the document but the D.C. on revision upheld the findings of the County Court on the grounds that the document unless admitted must be witnessed, preferably by at least two witnesses.

4. Unless there is specific provision to the contrary all contracts are assumed to give the herdsman the right to dispose of all milk.

5. Unless there is specific provision to the contrary all offspring of the stock belong to the owner.

> *Note*: It is not unusual for the owner to claim and to be awarded what should be the natural increase of a herd without proving that such increase occurred.

6. The herdsman is not responsible for any loss or damage to the herd, unless he directly caused it, provided that he takes all possible steps to inform the owner of any illness or loss without delay.

7. The herdsman is responsible for any damage done by the herd to crops or other property or for any contravention of grazing or quarantine rules. He is responsible also for building any necessary calf houses or kraals.

8. In disputes regarding remuneration, when no remuneration is specifically fixed in advance, courts assess the amount to be paid. Customs in this matter vary throughout the district.

> Note: In the past the cattle owners of any one area herded their cattle communally and each owner in the area had to take his turn as herdsman. There was, of course, no question of remuneration. This custom is no longer followed. Because holdings became more scattered or because owners were unwilling to undertake communal herding duties, it became customary to ask close friends or relations to herd stock. It was recognized practice to give this friend or relation a present such as a cow or calf as a token of gratitude, but no fixed remuneration was recognized. Nowadays cattle herding is a business almost exclusively in the hands of Bahima, and monetary rewards are becoming common.

> Quotation: (a) Gweri Sub-County 305/49: Kasungu s/o Sikirabanga (Muhima) v. Akuan s/o Eyapu:

> Kasungu agreed to herd Akuan's cattle for a specific period of four years in return for one head of cattle. The contract was written. Owing to sickness Kasungu resigned after four months. The Court fixed remuneration at 40s. for that period. Kasungu took milk for his own use 'because it was not recorded in the agreement' (see section 4 above).

> Quotation: (b) Kabulubulu Sub-County 187/51: B. Odungu v. Ekoyu:

> Odungu claimed 408s. for herding thirty-one head of cattle for one year and ten months, alleging the agreement was for two head of cattle a year. The agreement was not proved. Ekoyu had paid 28s. for Odungu's taxes in 1950 and had offered 30s. for 1951. The Court ruled that this offer was equitable.

> Quotation: (c) Kabulubulu Sub-County 25/50: Achela v. Mwanya Mugesera:

> Achela was given one cow to herd by Mwanya which produced five calves in the six years he herded it. The contract was for an unspecific amount. He was awarded 20s.

Other examples show 3s. per animal per year (Kyere); one cow for herding fifty head for a year, and one cow for herding fifteen head for a year (Kateta 76/51 and 78/51); 20s. a month (Amuria).

House-building

9. Contracts may be verbal or written.

> Note: Sections 9–12 refer to permanent or semi-permanent buildings only,

and the law is still vague on the subject as such houses have only begun to be erected in very modern times.

10. Contracts must always be witnessed by at least two witnesses. No witness fee is payable.

11. A time limit for completion of the work is seldom, if ever, specified in the contract and penalty clauses are unknown.

12. If a contractor fails to complete the work he must repay any money paid, keeping such amount as is adequate for work already done. If he has not been paid, a contractor may claim any reasonable sum for work already done in an uncompleted contract. The court has complete discretion to award any amount which is appropriate.

> *Quotation: D.C. 11/51: D.N.C. 4/51: Y. Kigwekyalwazi v. D. Eku-mekwap:*
>
> This was a claim for payment of 150s. or some lesser amount for bricks made according to a verbal agreement. The contract was never completed. The evidence showed that Kigwekyalwazi had only spent about three days on making the bricks and that their quality was poor. The claim was entirely dismissed.

13. Contracts for temporary houses are not made as in sections 9–12 above. On a given day neighbours are invited to assist by promise of beer or a small reward such as a meal of chicken.

It is unknown for a man to contract with one particular person for construction of a temporary house.

Medical treatment

14. Fees, varying from a few shillings to a goat and depending on the gravity of the illness, are always fixed in advance.

> *Note*: But fees may be much higher. Augusta Edwara of Orungo had a long illness which was not cured in Soroti hospital but was eventually cured by an *emuron* in Kabulubulu in Kaberamaido county. Payment of two head of cattle was made for this cure.

15. They are not, however, paid to the doctor (*emuron*) until a cure has been obtained. It is the mark of a bad doctor to ask for payment in advance.

But a patient usually makes a small gift in advance such as a small sum of money in return for the *emuron*'s efforts to find the right medicines, or a chicken to bless the medicine (*akokor aipukio ekia*).

16. If the patient does not recover, the doctor has no claim to the fee.

17. If the patient grows worse or dies, no compensation can be claimed from the doctor but any fees paid can be recovered.

> *Quotation: Amuria County 45/50: Kuju Sub-County 63/50: Abdi bin Oritai v. Sebastian Kayonjo:*
>
> Sebastian Kayonjo treated Abdi's child. He was paid two sheep, eight chickens, and 24s. before the child was cured. Unluckily the child died. Abdi therefore sued for return of this property and was awarded two sheep, eight chickens, and 22s. This judgement was upheld on appeal to the county court.

18. The patient is, however, at liberty to change his doctor provided he first informs him, and no claim will then lie by the doctor for payment of the fee.

Labour contracts

19. There are no regular private employers of labour gangs. Large land-owners employ labour for specific tasks such as weeding or harvesting.

20. Payment in such cases is usually by beer as in section 13 above, though monetary payment is becoming more common.

21. It is not unusual for a man to be employed in a particular homestead in return for food and tax obligations.

> *Quotation: Asamuk Sub-County 32/52: Court v. Echilu s/o Omorio:*
>
> Echilu was accused of keeping Reuben Okello in his house for three years without making his presence known to the chiefs. He was convicted and ordered to pay R. Okello's tax obligations for three years, 84s., and to pay a fine of 25s.
>
> *Note*: This was a criminal prosecution for the offence of hiding a potential taxpayer and is only quoted in this section because the Court held the view that the employer should meet the tax obligations of his employee.

22. A form of apprenticeship exists in the *asapan* initiation ceremonies during which an initiate serves in the house of his instructor, performing many menial tasks without remuneration until such time as he passes out at the initiation ceremonies (see p. 77).

> *Note*: Apprenticeship to a tradesman is almost unknown. Eria Mambule, a Muganda of Ngora, a carpenter, used to take pupils to work for him in return for their food until they became competent at the trade; he then paid them.

2. Sales

Sale of cattle

23. At least two witnesses are necessary for each transaction.

This rule does not, of course, apply to sales in cattle markets because such sales are recorded and permits issued for the movement of stock.

24. No witness fee is payable.

25. Payment can be by instalments if so agreed.

26. The animal in such cases remains the property of its old owner until such time as the final instalment is paid but it may be taken by the new owner at any time agreed upon between the parties.

27. The new owner can use all milk as soon as the cow is taken to his house even though he has not paid the final instalment.

28. If the beast dies in the new owner's hands, he must immediately pay any instalments still owing to the old owner.

29. Until the final instalment is paid the old owner has the right to take back the beast and to repay any instalments paid.

Sale of land, houses, and crops

30. See Chapter VI, Real Property.

Sale of other property

31. No witnesses are necessary to such transactions.

32. Ownership, when payment by instalments is agreed upon, is according to the rules in sections 25–29 above.

3. Pledges

Pledge of land

33. For pledge of land, crops and houses (mortgage) see Chapter VI, Real Property.

Pledge of female children

34. A female child may be pledged by her father or legal guardian as security for a debt or loan.

35. At least two witnesses are necessary. No witness fee is chargeable.

36. The girl visits the creditor's house from time to time as a token of the pledge but does not live there.

37. All marriage negotiations are conducted by the debtor (her father), and not by the creditor. (The loan or debt is usually repaid from the bride-price received.)

38. If the creditor has sexual intercourse with the girl he is liable to pay the usual compensation or to marry her, in which case the debt is set off against the bride-price payable.

Pledge of cattle

39. At least two witnesses are necessary. No fee is chargeable.

40. The beast is kept by the creditor.

41. Milk is the property of the creditor.

42. Calves are property of the debtor though they will be kept by the creditor until the pledge is redeemed.

43. If the cow dies while in possession of the creditor from causes which cannot be attributed to neglect by the creditor, the debtor has no claim against the creditor and must furnish a further pledge. If, however, death is due to the negligence of the creditor, the value of the cow may be set off against the debt owed by the debtor.

4. Loans

44. Loans must be witnessed. No witness fee is payable. Normally two witnesses are necessary but courts can accept one witness if other evidence is available.

Quotation: (a) D.C. Civil Appeal 16/51: D.N.C. 111/51: Ngora County 8/51: W. Opio v. E. Ekodeu:

W. Opio claimed a debt of 1,027s. and a bicycle from Ekodeu. The alleged loan had been made in eight instalments on eight separate occasions. Some of these instalments were not witnessed at all. Others amounting to 765s. were witnessed by only one witness at each transaction. The lower courts dismissed the claim on the grounds that Opio, being a business man, should have made a proper witnessed agreement or kept proper books. This decision was upheld by the D.C.

Quotation: (b) D.C. Rev. 6/52: D.N.C. 122/51: Serere County 112/51: Bugondo Sub-County 60/51: M. Ogabe v. K. Okiror:

Okiror sued Ogabe for repayment of a debt of 300s. The loan was witnessed by one man only. The evidence showed that other members of the same party agreed to buy bicycles together at Jinja. There was therefore a likely reason for the loan and Ogabe did apparently buy a bicycle. All courts ruled that the debt was valid and must be repaid.

45. Contracts may be written or verbal.

46. Unless specifically stated in the contract, interest is never charged.

47. Repayment of a loan in whole or in part must be witnessed.

Note: It is normal practice for the witness actually to take the money into his own hands from the debtor and hand it to the creditor.

48. There is no time limit for claiming repayment of a loan.

49. Debts are inheritable provided they are registered at the meeting held to dispose of the estate of a deceased person (Chapter IV, Inheritance, section 16).

CHAPTER VI

REAL PROPERTY

1. *Introduction*

1. '... *emameete akiro arai ikisila luikamunitos nukalupo kotoma Teso; bobo da etakani ebe kotoma obuku Ngora ikidioko alupo noi; ido itunga ipu; bobo da mam alup iyatasi, itunga kes iyatasi.* ...'

(There are no arrangements or laws concerning land in Teso; moreover it is clear that in Ngora county land is very scarce whereas people are many; and land does not increase whereas people do. ...)

(Extract from a judgement by the Chief Judge in D.N.C. 18/52 (D.C. 25/52), *S. Ecaat* v. *E. Iisa.*)

2. *Preliminary note:* A short account of the early economy of the Iteso before and during the migrations and of the impact caused by the introduction of cotton and ploughs is given in Part I. Details of agricultural and animal husbandry practice are contained in Part IV (pp. 135–47).

Teso District lies in what is scientifically known as a short grass/woodland area, although heights attained by these short grasses, mainly Hypparhenia species, are often in excess of nine feet. Long, low, gently undulating rises permeated by a vast network of swamps and rivers with rocky granitic outcrops, especially in the southern part, characterise the topography of the district. The soils vary from hard ironstone outcrops, usually on top of the slopes working down the slope through murram and easily erodable sandy mixtures, to the swampy black cotton soils which often overlay clays and swamp sands. Imperata cylindrica and Echinochloa pyramidalis along with papyrus are the most common swamp edge grasses. The general altitude is about 3,500 feet and the rocky outcrops referred to above stand anything from 100 to 600 feet above the surrounding country.

Rainfall averages 52 inches a year throughout the district and is characterised by a well defined dry season from October or November until March or April and a not so well defined dry season usually occurring in June and July.[1]

Customary land tenure is being subjected to many modern strains, among which may be noted the increase in houses made of costly and permanent materials; the advent of mechanical means of cultivation, involving the opening up by one individual of larger areas; the presence in certain areas of immigrant Bantu tribes who plant bananas, a permanent crop; and the modern tendency to mark graves with permanent monuments. (It was recorded in a land tenure survey by C. M. A. Gayer in 1939 that with constant rebuilding of huts and shifting cultivation the site of graves

---

[1] Uganda Protectorate, 1953.

is soon forgotten and that the question of burial places has little or no influence on land tenure. This is no longer true and title is often claimed on
the presence of ancestral graves.) The Agricultural Department has lately
encouraged the laying out of mixed farms in blocks, which will enable
tractors to be used on arable blocks and livestock to be grazed on resting
blocks; the blocks are often fenced with sisal to keep cattle in or out as the
case may be. Fencing with wire has not yet started but there are already
signs of a tendency to allow prominent persons to acquire more land than
they need for cultivation and, with increasing population, it is possible that
such land will be denied to others. Factors such as these coupled with an
uneven distribution of population, which has resulted in densities of about
200 to the square mile in south Teso compared with an average of only
about 50 in Usuku and Amuria, have caused substantial variations in
customary law of tenure throughout the district. Customary law itself
sometimes comes into conflict with Uganda statutory land law, more
particularly in matters of compensation on eviction for public purposes.

3. *Basis of land rights*: The process of settlement and land allocation has
been described in Part II (p. 69). Movement to new lands was by a
group of settlers of one or two age-sets. Within this group there would be
members of several different clans. In the new area settled by a group each
new settler claimed for himself and his family a piece of land, far in excess
of his own immediate needs, as his sphere of influence. As time passed his
family increased and adult sons and, later, grandsons were allotted land by
him within his original sphere of influence. From being a family head, he
became an extended family head, and land allocation is still on an extended
family basis. Each extended family has a recognized area of land within
which the extended family head after consultation may find land for members of his own group, or for group relatives by marriage or even for
strangers to the group.

In a sample area in Asuret taken for a survey in 1951[1] there were five
primary divisions of land controlled originally by the five extended families
who first settled there. Of these five different extended families, two belonged to the Ikarebwok clan, two to the Atekok clan, and one to the Ilalei.
From about forty years ago up to twenty-five years ago, nine newcomers
were allowed to settle and to use land allocated by one of the original
families. The families of these nine newcomers have now ramified and each
now has control over its division of land in which individual allocations are
made. Eight further families have come in in recent times. The difference
in seniority between these three groups of families is most marked.

Each extended family has its elected head responsible for land allocations
within its own particular area. S. Ejoku, who is head of the largest extended
family, which is one of the original families, is recognized as head of his
peers. He is the Land Authority (see section 4), who is consulted before

[1] J. Dean (personal communication).

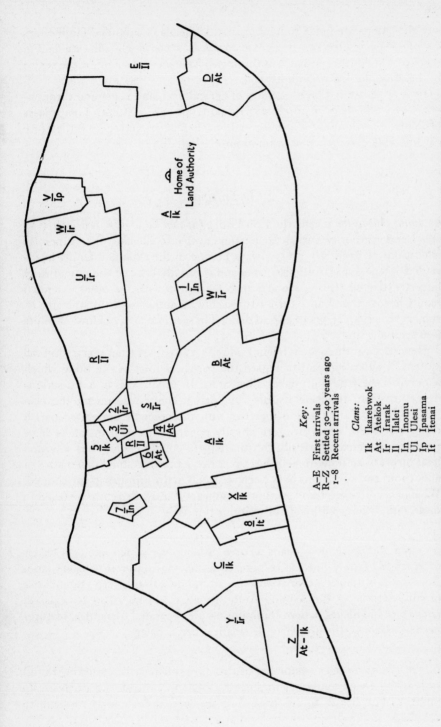

Diagram, not to scale, of a typical Land Authority area in Asuret comprising 3·7 square miles. (*From a map compiled by J. Dean.*)

any allocations are made to newcomers. All heads of extended families are called *apolok ka atekerin*. It is these *apolok ka atekerin* who allocate land in their area under the guidance of the *apolon ka ateker* chosen to be the senior in the area, the Land Authority.

In brief, extended family tenure of agricultural land is general throughout Teso. But ideas of purely individual tenure are existent. The process of change is at different stages throughout the district and there is therefore considerable divergence of opinion on the law.

2. *Definitions*

4. *Land Authority* means the clan leader (*apolon ka ateker*) recognized in any Land Authority area as the person entitled to allocate, or to supervise allocations of, land. He must always be one of the extended family heads settled in the Land Authority area and is usually head of the numerically largest extended family. He acts in consultation with the other extended family heads in the Land Authority area but his authority within the area is, subject to certain rights of appeal defined in sections 31–33 below, absolute (see section 3 above).

Nevertheless, there is a tendency nowadays to depart from this traditional system of allocation and to regard the parish council as the body which supervises the land and makes allocations. In origin, this is not a serious departure from tradition because by 'parish council' is meant the clan leaders of the parish acting together with the officially appointed parish chief. But wider departures are already apparent. Several instances have occurred in which a formally constituted sub-county council has allocated land direct to an individual or has overruled a parish council in a matter of allocation; such decisions have been recorded in the minutes of the council. Whenever the term 'Land Authority' appears it must therefore be taken to mean either the traditional authority or the parish council.

5. *Land Authority area* means an area of land over which one clan leader or extended family head is recognized as having power to allocate land. Boundaries of Land Authority areas usually follow administrative boundaries of villages (*ironya*), but a Land Authority area may be as big as a parish (*eitela*), or in villages, where communities are separated by natural features such as swamps, the area may be smaller than a village.

6. *Ownership* means a customary usufructory title nearly amounting to full ownership. In particular, it implies the right to cultivate, to excavate, to build, to bury dead, to cut trees (but see section 63 below), to lend, to subdivide, and to bequeath the land or any part of it. It does not imply the right to sell or rent the land.

7. *Newcomer* (*abwotunan*) is a person seeking to acquire title to land outside his own extended family land area.

8. *User* is a person who, after being an *abwotunan*, has been allowed to use land nominally in the ownership of another person or family.

9. *User rights* are the rights of a user. During the period of use, which may be for many years, these rights are almost identical with those of an owner. But a user may not bequeath land or bring in outsiders and will forfeit his rights if he leaves the land.

> *Note*: This term is coined to differentiate between the different status of families in one area. Thus in the area referred to in section 3 above the five original families are and always have been the 'owners'. The next nine families were originally 'newcomers', then they became 'users'. By now they may be termed 'owners'. The eight other families were 'newcomers' in recent times and may only now be considered as 'users'. They are not 'owners'. It is unfortunate that the term 'user' has in English acquired a special legal significance when used in relation to land. The term 'squatter', which I originally chose, has too many inappropriate associations.

10. *Unallocated land* means land which is not owned or used, i.e. unclaimed bush land. *Surplus land* means land which is considered owned but is not cultivated.

3. *Rights in land*

Ownership by inheritance or gift

11. Ownership may be acquired over land:
- (*a*) by inheritance,
- (*b*) by gift within the extended family,
- (*c*) by breaking new ground in unallocated or surplus land.

12. All land is inherited by the eldest son or next senior heir if there is no son (see Chapter IV, Inheritance, section 26).

13. The heir is responsible for subdivision of the estate as far as is practicable among his brothers.

14. No limit is imposed on subdivision but the heir always keeps a sufficient amount for his own needs and if there is no land left over for his brothers they must seek land elsewhere.

15. A father may subdivide his land in his lifetime among his sons provided that the heir is given enough for his use.

16. No woman can own land but a widow may claim all rights of private ownership on behalf of her son.

17. A widow who so wishes may remain in her house and cultivate the land she cultivated in her husband's lifetime.

18. Ownership does not entitle a man to sell or rent land. Mortgage is unknown.

> *Note*: (*a*) But a case of mortgage on a house recently came before the courts (D.C. 24/52: D.N.C. 143/51: *A. Kikungwe* v. *M. Waswa*). But both parties were Baganda. I have seen no case in which the parties were Iteso.

> *Note*: (*b*) Sales do take place but so far they are confined to improvements on land by construction of houses or by planting permanent crops.
> Thus one assessor recently bought a banana garden in Serere for 70*s*. Sales of houses are common but do not involve the right to cultivate nearby land. Sale of land has not yet been recognized in the courts.

> *Quotation: High Court 29/47: D.C. 30/47: D.N.C. 51/47: Y. Opolot* v. *Okwi:*

> 'The petitioner's sole claim to occupy the land in dispute appears to rest on some kind of transfer for a consideration from a Somali. The Somali, however, appears only to have cultivated the land upon sufferance and I cannot see what title he could have passed to the petitioner. . . .' (extract from High Court judgement).

> *Note*: (*c*) Renting of land is unknown.

19. An owner may lend any part of his land to any person and is morally bound to allow any members of his family group to cultivate any part which is not in his own use. The term 'in his own use' includes necessary fallow land.

20. When ownership lapses through the death of a man having no heirs, the land is usually divided by the Land Authority among neighbours.

> *Note*: This is given as the opinion of assessors but it is extremely unlikely that such circumstances would arise, and no such case has ever come to my notice.

Ownership by breaking new ground

21. Breaking new ground in unallocated or surplus land is subject to certain definite rules.

22. A newcomer (*abwotunan*), if a stranger in the Land Authority area in which he applies for land, must first find a sponsor and satisfy the Land Authority that he is of good character.

23. The sponsor may speak on the *abwotunan*'s behalf before the Land Authority; the *abwotunan* himself may not speak.

Note: Considerable care is taken in investigating antecedents and chiefs get in touch with the chief of the *abwotunan*'s home area. Two recent applicants at Obalanga were refused following an adverse report from the Kalaki chief. The *abwotunan* is sometimes made to cultivate part of his sponsor's holding, to ensure that his farming methods are sound.

24. (*a*) If inquiries reveal no objection, the Land Authority may allot a piece of unallocated or even, in cases of land shortage, of surplus land.

(*b*) An *abwotunan* may only be allotted as much land as he can cultivate and may not stake claims to further additional areas. An *abwotunan* who fails to cultivate land allotted may forfeit that land.

25. The land is allocated in the presence of as many witnesses as possible, usually from five to ten but often more. One witness is usually the parish chief, who is normally responsible for noting down the names of witnesses and is usually called as a witness if a dispute subsequently reaches the court.

26. No ceremony attends the allocation and no fee is customary. After the first harvest an *abwotunan* may, and usually does, provide beer and food for the clan leaders. Such a party is called *ebole*.

27. An *abwotunan* may be evicted by the Land Authority from his land for witchcraft or theft. His plots then revert to unallocated land or surplus land in the name of the previous owner.

Demarcation, disputes, and claims

28. No form of demarcation is obligatory.

Note: Plots are usually described in vague terms such as 'as far as the swamp and the side of that hill'.

Boundary marks do, however, exist; types noted are: euphorbia trees, fig trees, sisal, ditches, ant-hills, or paths.

29. Where disputes come before Land Authority or courts, the Land Authority or courts may order boundary marks to be erected.

Quotation: (*a*) D.C. 6/50: D.N.C. 13/50: *Y. Otim* v. *A. Otim*:

It was ordered that the two litigants, who had continually been quarrelling over a certain plot, should enter into a bond to keep the peace and that as part of the bond they should erect clear boundary marks of cairns or sisal hedges.

Quotation: (b) *D.C. 15/52: D.N.C. 85/51: E. Ogwang* v. *T. Odong:*

This was a dispute of long standing which had already reached the courts in 1945. In upholding the decisions of lower courts the D.C. ordered that E. Ogwang should erect boundary marks of cairns, fig poles or sisal to the satisfaction of the county court.

30. Where demarcation has been made either by order of the court or of the Land Authority or voluntarily, it is an offence to destroy boundary marks.

Quotation: Kateta Sub-County 118/51: E. Magino v. *A. Ocom:*

The land had already been awarded by the Court to Magino and Magino had planted trees to mark the boundary. A. Ocom uprooted these trees and was fined 5s.

31. All disputes and claims concerning ownership of land must be referred in the first instance to the village chief in consultation with the clan leaders of the village and thence to the parish chief in consultation with the clan leaders of the parish. There is no objection to clan leaders involved in the original dispute sitting as members of the village and parish councils.

32. Appeal lies from the parish council to the sub-county court and no court may hear a case which has not first been dealt with by the parish council.

Note: This procedure is the result of an administrative direction (No. 2/47 of 21 May 1947) and is rigidly followed. Thus Soroti County Court (187/49) of its own motion revised Katine Sub-County Case 216/49 and set aside the order because the case had not first been dealt with by the parish council.

It is a salutary provision, for local knowledge is required in all land disputes. The court invariably takes note of the decision of the parish council and usually records the decision of the parish council somewhere in the evidence.

33. A case may only be filed in the courts if the dispute is between two individuals and not against a clan leader in his capacity as Land Authority or against a chief in his capacity as chairman of a parish council.

Quotation: D.C. 47/52: D.N.C. 89/52: Bukedea County 76/52: Bukedea Sub-County 93/52: D. Opolot v. *E. Emong:*

D. Opolot sued E. Emong, a parish chief, 'for causing the village chief's house to be built on my three plots'. E. Emong had been chairman of the parish council which had made the allocation of land. The Court found that two of the three disputed plots did indeed belong to Opolot. Opolot unsuccessfully appealed in order to obtain the third plot. In the judgement of the D.N.C. appear the following words: 'This court does not understand why the sub-county court ever allowed Opolot to file this case against the parish chief in respect of this land; for it was the council which authorized the matter.'

Note: The commonest type of case is wilful trespass; complaints against occupation by a user are also common. Complaints concerning allocation by an heir to his brother are settled in the clan courts as this is a family affair.

34. Ownership may be claimed by the presence of ancestral graves.

Quotation: D.C. 19/51: D.N.C. 28/51: B. Osekeny v. Z. Ariko:

Osekeny claimed the disputed plots for several reasons, among which was the presence of ancestral graves and private mvule trees. Both these reasons were accepted and helped to establish his case.

35. Ownership may be claimed by the presence of private trees (see the quotation immediately above).

User rights

36. As stated above, a newcomer (*abwotunan*) may obtain his land by breaking new unallocated land or by being allotted land by the Land Authority from surplus land owned by another person (sections 21 et seq.) or he may be allowed the use of land by a relative or friend (section 19).

When an *abwotunan* has used the land for some time he may no longer be considered a 'newcomer' but a 'user'.

Note: No time can be laid down after which an *abwotunan* becomes a 'user', but if an *abwotunan* stays one or two years in a place he is unlikely to leave voluntarily and so becomes a 'user'. But in Asuret during the survey by J. Dean referred to in section 3 above the head of one of the original families spoke of one of the heads of the families who had been in occupation for about thirty years as a newcomer 'who might return to his original family land in Oregya'.

37. Provided he actually uses the land, a user may exercise nearly all rights of an owner.

38. A user may not be evicted by the owner who lent him the land or by the owner from whose surplus land the user was given land but only by the Land Authority.

Note: It not infrequently happens that an owner leaves his land for three or four years and that in that time the Land Authority allows another person to cultivate it. If the owner returns he cannot summarily eject the other, but normally, by appeal to the Land Authority, either the owner or the user will be found alternative plots.

39. User rights are not inheritable.

Note: This is said to be the rule. But in practice it is unusual for the children of a user not to be allowed to cultivate their father's land.

It follows that user rights can and do change into ownership rights (see sections 3 and 9 above).

An assessor at Mukura writing in English states: 'The trouble of allowing somebody to settle on the land is that if the children left on that land after their father's death are not strong minded, the new man may cause them to move away, he takes over the whole land for good.'

40. The distinction between owner and user, so apparent when the land is first allocated, soon becomes vague. The courts decide the many disputes which arise by equity and not by strict regard to rights of private ownership. Thus if an owner has delayed unduly to bring a case for recovery, or if the user has been in possession for many years, or if the user's relatives are buried on the land, or if the owner has other land elsewhere, the court may decide in favour of the user against the owner.

Quotation: D.N.C. 43/49: T. Emuge v. P. Chumale:

T. Emuge was the owner by inheritance and P. Chumale the user. But Chumale had used the land for sixteen years and taken it when it was vacant. Attempts were made to settle the dispute by the parish council but Emuge flouted the council. The D.N.C. found in favour of Chumale for these reasons.

4. *Official or public land*

41. Chiefs of the rank of sub-county and above may exercise user rights over certain defined land in the vicinity of their official house during their term of office only.

42. Parish and village chiefs are not normally transferred nor are they entitled to official houses.

If, therefore, such a chief owns his own land and house he retains both on transfer to another area and must be allocated new land for official use in his new area. He will not actually own such land as he will always return eventually to his own home.

43. But by a county council resolution in about 1943 official land was allocated by office to parish and village chiefs in Kumi, Ngora, and Bukedea only.

Quotation: (a)

Thus in a transfer of two parish chiefs in 1949 from Malera to Pigire, the Malera chief lost all title to the official land in Malera and was allotted new land to use in Pigire. But the Pigire chief continued to own his land in Pigire and acquired use of the official land in Malera as well.

Quotation: (b) *D.C. 47/52: D. Opolot* v. *E. Emong:*

In evidence E. Aide, ex-parish chief, stated: 'In 1942 the courts and councils agreed to select places where to build the homes of chiefs, so that when one was transferred his successor could come to his home. . . .'

44. It is customary to find all employees of the Local Government stationed at sub-county headquarters sufficient land to cultivate near their official houses but this practice is not universal.

45. No compensation is given for land taken for official use (roads, cotton stores, schools, sub-county headquarters, &c.), but compensation is payable for crops, if destroyed, and alternative land is found.

Note: This section is included to show what would probably be the result if an individual sued a chief in his official capacity for failing to provide compensation on eviction. The legal position is that the title to all land in Teso is vested in the Crown and is administered by Protectorate government legislation; Africans may occupy Crown land without lease or licence, but have no legal rights of ownership and may be evicted if the land is required for public purposes. In such cases the Government pays compensation based largely on the principles which would apply if the land had been compulsorily acquired under the Land Acquisition Act; in practice it is usually the African Local Government, not the Protectorate Government, which requires to evict people for public purposes; until 1955 the legal right of African local governments so to evict was not defined. It has been the practice for African local governments to pay compensation only for crops and buildings destroyed, although, as stated, efforts are usually made to find land elsewhere for those evicted.

46. A man may not cultivate over a public path between two villages but has the right to close a small path between houses which crosses his land.

Note: No cases concerning rights of way yet seen.

47. Certain areas are set aside for magico-religious purposes and may not be cultivated nor may trees be cut on them. (Examples are the *etem* groves in Usuku or Odeker near Kotiokot (Malera) where there is a source of clay used in ritual.)

5. *Grazing land*

48. Tenure of land which is used exclusively for grazing cattle and which is never cultivated is communal.

49. Certain areas are set aside by the Land Authority or by the parish council as grazing land and may not be cultivated. Such areas are usually swamp edges or areas of poor land away from cultivation.

Quotation: Achwa Sub-County 58/52: Court v. E. Tukei and others:

The accused were convicted of cultivating in the swamp contrary to the orders of the parish council and thereby preventing the grazing of cattle. They were ordered to fence their crops and not to cultivate any further and were fined 10s.

50. Cattle may be grazed on grazing land or on resting plots of owned agricultural land without any fee.

51. Any person who allows his cattle to damage a neighbour's crops must pay compensation as assessed by the court and a fine of 10s. Fencing of plots is not obligatory and the onus is on the herdsman to prevent damage by the cattle.

52. Grass for thatching may be cut by any person anywhere on private or unoccupied land and no fee may be charged. But *asisinit* grass may only be cut by the owner of the land on which it grows in Kumi, Ngora, and Bukedea counties.

53. Certain specified areas may be closed to grazing by order of the local council and any person found grazing cattle in the closed area may be fined.

Areas round dams are usually so closed by parish councils and demarcated with sisal.

Larger areas which have become eroded through over-grazing are closed by sub-county councils.

If non-native-owned cattle are likely to be involved orders are issued by the District Commissioner under the Cattle Grazing Ordinance No. 13 of 1945. But cases involving native-owned cattle in such areas are tried in the native courts.

54. When grass is dry, no person may burn grass without permission of his local chief.

Note: This is simply a precaution against the spread of bush fires and loss of grazing. When there is no danger of fire spreading, grass may be burnt without permission.

Quotation: (a) Orungo Sub-County 29/52: Court v. E. Okello:

The accused was convicted of burning grass 'at the wrong time of year thereby damaging grazing land'. He was fined 10s.

Quotation: (b) Asamuk Sub-County 25/52: Court v. Oreta Edosu:

The accused was convicted of 'setting grazing land on fire at the wrong time of year . . .' (*komam na erai apaki nakicweete amunaari inya luenyamete aituk . . .*). He was fined 50s.

Note: This rule is extended to make it obligatory to stop a bush fire which is destroying grazing (Achwa Sub-County 32/52).

6. *Water rights*

55. Natural water is free of access to any person whether or not it is situate on privately owned land.

56. No permission is required to dig wells or make small dams and no fee is payable.

57. Any such well or dam made on privately owned land remains the property of the owner if made by the owner or at the owner's expense.

Note: This is one view; exactly the opposite has been expressed, i.e. that wells become public even when made by an individual.

Certainly in Asuret, when E. Emuli made a dam of his own, slaughtering 108 head of cattle as payment for the labour and spending about 1,000s., the dam became public property and is used by all and sundry.

58. The local council may define places for the watering of stock and places for humans to draw water, and any person watering stock at the humans' watering place is guilty of an offence.

Quotation: Ochero Sub-County 136/51: Court v. Y. Kinaga:

Kinaga allowed eleven head of cattle to foul a tank in the part set aside for human consumption. He was fined 15s.

7. *Hunting rights*

59. Hunting rights are vested in certain persons (*apolok ka eriga*). The *apolon ka eriga* is usually a clan leader of an area which is usually a sub-county or an area of similar size but may be larger.

60. Rights of the *apolon ka eriga* are limited to choice of time for the hunt, choice of locality, organization of the hunt, and receiving a share of any animals killed. He has no proprietary rights over the land.

Note: Success for a hunt is ensured by the *apolon ka eriga* gathering the dung of as many species of animal as possible and boiling them together in a pot.

61. But long ago the *apolon ka eriga* may have had wider rights and even allocatory rights over his hunting grounds. One assessor writes:

Long ago there was forest land in which settlement was difficult or impossible because of wild beasts; there were leaders who controlled these forest lands: e.g.:

Omiat	*apolon ka eriga*		Achwa	
Egasu	,,	,,	Kapelabyong	in Amuria
Echungo	,,	,,	Obalanga	
Okomera	,,	,,	Morungatuny	
Omino	,,	,,	Olomet	in Kaberamaido.

If people wished to settle on their forest land, they first held a meeting and the *apolon ka eriga* explained where each group would go and settle and get water.[1]

8. *Forest rights*

62. Any person may gather fallen wood on any land.

63. Only an owner or user may cut trees on his land but any person may cut trees on unallocated land.

64. Certain trees because of their food properties or utilitarian uses are regarded as reserved trees and may not normally be cut down even by the person on whose land they grow. They are:

1. *Ekungur* (Butyrospermum parkii)
2. *Epeduru* (Tamarindus indica)
3. *Eloa* (Chlorophora excelsa)
4. *Etekwa* (Albizzia coriaria)
5. *Emurie* (Carrisa)
6. *Ekumi* (Diospyros mespiliformis)
7. *Ekoboi* (Terminalia)
8. *Ebule* (Ficus brachypoda or F. platyphylla)
9. *Elamai* (Ximenia americana)
10. *Ejinga* (Ficus sycomorus).

Quotation: Bugondo Sub-County 99/51: Court v. *M. Eseru:*

M. Eseru cut down an *ekoboi* tree and made a canoe out of it in 1950. He claimed permission was given by the D.C. but failed to prove this fact. He was convicted and fined 50s.

Note: There is a mixture of custom and governmental instructions in this law. The first four trees are reserved under the Forests Ordinance, 1947. But it is not unusual for persons to claim that they planted *eloa* or *etekwa* trees and to claim the right to cut them down and use the timber. Such claims are often upheld in native courts. But naturally sown *eloa* or *etekwa* trees are regarded as reserved. Other timber trees, *ekumi* or *ekoboi*, when ownership is claimed, are frequently felled, but naturally sown trees have a form of protection; see quotation above. Local carpenters are encouraged by Government to use local woods; this encouragement cuts across this law.

Some of these trees may also have medical or magical uses, which ensure their protection, in addition to their more practical uses as food or timber, e.g. *elamai* is protected as a cure for measles. Its leaves are pounded in water and the patient is washed in the liquid and the residue is rubbed in the hair. *Ejinga* cuttings are often planted round graves.

[1] E. P. Engulu (personal communication).

65. A chief who wrongly gives permission to cut a reserved tree may also be prosecuted.

Note: This law is based on one example, also from Bugondo (115/51), in which a chief was maliciously prosecuted on this charge. He defended himself by proving that his superior, since deceased, gave the permission at a time of food shortage when the Iteso needed canoes to pick water-lilies for food.

66. Trees planted by hand remain the property of the planter or his heir even if the land on which they grow has, through the planter's absence or some other reason, ceased to belong to him. But if he leaves the area he must detail some person to look after the trees and certify that they are his.

Quotation: Mukongoro Sub-County 81/51: Owachi s/o Adupa v. Lebo s/o Kapule:

Owachi sued Lebo for destroying 100 cassia trees, his private property. The Court awarded 20s. compensation (the trees were young ones) and Lebo was fined 15s. for destroying the trees.

Note: The usual trees so planted are cape lilac and cassia. There are considerable quantities in Kumi, Ngora, and Bukedea. Mvule trees are also planted. The larger trees are sometimes named individually after the planter or after the owner of the house near which they were planted.

67. Private trees may be bought and sold at the owner's discretion and sale conveys no title to land on which the tree grows.

68. No person may cut trees in a Local Government plantation without first obtaining permission of the sub-county chief and paying the prescribed price per pole.

Note: This section is included here because offences against it are invariably tried in the native courts. It is, of course, an offence under the Forests Ordinance, but native courts are not empowered to hear cases under that ordinance.

9. *Houses*

69. *Aanyu airabet ebe mam erai eipone toma apakio ber nu aiwosa alupoko naarai aiboisit ngin na Magoro erai nadidingiari noi kwangin aanyu airabet ebe E. Elungat nges ekolono kanu aiduku ireria iarei kanu amaria alupok kwabo ti nges edukit ere ediopet kanuka angor aarei nuejatatar.*

(The Court sees that it was not the custom in the past to sue for land; for this place, Magoro, is very small: so the court sees that E. Elungat is at fault for building two homesteads through lust for land whereas he should only have built one for the two wives he has.)

Extract from the judgement in Usuku County Court 21/51, *E. Elungat v. E. Ekelot.*

70. Original permission to build a house whether permanent or temporary must be given by the Land Authority.

71. No permission to rebuild on the same site is necessary even if a permanent house is built instead of a temporary one.

> *Quotation: D.N.C. 131/50: Bukedea County 129/50: Court v. M. Waswa:*
>
> M. Waswa was fined 50s. in the lower courts for building a permanent house on the site of a temporary one. The D.N.C. reversed this decision and acquitted Waswa.

72. Houses may be bought and sold. The sale implies transfer of the land on which the house stands but no more.

73. But the presence of a house is often a valid ground for claiming title to the land nearby.

74. Mortgage is unknown, but see section 18 above, where a case between two Baganda is quoted.

CHAPTER VII

CRIMINAL, APPLIED, AND LOCAL LAW

1. *Criminal*

Offences against the person

1. NATIVE courts are debarred from hearing homicide cases by section 10 of the Native Courts Ordinance but cases of blood-money, payable as a result of homicide, can be heard.

> *Note*: Formerly cases of homicide were settled by taking the life of the killer or of a member of his extended family or clan; or by the gift of a girl by the relatives of the killer to the clan of the deceased; or by payment of cattle equivalent to prevailing bride-price rates to enable the deceased's clan to replace the life lost by taking a girl in marriage from another clan. This last method of settlement still prevails.

2. Blood-money is fixed at five head of cattle or 500s.

> *Note*: This amount is fixed by council resolution and is the same as the maximum permitted bride-price.

3. Blood-money is payable by the killer to the heir of the person killed in all cases of homicide in which the killer is not executed. If the killer is executed no blood-money is payable.

> *Note*: This rule was held to refer only to legal executions, but by High Court Revision 44 of 1952 must be taken to include any atonement by death.

> *Quotation: High Court 44/52: D.C. 23/52: D.N.C. 114/51: Y. Okitoi v. P. Aisu:*
>
> Aisu's father, Otaget, ran amok and killed a child aged five years and wounded several other persons. He was set upon by an angry crowd and done to death. Certain persons were prosecuted for his murder but in the preliminary inquiry in the District Court the magistrate did not commit them for trial and they were discharged. In this case Okitoi sued Aisu, as heir of Otaget, for customary blood-money. The District Native Court (a full bench of seventeen including all county chiefs) ruled that although Otaget had been killed it was not by legal execution and that Aisu must pay customary blood-money of five head of cattle to Okitoi, father of the murdered child. He in turn could claim blood-money from the killers of Otaget if they could be traced. With modifications this finding was upheld by the D.C. but reversed on petition to the High Court, which ruled that no blood-money was payable since Otaget had atoned for his crime with his life.

4. It is immaterial whether the killing amounted to murder or manslaughter or whether it was accidental; provided it was caused by the direct agency of the person sued for blood-money, he is liable to pay blood-money.

5. If the person liable to pay blood-money under section 3 above is unable to pay by reason of poverty or any other reason or if he absconds or if he dies without paying, the debt must be paid by his nearest relative within the extended family (*ekek*).

6. Blood-money debts are not cancelled by the death of the judgement creditor and can be claimed by his heirs without time limitation.

7. Assault is punishable by fine or imprisonment or both and by compensation.

8. Compensation for a tooth has been fixed by council resolution at 100s. Compensation for other hurts have not been fixed but examples show:

D.N.C. 25/52. Loss of one eye: 200s. compensation and a year's imprisonment.

D.N.C. 28/52. Loss of hearing in one ear: two head of cattle compensation and three months' imprisonment.

D.N.C. 93/51. Loss of fingers of one hand and broken arm: Three head of cattle compensation and three months' imprisonment.

(*Toma obaren 3 epedori loewosan adumun aberu naingarakini* . . .'and with the three head of cattle the plaintiff can get himself a wife to help him . . .'.)

9. Cases of assault are never heard until the complainant has been discharged from hospital or has ceased to receive any medical treatment and the time spent in hospital or attending at an aid-post is always taken into account in assessing compensation. Unproved documentary evidence on this point is usually accepted.

10. By administrative direction cases of defilement of girls under 14 years of age are triable by magistrates' courts only unless referred to native courts. Cases of rape or indecent assault are treated as civil actions rather than criminal offences (see Part VI, Chapter III, sections 23 and 24, although fines are often awarded in addition to compensation).

Offences against property

11. Cases of cattle theft are triable only in the county courts. The penalty for cattle theft is two years' imprisonment and fifteen strokes.

fallen sick after a visit to Ibulaya's house. It was later found from medical examination that she was suffering from whooping-cough. Iningo was fined 50s. and ordered to pay 50s. to Ibulaya.

Quotation: (b) *Obalanga Sub-County 132/51: Etapu Enyadu* v. *R. Amorokin:*

R. Amorokin threatened to kill Etapu. He was imprisoned for three months.

Quotation: (c) *Asamuk Sub-County 153/53: Lakeri Anyalo* v. *Idi bin Salim:*

The charge was 'for calling me a wizard and saying I sleep with dogs' and the sentence was three months' imprisonment.

Note: Visible practice of witchcraft as in sections 16 and 17 is now regarded as a criminal offence and the punishment is almost invariably imprisonment with or without corporal punishment. Accusations of witchcraft or threatening statements are regarded as civil actions although punishment is often awarded by the courts.

2. Applied laws

20. Native courts are empowered (1954) by warrant to administer the following Protectorate Government laws:

(a) Poll Tax Ordinance.
(b) African Local Government Tax Ordinance.
(c) Native Authority Ordinance, 7 (a) and 7 (b).
(d) Census Ordinance.
(e) Cattle Traders Ordinance, 3, 7, 9, 10.
(f) Hide & Skin Trade (Control) Ordinance, 4, 11, 15 (i) and (ii).
(g) Diseases of Animals Rules, 9. Rules C. 12 and 13.
(h) Witchcraft Ordinance (County Courts and D.N.C. only).

Note: Cases under the Poll Tax and African Local Government Tax Ordinance are common. Cases under remaining ordinances are rare.

21. Although not specifically empowered, native courts commonly hear cases under the following Protectorate Government laws:

(a) Traffic Ordinance (offences relating to bicycles).
(b) Distribution & Price of Goods Ordinance (offences relating to price labelling and controlled prices).
(c) Waragi Ordinance. (Though it can be argued that native courts hear such cases under Native Authority Ordinance Section 7 (b) (2).)

3. Local laws

22. By section 3 of the Native Law Ordinance legislative resolutions of the Teso District Council when approved by the Provincial Commissioner have the force of law. By section 9 (2) of the African Local Governments Ordinance laws so made continue in force in spite of the revocation of the Native Law Ordinance. Resolutions thus approved are set out in sections 24–27 below.

23. By section 6 (4) of the African Local Governments Ordinance legislative resolutions of the Teso District Council take the form of by-laws. By-laws so made are set out in sections 28–31 below.

24. *Preservation of law and order.*

(*a*) Any person convicted of gambling is liable to a fine not exceeding 30*s*.

Note: Though it is not laid down, courts usually take any gambling money found with the gamblers as well.

(*b*) No person may hold a dance without permission of the county chief.

(*c*) A parish chief must be present at every dance.

(*d*) Leaders of songs will be chosen by the supervising parish chief in rotation and must obey all his orders.

(*e*) Dances may be held only in daylight hours.

(*f*) Heavy sticks and spears may not be carried.

(*g*) If a quarrel arises, its originator, the supervising parish chief, and song leaders are liable to fines.

(*h*) No beer may be provided at dances.

Note: No specific punishments are listed.

Quotation: Obalanga Sub-County 46/50: Court v. Emechu s/o Eyamu:

Emechu held an *ekuma* dance without permission at which there was a quarrel and disturbance. He pleaded guilty and was imprisoned for three months and fined 50*s*.

Examples of offences against (*c*), (*d*), (*f*), and (*h*) have not come to my notice.

(*i*) Every person must report the presence of a visitor at his home. Failure to report renders host and visitor liable to a fine of 1*s*.

Note: The report must be made to the village chief in respect of visitors from outside the sub-county who come to stay a night or more.

(*j*) Any person escaping from lawful custody is liable to imprisonment not exceeding three months.

(*k*) Any person who smokes, possesses, or cultivates bhang is liable on conviction to imprisonment for a maximum period of six months.

Note: Courts always award the maximum penalty.

25. *Agriculture and soil conservation.* The following rules are to be observed:

(*a*) Not more than six cotton seeds to be planted in each hole.

(*b*) Gaps in cotton to be filled by re-planting.

(*c*) The rows of cotton not to be more than 3 feet apart.

(*d*) Each cotton plant not to be more than 1 foot apart.

(*e*) Fields to be not more than 35 yards in width.

(*f*) Grass strips at least 9 feet in width to be left between all fields.

(*g*) No cultivation within 15 feet of any road and within 3 feet of any track.

(*h*) No one to trail a plough along a path and cut a furrow.

(*i*) No ploughing up and down the slopes of a hill.

(*j*) No planting of cotton (and other crops) in rows up and down the slopes of a hill.

(*k*) No cultivation in and near swamps normally used as grazing areas for cattle, except when prior permission obtained from the parish council.

(*l*) No ploughing to be left to children.

The penalties for breaches of the foregoing rules are: a fine not exceeding 3*s*. for the first offence and a fine not exceeding 5*s*. for the second or subsequent offences. But heavier fines are often awarded.

(*m*) Clan leaders are responsible for encouraging people to plant cassava for the provision of sticks for planting.

(*n*) Any person failing to weed his cassava plot is liable to a fine of 1*s*. for the first offence and 2*s*. for each subsequent offence.

(*o*) Any person convicted of eating the contents of his famine granary without permission is liable to a fine of 10*s*. and must purchase grain to refill it.

(*p*) Grass at the side of paths and tracks is not to be dug up but cut short. Penalty for non-compliance: fine of 3*s*. for the first offence and 5*s*. for each subsequent offence.

(*q*) Any person who drives stock on to dam walls or who allows stock to pass on to dam walls is liable on conviction to a fine of 5*s*. for the first offence and 10*s*. for each subsequent offence and may be ordered to make good any damage done.

26. *Veterinary*.

(*a*) Unlawful movement of cattle without a permit is punishable by a fine not exceeding 50*s*.

(*b*) If the movement is from an area in quarantine, the fine is not exceeding 70*s*.

(*c*) If a person ill-treats an ox or uses young oxen for ploughing he is liable to a fine not exceeding 10*s*.

(*d*) If cattle stray through the owner's negligence in not looking after them properly or providing a kraal, the owner is liable, in addition to compensation due for crops, to a fine of 10*s*.

27. *Public health.*

(*a*) Every person must keep his house and compound clean. Penalty: a fine not exceeding 5*s*.

(*b*) Any woman or girl convicted of prostitution is liable to be sentenced to imprisonment not exceeding two months and to be repatriated if her home is in another district.

(*c*) If on examination by a doctor she is found to be suffering from venereal disease the penalty may be enhanced to imprisonment not exceeding six months.

Note: (*b*) and (*c*) are never enforced.

28. *Beer by-law, 1951.*

A BYE-LAW TO CONTROL THE BREWING AND DRINKING OF BEER

Passed by the Teso District Council with the approval of the Governor.

(1) This bye-law shall be called the Brewing and Drinking of Beer Bye-law 1951.

(2) No person may brew beer in excess of his or her own personal requirements without first having obtained the permission of a Parish or Village Chief.

(3) No person shall give beer to a person who appears to be under the age of sixteen years.

(4) Any person disobeying the provision of section (2) or (3) above shall be guilty of an offence and shall on a first conviction be liable to a fine not exceeding Shs. 5/- and shall on any subsequent conviction be liable to a fine not exceeding Shs. 20/- or to imprisonment for a period not exceeding one month or to both such fine and imprisonment.

(5) If at any drinking party a dispute arises as a result of which any act of violence is done, the person who in the opinion of the court started the dispute shall be guilty of an offence and shall on conviction be liable to a fine not exceeding Shs. 150/- or to imprisonment for a period not exceeding 4 months or to both such fine and imprisonment.

(6) If at any drinking party a dispute arises as a result of which any act of violence is done, the person who provided the beer shall be guilty of an offence and shall on conviction be liable to a fine not exceeding Shs. 50/- or to imprisonment for a period not exceeding one month or to both such fine and imprisonment.

(7) If at any drinking party a dispute arises as a result of which any act of violence is done all persons present at the drinking party shall be guilty of an offence and shall on conviction be liable to a fine not exceeding Shs. 30/- or to imprisonment for a period not exceeding one month or to both such fine and imprisonment.

29. *Cassava by-law, 1951.*

A BYE-LAW TO CONTROL DISEASE IN CASSAVA

Passed by the Teso District Council with the approval of the Provincial Commissioner, Eastern Province.

(1) This bye-law shall be known as the Diseased Cassava Bye-law 1952.

(2) Any member of the Agricultural Department finding diseased cassava in any area within his jurisdiction shall make a report of such diseased cassava and the name of its owner to the Sub-County Chief in whose jurisdiction the diseased cassava is found.

(3) The Sub-County Chief, if satisfied with the correctness of this report, shall order the owner to uproot and to burn the diseased cassava within seven days.

(4) Any person who fails to carry out the order contained in section (3) above shall be liable on conviction to a fine not exceeding Shs. 5/- and shall be ordered to uproot and to burn the diseased cassava within seven days of such conviction.

(5) Any person who fails to carry out the order contained in section (4) above shall be liable on conviction to a fine not exceeding Shs. 20/- or to imprisonment not exceeding one month or to both such fine and imprisonment and the diseased cassava shall be uprooted and burned by a member of the Agricultural Department.

30. *Education tax by-law, 1952.*

A BYE-LAW FOR THE COLLECTION OF EDUCATION TAX

Passed by the Teso District Council, with the approval of the Provincial Commissioner, Eastern Province.

(1) This bye-law shall be known as the Education Tax Bye-law, 1952, and shall come into operation on the 1st January, 1953.

(2) Subject to the provisions of section 6 of this Bye-law every male African in Teso over the apparent age of 18 years shall be liable to pay an Education tax if he has not paid an African Local Government tax outside Teso in the year of collection.

(3) The rate of such tax shall be Shs. 5 per annum.

(4) The proceeds of such tax shall be devoted to such educational projects as the District Council with the approval of the Provincial Commissioner shall determine.

(5) The tax shall be due and payable on the 1st January every year.

(6) Any person permanently exempted from paying African Local Government tax shall be deemed to be permanently exempted from paying Education tax and any person temporarily exempted from paying African Local Government tax shall be deemed to be temporarily exempted from paying Education tax.

(7) A receipt for the amount of tax paid by each tax payer shall be issued by the Sub-County Chief to whom the Education tax is paid.

(8) Any person who refuses or neglects to pay his Education tax shall be guilty of an offence and shall be liable on conviction to a fine not exceeding Shs. 10 or to imprisonment not exceeding 14 days. Such punishment shall in no way cancel the obligation to pay the Education tax.

31. *Ferries by-law, 1952.*

A BYE-LAW TO CONTROL THE LICENSING AND OPERATION OF FERRIES

Passed by the Teso District Council, with the approval of the Provincial Commissioner, Eastern Province.

(1) This bye-law shall be known as the Teso Ferries Bye-law, 1952.

(2) (i) No canoe shall be plied for hire on any ferry declared to be a public ferry under Section 2 of the Public Ferries Ordinance unless a licence so to do has been issued in respect of such canoe by the African Local Government of the district in which the owner of such canoe resides.

(ii) for the purposes of this section a licence issued in Mbale or Busoga Districts shall be valid in Teso District for such places as are mentioned in the licence;

(iii) a licence under this Bye-law shall be in the form in the Schedule hereto and shall remain in force till December 31st following the date of its issue.

(3) A fee of Shs. 10 shall be paid for each licence.

(4) A sub-county chief shall before issuing a licence first inspect the canoe and satisfy himself that the canoe is totally seaworthy.

(5) Each licence must stipulate the maximum number of passengers, bicycles, cattle or goats to be carried in the licensee's canoe.

(6) No licensee shall permit a drunk person to board his canoe.

(7) No ferry shall operate before sunrise or after sunset.

(8) The person in whose name any canoe is licensed shall be responsible for ensuring that poles of ambach or other light buoyant material shall be carried in the canoe. Such poles must be sufficient to support the number of passengers for which the canoe is licensed.

(9) Any person who breaks any of the provisions of this Bye-law shall be liable to a fine of not more than Shs. 200 or imprisonment for a period of not more than 3 months, or to both such fine and imprisonment.

Schedule I

LICENCE TO OPERATE A FERRY UNDER THE TESO
DISTRICT COUNCIL FERRIES BYE-LAW, 1952

1. One canoe, licensed in the name of ....
is hereby permitted to operate a ferry between ....
and ....subject to the following conditions:—

(1) The ferry shall at no time carry more than:—

.... Passengers.

.... Bicycles.

.... Cattle.

.... Goats.

(2) The licensee shall not permit a drunk person to board the canoe.

(3) The ferry shall not be operated after sunset or before sunrise.

(4) The licensee shall be responsible for ensuring that poles of ambach or other light buoyant material will be carried on the canoe; such poles must be sufficient to support the number of passengers for which the canoe is licensed.

2. This licence is only valied for the..
landing in Teso district and the landing of ....
in ....district.

3. I hereby certify that I made an inspection of ....'s
canoe on ...., and that in my opinion it was seaworthy and fit to carry the number of passengers specified above.

4. This licence expires on 31st December, 19........

....

Sub-county Chief.

CHAPTER VIII

COURTS

1. *Clan courts*

1. THE way in which members of several different clans would move out as one age-set group from their *etem* area to settle a new *etem* area has been described in Part II (p. 68). The head of each clan group in an *etem* area used to have recognized judicial authority to settle disputes within his own group. To some extent this authority remains. Disputes concerning members of other clans within the *etem* area were decided by a larger tribunal consisting of all the clan leaders of the *etem* area. These leaders used to meet at the recognized *etem* meeting-place, a grove or prominent tree or rock, to discuss matters of *etem* concern and to hear individual disputes. *Etem* areas, as has been described elsewhere, corresponded roughly to the administrative divisions now known as parishes (*itela*). These traditional courts still exist and have been referred to elsewhere as clan courts. This term is used because the court is composed of the clan leaders of a modern administrative division, who are chosen in proportion to the strength of the clans in that division. Each clan is represented, unless it is very small, and a large clan may have several representatives. It should, however, be understood that these courts have now lost their traditional form. Clan leaders are nowadays appointed in the manner described in Part II (p. 67), and are to all intents and purposes minor and unpaid government chiefs. The procedure of clan courts is nowadays modelled on that of the official native courts established at sub-county level and above.

2. The territorial jurisdiction of clan courts now conforms to the modern administrative divisions of parish and village.

3. Village clan courts are made up of the clan leaders in the village. Five is an average quorum and from 7 to 12 an average total of members. The village chief sits as chairman.

4. Parish clan courts are composed of the clan leaders in the parish. The total number averages 14 to 30 and the average quorum is 5 to 10. The parish chief is chairman.

> *Note*: In one parish court (in Kumi) there were 14 members: 2 Igoria, 2 Irarak, 7 Ikomolo, 3 Ikarebwok.

5. If both parties live in one village, the dispute would normally come before the village clan court, and if they lived in different villages but in the same parish, the dispute would normally come to the parish clan court in the first instance.

6. Clan courts are in effect arbitration tribunals and they hear only civil cases and have no penal sanctions; but all decisions of clan courts are implicitly (and often openly) recognized by constituted native courts. Evidence of clan court decisions is often recorded in the native court records, and in land disputes it must be so recorded.

7. There are no fees payable in clan courts.

8. Appeals from village clan court to parish clan court and thence to a constituted native court are recognized. No appeal fee is payable.

2. *Constituted native courts*

9. Forty-six sub-county, eight county, and a District Native Court are established in Teso by warrant of the Provincial Commissioner under the Native Courts Ordinance.

10. The territorial jurisdiction of these courts coincides with the administrative boundary of the sub-county, county, and district except that the District Native Court has jurisdiction to twenty miles within Karamoja to enable it to hear cases of cattle theft and of affrays resulting from cattle thefts.

11. The courts have personal jurisdiction over all natives in cases in which both parties are native.

12. In criminal cases sub-county courts have powers of imprisonment up to six months, of fine up to 500s. or twelve head of cattle or sixty goats, and of whipping not exceeding ten strokes. County courts can imprison up to one year, fine up to 1,000s. or twenty-five head of cattle or 125 goats, or order a whipping not exceeding fifteen strokes. But for cattle theft only county courts may award up to two years I.H.L. subject to confirmation by the District Native Court.

The District Native Court can imprison up to two years, fine up to 2,000s. or fifty head of cattle or 250 goats, and order a whipping not exceeding twenty-four strokes.

13. In civil matters the District Native Court has unlimited jurisdiction. County courts may only hear cases in which the subject-matter does not exceed 2,500s. or fifty head of cattle or 250 goats. The limit for sub-county courts is 1,000s. or twenty head of cattle or 100 goats.

14. Appeals lie from the sub-county court to the county and from the county to the District Native Court. If the case originated in the county court a further appeal lies to the District Commissioner but no appeal to the District Commissioner lies if the case started in the sub-county court and has been heard on appeal by the county and District Native Court. In all cases parties have the right of petition to the District Commissioner or to the High Court for revision.

15. The constitution of each grade of court is laid down by the Provincial Commissioner in Directions to Native Courts, Eastern Province. Each court has a panel of unofficial members appointed by the Provincial Commissioner, or by the District Commissioner in the case of sub-county courts. The District Native Court is presided over by a permanent judge (*Ekeraban*). A quorum of court members consists of three county chiefs or deputies and three unofficial members.

County courts are presided over by a permanent county judge or by the county chief or his deputy. A quorum of members consists of three sub-county chiefs or their deputies and three unofficial members.

Sub-county courts are presided over by the sub-county chief or his deputy with two parish chiefs or deputies and two unofficial members forming a quorum.

3. *Procedure and records*

16. Clan leaders (*apolok ka atekerin*) are agents and representatives of the chief in whose area they live, and reports of crimes may be made either to a clan leader or to a chief.

17. A clan leader to whom such a report is made may arrest a suspected party and take him before the chief. A clan leader may also search a house if there is reasonable ground for suspicion of an offence. They are frequently sent by chiefs to effect an arrest or to make an investigation.

18. Persons arrested may be released on bail or surety. The surety offered is payable direct to the complainant by the third party if the accused person absconds. Surety may also be offered in kind by the person arrested. In that case the article is held by the court.

19. Administrative orders confine remand to certain more serious offences only and to adultery.

20. Procedure in court is standardized. The president calls out the case. The plaintiff states his case and names his witnesses, usually calling on one as seconder to the charge. The defendant then replies and names his witnesses, though sometimes all the prosecution witnesses are heard first before the defendant makes any statement. Both parties remain standing before the court throughout the hearing of evidence. Any member of the court can act as advocate for either party and cross-examine any witness. No form of oath is used. The evidence of each witness is recorded by the court clerk in brief and signed or thumb-printed by the witness. At the conclusion of the hearing each court member states his opinion openly. The president thereupon pronounces his judgement and sentence and signs the record. The record is then signed by all other court members.

Procedure in clan courts is similar though no written records are kept.

21. Sentence consists of fine, I.H.L., or corporal punishment.

Rules governing the infliction of corporal punishment are contained in the Native Courts (Eastern Province) Rules, 1949. The offences for which corporal punishment may be awarded are listed in an administrative order from the District Commissioner on the reverse of court warrants. The offences are similar to those for which corporal punishment is awarded in magistrates' courts except that cattle theft is included. A person sentenced to imprisonment is always committed to the prison of the county in which the court is situated. The president of the court must sign the committal warrant.

> *Note*: Nearly all disputes were and still are considered the concern of the two parties and were settled by compensation only. The idea of punishment for a wrong done to the community is still new and alien. There are not therefore any records of penal sanctions imposed in olden days though it is alleged by some that witchcraft was punishable by death by spearing. Uncompensated killings also bestowed the right to take a life in exchange.

22. The Native Courts (Eastern Province) Rules, 1949, require all con-stituted native courts to keep case registers showing certain essential details about each case. In addition the District Native Court and county courts are required to keep case files with a full record of the evidence. In practice sub-county courts also keep case files.

23. In addition to case registers and case files each court is required to keep or use the following records:

(*a*) Court fee receipts: issued to plaintiff as summons to be served on defendant.

(*b*) Court fine receipts: issued on payment of fine.

(*c*) Debt receipt: issued when any compensation or debt, whether in cash or in kind, is paid. It must be signed by both parties and by the court.

(*d*) Appeal result notices: issued by the appellate to the lower court to convey the result of appeals.

BIBLIOGRAPHY

THIS bibliography contains:

(i) All published works known to me which are devoted exclusively to any aspect of the Teso people's life or environment.

(ii) Certain unpublished but completed works devoted exclusively to any aspect of the Teso people's life or environment which I consider of exceptional interest or which I have quoted in the text. Copies of some of these works, including those of the late Father J. Kruyer and of the Amootoi ka Etesot Society which are extensively quoted, can be found in the Teso District Office.

(iii) Published works devoted to other subjects but containing material on the Teso people or country. In such cases I have indicated the numbers of the relevant pages in brackets; in some works, however, such as *Tribal Crafts of Uganda*, by Trowell and Wachsmann, or *The Lango*, by Driberg, the references to Teso are far too numerous to list.

(iv) A few published works devoted to other subjects which I consider contain valuable comparative material on tribes closely allied to the Iteso. Works in this class are indicated by an asterisk.

Official publications of the Uganda Government have not been included unless reference is made to them in the text. Annual reports of Uganda Government departments often contain statistical information relating to Teso.

ABBREVIATIONS

Africa	*Journal of the International African Institute*
E.A.A.J.	*East African Agricultural Journal*
E.A.M.J.	*East African Medical Journal*
J.A.A.	*Journal of African Administration*
J.R.A.I.	*Journal of the Royal Anthropological Institute*
U.J.	*Uganda Journal*

African Studies Branch, Colonial Office, 1952. 'A Survey of the Development of Local Government in the African Territories since 1947: IV. Uganda', *J.A.A.* 4. (References to Teso, pp. 28–31.)

Amootoi ka Etesot Society, undated (*c.* 1946). 'Origins of the Iteso', manuscript in Ateso.

BERNARDI, B., 1952. 'The Age-system of the Nilo-Hamitic Peoples', *Africa*, 22.

CLARK, DORIS, 1950. *'Karamojong Age-groups and Clans', *U.J.* 14.

COOK, SIR A. R., 1945. *Uganda Memories*, Kampala, Uganda Society.

COUTTS, P. G., 1950. 'Musical Instruments of Usuku', *U.J.* 14.

DE COURCY IRELAND, M. G., HOSKING, H. R., LOEWENTHAL, DR. L. J. A., 1937. *An Investigation into Health and Agriculture in Teso*, Entebbe, Government Printer.

DRIBERG, J. H., 1923. *The Lango, a Nilotic Tribe of Uganda*, London, Fisher Unwin.

DUNDAS, HON. K. R., 1913. 'The Wawanga and other Tribes of the Elgon District', *J.R.A.I.* 43. (Notes on Teso, pp. 62–63.)

EKADU, REV. Y., 1954. 'Kumam History', manuscript in Kumam.

ENGULU, E. P., 1937. 'Clan Taboos and Table of Relationships', manuscript in Ateso.

GULLIVER, DR. P. H., 1952 (i). 'The Karamajong Cluster', *Africa*, 22.

—— 1952 (ii). *'Bell-Oxen and Ox-Names among the Jie', *U.J.* 16.

—— 1953 (i). *'The Population of Karamoja', *U.J.* 17.

—— and PAMELA, 1953 (ii). *The Central Nilo-Hamites*, London, International African Institute.

—— 1954. *'Jie Agriculture', *U.J.* 18.

—— 1955. **The Family Herds*, London, Routledge & Kegan Paul.

HENDRIKSEN, REV. FR. A. M., undated. 'Ateso Grammar', manuscript (cyclostyled).

HILDERS, REV. FR. J. H., and LAWRANCE, J. C. D., 1956. *An Introduction to the Ateso Language*, Kampala, Eagle Press.

HOBLEY, C. W., 1902. *Eastern Uganda*, London, Anthropological Institute of Great Britain and Ireland. (Notes on Teso, p. 57.)

HOSKING, H. R., DE COURCY IRELAND, M. G., and LOEWENTHAL, DR. L. J. A., 1937. *An Investigation into Health and Agriculture in Teso*, Entebbe, Government Printer.

HUNTINGFORD, G. W. B., 1953. *The Northern Nilo-Hamites*, London, International African Institute. (Brief note on Teso, p. 12.)

JOHNSTON, SIR H. H., 1902. *The Uganda Protectorate*, London, Hutchinson. (Notes on Teso, pp. 713, 853, 855.)

KAGOLO, B. M., 1955. 'Tribal Names and Customs in Teso District', *U.J.* 19.

KENNEDY, F. R., 1937. 'Teso Clans', *U.J.* 5.

KIGGEN, REV. FR. J., c. 1928. *Grammar nak' Ateso*, Ngora, Mill Hill Mission.

—— 1953. *English–Ateso Dictionary*, Ngora, Mill Hill Mission.[1]

KIRKPATRICK, CAPT. R. T., 1899. 'Lake Choga and Surrounding Country', *Geographical Journal*, 13. (Reprinted *U.J.* 10 (1946).)

KITCHING, REV. A. L., 1912. *On the Backwaters of the Nile*, London, Fisher Unwin.

—— 1915. *A Handbook of the Ateso Language*, London, S.P.C.K.

KRUYER, REV. FR. J., undated (c. 1920). 'Notes on the Teso Tribe', manuscript.

LAWRANCE, J. C. D., 1953 (i). 'Rock Paintings in Teso', *U.J.* 17.

—— 1953 (ii). 'The Karamojong Cluster—A Note', *Africa* 23.

—— 1955. 'A History of Teso to 1937', *U.J.* 19.

—— and HILDERS, REV. FR. J. H., 1956. *An Introduction to the Ateso Language*, Kampala, Eagle Press.

LEHMANN, DR. H., and RAPER, Dr. A. B., 1951. 'Distribution of the Sickle Cell Trait in Uganda,' *U.J.* 15.

LOEWENTHAL, DR. L. J. A., DE COURCY IRELAND, M. G., HOSKING, H. R., 1937. *An Investigation into Health and Agriculture in Teso*, Entebbe, Government Printer.

—— 1939 (i). *Abstract of a further Survey of Health in relation to Agriculture in Teso, Uganda*, Entebbe, Government Printer.

—— 1939 (ii). *Effect of Various Dietary Supplements on the Growth of School Children in Uganda*, Entebbe, Government Printer (pp. 16–18 concern Teso).

LUDGER, BROTHER K., 1952. 'Control of Crime in Primitive Society—An example from Teso', *U.J.* 16.

—— 1954. 'Rainmakers in Teso , *U.J.* 18.

---

[1] A companion Ateso-English Dictionary is shortly to be published.

LUKYN-WILLIAMS, F., 1936. 'Teso Clans', *U.J.* 4.

McGOUGH, REV. FR., F.J., undated. 'Ateso Grammar', manuscript.

'MILL HILL FATHERS', 1952. 'Derivations of some Teso Place Names', *U.J.* 16.

'MISSIONARY PRIEST', 1955. 'The Teso Tribe of Uganda', *Daystar in Africa* (Journal of the Franciscan Sisters).

RAPER, DR. A. B., and LEHMANN, DR. H., 1951. 'Distribution of the Sickle Cell Trait in Uganda', *U.J.* 15.

ROSCOE, REV. J., 1915. *The Northern Bantu*, Cambridge, Cambridge University Press. (Notes on Teso, pp. 259–73.)

—— 1924. *The Bagisu*, Cambridge, Cambridge University Press. (Notes on Teso, pp. 91–96.)

ROSS, J. G., 1954. 'A Study of Zebu Cattle in Teso District', manuscript.

SCHUT, REV. FR., undated. 'The Iteso alias the Bateso', manuscript.

SCOTT, R., and THOMAS, H. B., 1935. *Uganda*, London, Oxford University Press.

SELIGMAN, C. G., 1930. *Races of Africa*, London, Thornton Butterworth Ltd.

STEPHENS, A. L., 1942. *Problems of Rural Reconstruction in Teso*, Entebbe, Government Printer.

STEPHENS, J. E. M., 1953. 'Derivations of Teso Place Names', *U.J.* 17.

TARANTINO, REV. FR. A., 1949 (i). *'Notes on the Lango', *U.J.* 13.

—— 1949 (ii). *'Lango Wars', *U.J.* 13.

THOMAS, H. B., 1939. ' "Capax Imperii"—The Story of Semei Kakunguru', *U.J.* 6.

—— and SCOTT, R., 1935. *Uganda*, London, Oxford University Press.

TOTHILL, DR. J. D., 1938. *A Report on Nineteen Surveys done in Small Agricultural Areas in Uganda*, Entebbe, Government Printer (pp. 140–66 and 182–7 concern Teso).

—— (editor), 1939. *Agriculture in Uganda*, London, Oxford University Press.

TROWELL, M., and WACHSMANN, DR. K. P., 1953. *Tribal Crafts of Uganda*, London, Oxford University Press.

TURPIN, C. A., 1916 (Secretariat Archives). 'The Occupation of the Turkwel River Area by the Karamojong Tribe', *U.J.* 12 (1948).

Uganda Protectorate: Official Publications:
    Uganda Protectorate Intelligence Report No. 34, 1908 (i).
    Uganda Protectorate Intelligence Report No. 35, 1908 (ii).
    Handbook of Uganda, 1913.
    Report of the Teso Informal Committee, 1937.
    Annual Reports on the Kingdom of Buganda, Eastern Province, Western Province, 1939–46, 1949.
    Teso District Plan, 1953.

WACHSMANN, DR. K. P., and TROWELL, M., 1953. *Tribal Crafts of Uganda*, London, Oxford University Press.

WALSHE, REV. FR. C. I., 1947. 'Notes on the Kumam', *U.J.* 11.

WASWA, S., 1950. 'Kakunguru mu Bukedi', manuscript in Luganda.

WATSON, J. M., 1937. 'Survey of Kasilang Atongole', manuscript. (Department of Agriculture, Entebbe.)

—— 1941. 'Some Aspects of Teso Agriculture', *E.A.A.J.* 6.

—— 1949. 'The Wild Mammals of Teso and Karamoja', *U.J.* 12–16.

WHEATE, DR. H. W., 1950. 'Leprosy Survey in Teso', *E.A.M.J.* 27.

—— 1951. 'Leprosy in Teso District', *E.A.M.J.* 28.

WILSON, P. N., 1954. 'Kasilang Erony Survey, 1953' (to be published).[1]

---

[1] Part of this survey, 'The Flora of Kasilang Erony, Teso,' by P. N. Wilson and J. M. Watson, is published in *U.J.* 19.

Wilson, Dr. W. A., undated (*c.* 1947). 'Teso-Karamojong–English Vocabulary', manuscript (cyclostyled).

Wright, A. C. A., 1942. 'Notes on Iteso Social Organization', *U.J.* 9.

—— 1946. 'A Rain-making Ceremony in Teso', *U.J.* 10.

—— 1951. 'Blood Grouping and the Tribal Historian', *U.J.* 15.

INDEX

PRINTED IN GREAT BRITAIN
AT THE UNIVERSITY PRESS, OXFORD
BY CHARLES BATEY, PRINTER TO THE UNIVERSITY